Chestnut, Cherry & Kiwi Fruit Sponge

Lisa Rose Wright

Chestnut, Cherry & Kiwi Fruit Sponge
Copyright © Lisa Rose Wright 2021

The right of Lisa Rose Wright to be identified as the author of this work has been asserted by her in accordance with the Copyright Designs and Patents Act 1988

All rights reserved. No part of this publication may be reproduced, transmitted, or stored in a retrieval system in any form or by any means, without permission in writing of the author.

Any queries please contact me at
lisarosewright@msn.com

Cover design by 100 covers at https://100covers.com
All photographs © Lisa Rose Wright

ISBN: 9798465168311

For Mum, and Dad –
my inspiration, and my guide.
You always taught me to aim high and not be afraid.

CONTENTS

SUMMER IN GALICIA	1
JULY 2014	23
AUGUST 2014	43
SEPTEMBER 2014	61
OCTOBER 2014	78
NOVEMBER 2014	95
DECEMBER 2014	113
JANUARY 2015	130
FEBRUARY 2015	146
MARCH 2015	160
APRIL 2015	177
MAY 2015	194
JUNE 2015 Part I: Departures	210
JUNE 2015 Part II: Arrivals	227
JULY 2015	240
AUGUST 2015	252
SEPTEMBER 2015	265
OCTOBER 2015	279
NOVEMBER 2015	294
DECEMBER 2015	308
JANUARY 2016	324
FEBRUARY 2016	337
MARCH 2016	351
APRIL 2016	362
MAY 2016	375
JUNE 2016	388

Coming next: *Pulpo, Pig & Peppers*	400
THE RECIPES	402
A GLOSSARY OF ENGLISH WORDS	418
ACKNOWLEDGEMENTS	422
ABOUT THE AUTHOR:	423

Author's note

Welcome to the third, bumper book of our adventures in beautiful green Galicia. As ever, all of our adventures in here are true, even the more bizarre ones. S often has a slightly different version of the truth to me – in many things, and I now have a second memory holder, who has yet another version of events – Mum. But this is still my memoir and therefore events happened as *I* remember them... most of the time. These final letters home have been faithfully transcribed, though some have once more been abridged to spare you, the reader, from total boredom or confusion (I hope).

Every person and animal in this book is real, although some names have been changed or omitted to prevent any unnecessary law suits.

Lisa

I hope you enjoy this third volume of our adventures in Galicia. If you are curious about this place we call home and would like to see more, just download my free photo album which accompanies this book.
https://www.flipsnack.com/65E9E6B9E8C/album-3-cherry.html

Or follow me on my facebook page:
http://www.facebook.com/lisarosewright.author

Part I

A final year to write home about

SUMMER IN GALICIA
A Casita do Campo

"That's my job done, it's over to you now."

It was my youngest brother ringing from England.

"What? She's agreed? How on Earth did you manage that?"

My husband Stewart (or S as he is better known to my readers) and I had been living in Galicia for eight years, and for at least seven years and nine months we had been trying to persuade my mum to move out here permanently. Despite her visiting us frequently, and for longer and longer periods of time – and thoroughly enjoying herself – she was adamant. She wouldn't leave her home of 63 years nor her friend and next-door neighbour, Aunty Jean.

For a couple of years Mum had had some health problems: one of these ended with her being whisked to hospital in an ambulance after she collapsed on the bathroom floor. On that occasion a neighbour had found her, but we were increasingly concerned. My brothers both lived over an hour away and Mum had steadfastly refused to move in with either. Mum was (and still is) a very independent lady. She was not going to agree to move in with us either.

It was my brother who had suggested we find a house for her and introduce it as a *fait accompli.* "She's bound to say yes then," he'd said.

"Okay, but it's up to you to persuade her," I'd countered.

Now it looked like he had.

"There was a party," my brother continued, laughing. "I overheard Mum telling someone that she was moving to Spain and didn't care what anyone said."

"But, that's incredible. Contrary woman! No one has ever said anything about her moving here, other than it's a good idea! Anyway, we'd better get house hunting seriously. Maybe we can show Mum a few places whilst she's over."

I couldn't say any of us had really had any input into changing Mum's mind, but the decision was made and Mum was suddenly raring to go.

§

That spring, 2014, Mum was to stay with us for six weeks. She arrived at the end of March on a wild and windy day and left in the middle of a hot and sunny May. We had a wonderful time seeing friends and visiting fiestas, eating and drinking, laughing and working.

Diary Saturday 5th April Cloud and Sun
Thankfully warmer than yesterday for our dinner party. Mike and John arrived early of course, John and Fiona a little while later. S set up the table outside in the horno area. Mum helped me make the ravioli starter.
Salmon and smoked salmon ravioli (homemade). Rabbit, marmalade, and chorizo stew with roast potatoes and squash. Orange almond cake with marmalade cream.
Mum did all the washing up for me which was fabulous... could get used to that!
Sowed new potatoes. First cuckoo. Full house - 8 eggs (John and Fiona bought two dozen).

CHESTNUT, CHERRY & KIWI FRUIT SPONGE

Diary Thursday 10th April Mist then sun then thunder and lightning!
All to Monforte de Lemos. Found the swimming baths. Very deep and very busy. Mum stayed in the shallower pool. Nice hydro-massage and sauna. Be happy when Chantada reopens though.
Lunch at the Capitol. Excellent and I feel we really deserved it after our exercise.
Wandered around Monforte. Saw a pair of buttercup-yellow, soft, suede sofas. A three and a two-seater which would be perfect for our Big Barn, so we bought them!
Drove around town looking for possible houses to buy.

We had been putting feelers out for properties for a while, in the hope that Mum would agree to move. Our criteria were simple: close to us, a manageable size, and with as few stairs as possible. Mum's criteria were even simpler: some outdoor space, and a view.

My childhood home in the English Midlands was one of the best located council homes I've ever come across. There were 26 semi-detached houses built around a large central grass oval. This meant that no one was overlooked at the front. To the rear of our house there were rolling fields, with cows and copses of oak and sycamore trees as far as the eye could see.

Beating that was going to be a tall order.

Diary Monday 5th May Humid
L planted out 6 peppers and 4 courgettes plus one pumpkin and one squash.
Mum sewed and repaired my tops and jeans, and planted out 3 further peppers in tubs for me. S mowed the lawns and mulched our new hazel trees.

SUMMER IN GALICIA

Lunch: Roast chicken salad.
Mum sowed basil and butternut squash for me, then processed a huge barrowload of spinach from Carmen. L had an English lesson with Maria.
Cleared out the Big Barn for the sofas we bought in April.

We had looked at a promising house a few years ago. CJ's friend, 'Rainman' Pete, was selling his place. It was small and manageable, sitting in its own pleasant plot with views across the Miño valley. But it was in a tiny village, remote from any shops and just too far from us for our liking.

Then there was mad Maria. I had no idea why she was called that at the time. We visited her house with Mum that spring. It was nearby but had no garden attached to it, no view, and a back wall which had collapsed into the street. We politely declined. But that wasn't the end of the matter. Maria began to stalk us. On the streets, turning up at the house, then ringing me constantly - asking when we were going to buy the house but never giving a price. It was months before she backed off, having found alternative prey.

Diary Thursday 15th May Hot
Up, fed and watered all. Off to Carballiño to the new swimming pool we found as Chantada is still closed. Will have visited all the local pools soon. Good swim followed by lunch at a local pizzeria. Excellent.
Visited the monastery at Oseira. They do guided tours which was very interesting. Mum bought up the shop and wanted to take the tiny monk she met home 'to put on her shelf'. He was from Madrid and spoke excellent English.
Last night drinks in town. We will miss her, and she us I think.

CHESTNUT, CHERRY & KIWI FRUIT SPONGE

The best property we had seen to date was a tiny bungalow in our nearby town of Taboada. It was just four small rooms, but sat on a good-sized plot with open views to the front across the valley. It was also only a two-minute walk into town with its many cafes and shops. We had driven there with Mum.

"No."

"Why ever not?" I'd asked. "It's perfect."

"The cemetery is there," she replied, pointing.

I admit that the end of the cul-de-sac on which the property sat did terminate (literally) in the town's cemetery. But it couldn't be seen from the bungalow, and anyway the neighbours were quiet.

The bungalow needed a fair bit of work doing, though it had town sewerage and water laid on. The roof was old and sagging, the walls were thin brick so would need insulating and cladding to keep the heat in, the bathroom was ancient and tired, and the kitchen non-existent. The owner refused to drop a penny from his unrealistic asking price. We persisted, asking Paco, a *Galego* friend, to talk to the owner.

Diary Saturday 17th May Hot
S in the Big Barn fitting new beams for the mezzanine level. L knocking plaster off the south wall outside. Then needed a shower (again). Feels like it's summer in Galicia. Rang Paco regarding the bungalow chap reducing his price. No go, he says. Oh well, Plan C, or D!

With Mum's objections ringing in our ears, and the too high price, we walked away from the bungalow.

SUMMER IN GALICIA

Tuesday 20th May 2014. Wet! (Because I decommissioned the cocina yesterday - serves me right for thinking it's summer.)
Dear Mum,

Thought I'd start dating my letters properly, though it won't last as we had to look through the diary to find the date.

Well, it seems odd without you. S made you a tea and forgot me, I set the table for three at lunch, and I swear you were walking about in the night! You'll have to hurry back!

As I said in my text, Buffy has 4 beautiful chicks. They are very easy to distinguish: A big brown one with a black stripe on its head, a large yellow one, a white one with a brown 'clown's' face, and a jet black one. The eggs were from Carmen's sister's hens so they will probably be big chickens. (She had Colin, our huge brown male a couple of years ago if you remember.) We are on the letter 'E' this year so think of some names... S says Edwina - for Edwina Curry and her salmonella in eggs gaff. Haha.

So far, the new chicks have tried slug, snail, and ant eggs all successfully. Yesterday we lifted the chicks back indoors in the evening, but today Buffy had them inside by herself. She stood at the top of the ramp shouting encouragement. It was quite funny to watch as they ran up the ramp then got confused and jumped back down again time after time until one found the

CHESTNUT, CHERRY & KIWI FRUIT SPONGE

entrance and disappeared inside. It was like watching a Pacman game.

Two of Billie Jean's eggs have broken (infertile I assume) so she is on 5 now. She started sitting the day you went home.

I have been continuing to knock off the mortar on the back wall. The stone wall looks quite good but where it abuts the older wall it's not tied in at all, just a dead straight line so may look a bit strange. I shall see.

S is fixing the last of his beams for the mezzanine floor in the Big Barn. It's going to be a fabulous space. I'm looking forward to moving in there and sitting on my nice new sofas.

Wednesday: Still wet and quite cold. I'm sure one of my courgettes was frosted last night! I've fleeced them but the tomatoes will have to fight for it. We walked into town last night for a drink muffled up like winter - the wind was icy and we have no excuse to take the car now you are gone.

Everyone asked about you. Luisa was sorry you had left and has decided she will find a house for you! We wandered the streets looking at a few I'd found online but nothing suitable for a discerning, soon-to-be 83-year-old lady.

Seems funny having to write again after so long. I almost couldn't remember the address!!

Love you tons and tons and looking forward to your next visit. Will stockpile the sewing but not the washing up, haha. XXXXXX

SUMMER IN GALICIA

It had been good to have Mum with us for so long but we were no nearer finding a house for her. I was beginning to despair. It was down to us to make this work.

Diary Thursday 22nd May 4°C overnight and very windy.
Both into town to book the car in for its pre-ITV check. Wandered around searching for a couple more houses I'd seen on the internet. One looked promising but, although it's not far away as the crow flies (just across the river), it is a long way by road and I can't see Mum walking to us across the fields.
Lunch: Baby squid in tomato sauce and first new potatoes, roasted. Crumble and custard.

Our friend Pepe said he had a house to sell. It was twice the size of our 250 square metre property and came with 13 acres of land. We felt it was not quite suitable for a soon-to-be 83-year-old. Another friend in town offered us a plot of land for 28,000 euros but we felt it was a bit of a tall order to build a home from scratch for a soon-to-be 83-year-old.

Sunday 31st May (I know that cos it's Monterroso market tomorrow). Sunshine!
Dear Mum,
 Glad it's sunny, after a very soggy cold week. My wild strawberries may actually ripen now instead of going mouldy! I have lots of redcurrants on so am going to try the ice cream recipe you sent but with elderflower and redcurrants instead of gooseberries. The male kiwi is full of flowers this year but the female ones haven't opened yet. They had better hurry or it will all be

CHESTNUT, CHERRY & KIWI FRUIT SPONGE

over before they are ready! (Oops, just reread that, it sounds rude haha).

One of the chicken eggs got broken today (big fat brown one sat on it I think), later I heard a chuntering and saw a very small egg near the top gate. It was the plastic one we put in the laying box to encourage them to use it. It must've got egg yolk on it and someone (big fat brown one again?) had carried it out of the pen and down the steps! Lucky she didn't swallow it!

Monday: Just realised I'm wrong. I must have written the above on Saturday as Monterroso was Sunday! Think I'll give up trying to do dates.

Anyway, Monterroso was quite quiet this month. Jayne was there and asked when you were coming and I had to tell her she had missed you. Gala accused me of swapping your ticket home as she was sure it was the 11th of next month you went back! We will just have to hurry and find this house for you.

PS: You wanted our overheads...

Council tax 43€ a year plus 60€ a year rubbish collection (new tax), electric 240€ a year, water zero unless we need a new pump or we test it (then around 40€), mobile phone 15€ a month, car tax 36€ a year, MOT 40€ (passed!!), firewood around 400€ a year (minus £200 from S' UK government fuel allowance), gas around 80€ a year.

SUMMER IN GALICIA

I've made my elderflower cordial for the ice cream. Need a redcurrant, blackcurrant, and strawberry picker. There are so many on now the weather has changed. I managed to give Carmen some redcurrants this morning - I think I caught her by surprise!

I only have one patch of mortar left to do on the first section of the back wall. I'm doing it slowly but it's a good way to get a suntan!

Just going to make my bread to leave in the fridge overnight to raise. It works well and has a lovely taste.

Oh, and the swimming pool at Chantada finally reopened last week after almost six months. They weren't charging, to encourage folk to return, so that was good.

Still missing you and your help. Love you tons and tons and tons

xxxxxxx

We had often said that Mum could afford to live in Galicia on the savings she made from her UK overheads; which included £120 council tax - a month - and much higher electricity and water rates (it's not difficult to be higher than zero mind). But cost was never an issue - finding a house was. And now the clock was ticking.

Diary Thursday 12th June Hotter
Up late again! Watered everything then went into town. S was shaping the plasterboard for the downstairs snug wall in the Big Barn, cutting around the beams and the 'standing stones'.

CHESTNUT, CHERRY & KIWI FRUIT SPONGE

Lunch: Ribs, rice, carrot, onion, ginger and garlic stir fry. Last of the berry tart.
I continued knocking the mortar off the south wall in the heat.
Evening. Watered the allotment and chatted to Carmen. She says there may be a house for sale in the village!

As I was chatting to our wonderful neighbour, Carmen, that evening, I mentioned our quest.

"*Hay número tres,*" she said.

"Number three?" I repeated, puzzled.

"*Si, allí. Abajo.*" She pointed eastwards toward the other end of our village. "Pepe lives in Barcelona, it's his parents' house. I'm sure he'd be happy to sell it."

I was stunned. She was telling me there might actually be a house we could buy in our tiny hamlet of six?

"Go and look," said Carmen.

"But we don't have a key."

"Oh, the door isn't locked, hasn't been for years."

That evening, feeling like inept cat burglars, we snuck down the slope to the house armed with torches. There were two doors: a huge, solid, glazed blue door leading into a kitchen, which was locked, firmly; and just beyond it, up four steps, a stable door, also painted blue.

This second door led into a bedroom – and the man trap just inside almost got me.

I stepped onto a piece of linoleum at the foot of the bed and squealed as it sagged beneath my eight stone weight. Carefully pulling up a corner of the carpet, we found that it concealed a two-foot square hole in the floorboards. I resolved to be far more careful in future.

Once inside, and avoiding holes in the floors, the place opened out. It was much bigger than I'd envisaged.

SUMMER IN GALICIA

There was a tangle of ivy, brambles and grapevines covering a good three-quarters of the outside house wall, leaving only the two doors exposed. I had expected a couple of rooms inside. Instead, the bedroom led into a large, square dining room complete with old, mouldy furniture and a plastic potty sitting on a low chair. Off this room were five further doors.

To the right, down four steps, was the kitchen we'd spied through the first door. It was a long room with a Galician range cooker in the middle, built into a brick surround the same as ours. Although slightly smaller than our kitchen, it was still a good size – and a mess of rotten wood and damp, peeling plaster.

Past the top of the kitchen steps, on the right, was a door leading to a small dim room littered with wine bottles and the remnants of a fire pit in its centre. Ahead was another dark room – this one long and narrow, with ivy winding through the exposed roof tiles. An old ironing board gave the only hint as to the room's previous use.

To the left of the bedroom was a large room set in a rhomboid shape. In the middle of this room was a bed piled so high with clothes that in the gloom I was sure there was a body in it. In the corner was a large wooden cupboard. From the window, if one parted the vines, ivy, and thickets of brambles growing up and over the roof, there was a far-reaching view eastwards, along the valley, across fields and copses.

The final door from the dining room led down two steps to a second bedroom with, luxury, an en suite bathroom. The doorway was even shorter than me, at less than five feet high, and the floor beyond was rotten and holed, but the windows gave out onto a balcony and a large, open-sided barn called an *alpendre*.

CHESTNUT, CHERRY & KIWI FRUIT SPONGE

Unwilling to explore further without permissions we walked the 50 metres back to our house chatting about the possibilities.

At home we both drew a plan of the property. S had an extra room on his plan. He swears to this day that the extra room was there when we viewed the place that first time. No matter. It looked, on paper at least, just what we wanted. Now all we had to do was buy it.

I was dreading going through the whole bureaucracy thing again. Our house, *A Casa do Campo,* had taken us six months and numerous heartbreaks to buy. We had withstood an enforced change of estate agent, a reduced amount of land, and an increased price before it was finally ours. Three years later we got married in Galicia – that had also been a nightmare of red tape, delays and frustrations. I really didn't want to have to go through that sort of stress again – but we wanted a house for Mum and this was the one.

I spoke with Carmen again a few days later. She didn't have a contact number for the owners but thought 'our' Pepe, whose family had owned *A Casa do Campo,* may have.

Diary Tuesday 17th June Hot
Watered, and pinched out the side shoots on the tomatoes which took most of the morning. Decommissioned the stove in the hallway upstairs. Oiled it and moved the furniture to its summer configuration.
S cut and dragged twigs back from the finca below ours which Manuel had told us to take.
Lunch: Smoked mackerel rice salad with broad beans, sun-dried tomatoes, onion and parsnip. Last of my trifle. CJ's home-smoked mackerel was heavenly.
To Taboada in the evening. Pepe was in Bar Gema so I asked him about the house

SUMMER IN GALICIA

Pepe, it turned out, was best friends with the Pepe (another one) who owned number three. They had grown up together. At that time there had been so many more people in our tiny village. I imagined it ringing with the sounds of children playing, running in and out of each other's houses and generally having a great time.

Pepe asked if we wanted the owners' phone number or preferred him to ring for us. We had been in Galicia long enough to know that wheels are always oiled by a personal recommendation so I asked Pepe to ring, knowing he would give us a good reference.

Wednesday 18th June. Very, very hot!
Dear Mum,

I've been mortaring the back wall and boy was it hot with the rubber gloves on - sweat was dripping down my arms... yuk!

Mind you, my tan is coming on. It's a good place to go topless as no one can see me up there. Hope my tan lasts for our hols in November so I can show off in my posh new birthday bikini with the frilly tassels you bought me. Haha!

We walked into town for a drink last night. Everyone sent their love. We met Pepe in the Gema (our neighbourhood bar). He was amazed you were over 80 and said you didn't look it (true). He asked if you were moving over and I said yes!

They have canaries in the bar which have had babies. So cute! They reminded me of my canary, Lemon, that brother

CHESTNUT, CHERRY & KIWI FRUIT SPONGE

bought me years ago, singing away.

Our black chick is a boy, I think. The other day I thought there was a blackbird in the pen but it was him. They have all been out into the other pen today with mum. Will let them into the wide world with the others tomorrow and see how they get on.

I think I told you Billie Jean didn't get any chicks. The eggs were infertile. We brought her back up top but she is keeping very close to Buzz as the others are bullying her (need to get the pecking order sorted again). Today I heard a commotion in the house and could see Buzz in there. BJ was on the nest and Buzz was standing guard with his back to her to stop anyone else coming in. How sweet is that?

Do you remember the little tomato seedling you refused to throw away, and put in a tiny pot? Despite ignoring it, it grew so I potted it up and gave it to S. Now it is as big as the ones on the allotment. S says to tell you he is taking good care of it for you.

Thurs am: VVV hot

This will be late I'm afraid as Leo and Margaret called for eggs this morning so I am late going into town (and hurrying, hence the scribble!)

Love you tons and tons.

xxxx

Too hot to be out really. Huge tub full of blackcurrants and raspberries today!

Xxxxx

SUMMER IN GALICIA

I didn't mention the house in my letter to Mum. Knowing how slowly things happen in Galicia, and the many possible pitfalls to come, I decided to wait until we knew more.

It turns out I didn't have long to wait.

Diary Friday 20th June Storm clouds pm but just drizzled a little
S fitting the plasterboard ceiling above the mezzanine in the Big Barn whilst I made lunch and egg custards.
Lunch: Trout and ginger quiche with garden salad. Raspberry egg custard.
Jetwashed the south wall outside at the top and got extremely muddy. Granite in my hair, down my socks and in my belly button.
Bathnight thankfully. Open evening in Chantada so wandered around looking at shops and partaking of free tapas after our swim.
Pepe rang to say number three is definitely for sale!

The very next evening, a Saturday, we heard a knock on the gate as we were finishing for the evening.

A short, stocky Galician man was standing there with a smiling, attractive woman next to him. They introduced themselves.

"You want to buy my house," he said. Typical, direct Galician.

"Er, well, maybe." Typical indirect English.

"Do you want to see it?" asked his wife, Mercedes, seeing my hesitancy.

"Yes, please."

We wandered down the track and through that same blue door into the bedroom. Both Pepe and Mercedes skirted the old linoleum without hesitation and I did the same.

CHESTNUT, CHERRY & KIWI FRUIT SPONGE

"It's ready to move into," announced Pepe, artfully throwing a dining chair across a vast hole in the floorboards to hide it.

I started to laugh but Mercedes was shaking her head at her husband. I turned the laugh into a cough and we carried on. They pointed out the bedroom they'd used after they had married, the *chorizo* smoking room with the fire pit, the glass '*pendentes*' or ceiling lights and the huge and ancient TV in the kitchen. The house had been empty for 25 years and it showed.

Everything depended on the price.

We walked back to our gate chatting.

"So, do you want it?" asked Pepe.

"How much?" I countered.

Pepe thought. This is the tricky bit for a *Galego*. They are genetically unable to give a direct answer. His reply was; "How much will you pay?"

We had discussed this. We knew the cottage would be costly to renovate and have little resale value due to its location, though it was perfect for our soon-to-be 83-year-old.

I hesitated. Galicians still think in terms of pesetas for large value items. Often house prices will be advertised in increments of 6000 euros, or one million pesetas. Plus, the price sounds more in pesetas. "Two million?" I was trying to sound confident but my voice had a questioning edge.

Pepe looked disappointed and opened his mouth to speak. Mercedes elbowed him none too gently in the ribs, and said, "Yes."

"I will speak to the notary tomorrow," she continued. "We can visit the following day."

Wow!

"Tomorrow is Sunday," I pointed out.

"No matter. Monday then." Mercedes was definitely the business person around here. "We have the paperwork ready. I will ring you." With that they left.

SUMMER IN GALICIA

On Monday morning, Mercedes rang.

"The appointment is tomorrow at twelve noon at the notary in Melide," she said. "Bring your passports."

Talk about quick! We had just time to ask our friends Leo and Margaret to come with us to help translate if we hit any problems.

"Of course," said Leo. "But this will only be to show your passports, not to actually buy anything so quickly." We decided to take the money anyway. We would pay in cash, but no black money had been discussed so it would all be properly notarised.

At 11.45am on Tuesday the 24th of June 2014 we met Leo and Margaret in Melide and all trailed round to the owners' beautiful house. They greeted us warmly. Margaret chatted easily in Spanish, her lovely Canadian accent causing Mercedes to occasionally frown in confusion. But Mercedes had taught herself *Vasco*, the impossible language of the Basque country, so she could decipher anything. Leo and Pepe could have been brothers – both short and solidly Galician in shape, they discussed farming and livestock issues of the day. After coffee we made our way to the notary's office in town.

The notary told us the tiny garden at the house couldn't be registered as it doesn't belong to anyone. We didn't care. The garden was originally an access to someone's fields beyond. Pepe pointed out that there was now another, easier, access to that field. From what we had seen of the 'garden' no one had passed that way by tractor, nor on foot, for dozens of years.

Other than this minor hitch, all went smoothly. The papers were signed, the notary counted the cash and agreed with all parties that this was the price for the property.

"Now he will leave the room so you can pay the black," whispered Leo.

CHESTNUT, CHERRY & KIWI FRUIT SPONGE

I started to explain there wasn't any illegal 'black' money to be paid but the notary was standing up.

"Please sign here," he said.

I smiled as our friend sat open mouthed, shock on his face. Then again, Leo hadn't seen our new *Casita* yet.

For myself, I was still in shock at the speed of the whole process. It could not have more different from buying our own house all those years earlier. That had involved months of stress. From viewing to buying the *Casita* had taken us an unbelievable four days.

Pepe and Mercedes wanted to buy us all lunch but Leo and Margaret had things to do. We on the other hand had no commitments, other than another house to renovate. We had a lovely meal with two lovely people, and I broached the one subject we hadn't mentioned.

A key.

"Oh, I don't have one," said Pepe, looking at his wife. "I never have had."

Oh well. We knew we could get in the bedroom door; we would sort out the locked kitchen door when we got to it.

We were happy, we had a house for Mum. And now I could tell her our news - in my own roundabout way...

Tuesday 23rd June 10pm. Cloudy but huge thunderstorms, Sat, Sun, Mon. Electric off overnight.
Dear Mum,
What a busy week we are having! Saturday, we had that thunderstorm whilst I was talking to you then unexpected visitors arrived — but more about that later on.

SUMMER IN GALICIA

On Sunday we had friends over for dinner. Kath and Jorge (who did such a good acting job when collecting you for our wedding) and Debs and Al from south of the Sil. If you remember they came to Lugo with us last Christmas, we met them at Barbara and Martin's plant and artisan sale the year before. Debs weaves the most wonderful baskets. Our Dutch friend Geert arrived about 1pm so I invited him to stay for lunch too. Poor Geert has only been back home a few days after a month away so he missed the sun earlier in June. He thinks it's always raining here! It was a lovely afternoon; they didn't leave until 7pm. Then we had another big storm.

On Monday we had just finished morning tea when CJ arrived, so more tea and chat. I gave him your paper about hip replacement exercises. He still doesn't have a date, which is annoying for him.

This morning we met Leo and Margaret in Melide. You met them last year if you remember. Leo is Galician and Margaret is Canadian. Lovely couple, they have been married forever and still get on so well together. They had kindly agreed to act as translators for us. We all met Pepe and Mercedes, our visitors from Saturday, at their house (very nice, very grand).

After we had sorted everything out, they took us for lunch in Melide then to see their farm near Palas de Rei. We didn't get home

CHESTNUT, CHERRY & KIWI FRUIT SPONGE

until 5pm but no thunderstorm tonight as yet.

Did I say, on Monday evening we had a heck of a storm and then the electric went off so we had to go into Taboada for water from the fountain (our electric water pump doesn't work of course without power). Found out it was the sardine fiesta for San Juan which we had forgotten about. Someone found us a sardine or two left over and a glass of vino! When we got home, we found it was just a blown fuse anyway. Oh well.

Oh, yes, I haven't told you what we were doing today have I? Must be getting forgetful...

We bought a house.

In this village to be exact.

Carmen told us a while ago that it might be for sale but she didn't have a phone number. Turns out Pepe, whose family owned our house, was good friends with the owner. We were chatting in the bar, as one does, and he said he would ring them for us. They said they would sell and came over unexpectedly on Saturday.

We had a look at the house with them Saturday evening and made an offer which they accepted, and as they had all the paperwork ready to go, we visited the notary today and signed. 'Ya ésta'. Done!

Now we are the proud owners of not only 'A Casa do Campo' but 'A Casita do Campo too'! (The Country House and the Country Cottage). The neighbours think we are crazy but that is nothing new.

The house has been empty a while and is rather derelict. The garden looks like something out of Sleeping Beauty - after the 100 years. But the house has a lovely view down the valley and will be a nice two bed cottage... eventually.

Now we just need a tenant!! Do you know anyone who might be interested?

Bring your gardening gloves at Christmas, we will need your input on design and planting. There are some good chestnut doors like ours to clean up and of course a few renovations to do, so plenty to keep you (and us) busy.

Look forward to speaking with you on Saturday - as I say it's been a busy week and it's still only Tuesday!

Love you tons and tons

Merry Christmas! Hope you like your present!

XXXXXXXXX

I still couldn't believe how quickly everything had happened. One minute we were the owners of one almost, but not quite, renovated stone house. Now we had two houses to renovate. It wasn't as if we didn't know what we were letting ourselves in for - after all we *had* done this all before. It was still daunting though, when I thought back to all the hard work we had put into our own house over the years.

JULY 2014
A Casa do Campo

We first saw *A Casa do Campo* on a damp and misty November morning in 2006. It had been in a similar state of disrepair to *A Casita do Campo* in 2014. Over the intervening years we had self-renovated our large, stone farmhouse, beginning with the essentials: sewerage, water, and a roof.

We moved into our Galician home in August 2007. That first year S dug and laid a brand-new sewerage system, as the house had none, and started renovating the saggy and leaking roof. By the end of the following year, we had a bedroom, a bathroom with hot running water, a new-old roof and a guest room for Mum who stayed with us, *casa nosotros*, for the first time that Christmas. In 2009 we renovated a second bedroom and a central living space. We also spent time trying to foil Spanish bureaucracy into letting us marry here in Galicia.

The beginning of our third year saw us renovating our bright sunroom with its huge picture windows overlooking the river at the bottom of our little valley. My domain, the kitchen, was also completed that year – the year we managed to tie the knot in our tiny town of Taboada, 2010.

Since then, we had renovated a third bedroom, in the attic space, and a large storeroom-pantry on the ground floor. We had done much needed maintenance around the property; pruning trees and growing more of our own food to eat and were also able to spend more time out and about, enjoying the area and relaxing. I was now working my way around the house mortaring the exterior stonework while S had started work on the 'Big Barn' – our final project.

A double height masterpiece, the Big Barn had been a cow barn for many years. Jetwashing the walls had removed the smell and a considerable amount of cow shit – most of which was transferred to me during the process. We had put in a huge new beam with the help of S' friend and best man, Les, and his partner Judith. I had mortared the two stone walls we were leaving exposed, and plastered the third wall. We had plasterboarded half of the ceiling with the help of our friend CJ's scaffolding, fitted new floor beams for the mezzanine and new roof supports using two tall chestnut trees from our own woodland. S had also fitted a large skylight window and started to plasterboard the remaining walls.

There were still wooden floors and a wood-burning stove to fit, the mezzanine to complete, a staircase to build, beams to clean and lots of odds and ends which we knew from experience took the most time.

Now we had bought another house.

We needed to get on with renovating the *Casita* before the place fell down or succumbed to the encroaching wilderness, disappearing finally and inevitably into the undergrowth.

In short, we needed help.

Tuesday 1st July 2014 (I'm sure for once).
Dear Mum,
Not such an exciting letter this week!
We did collect the deeds for the Casita yesterday. Still can't believe how quick and easy it was when I think of how long it took us to buy this house and all the trouble and heartache we had. Goes to show it's best to

CHESTNUT, CHERRY & KIWI FRUIT SPONGE

just put the word out than to go through an estate agent. Being honorary Galicians helps too of course!

I've had fun cleaning out some of the junk from the house - loads of old clothes and 20-year-old pills, plus some interesting jars... one of honey and three of possibly fat for rubbing on the chest! I've filled the village bin now so we will have to wait for it to be emptied (now they are charging us a rubbish tax, we may as well use it... especially as they are charging us for the Casita too.)

Unfortunately, it's still raining off and on so S can't get onto the roof to strip it. Surely it will be sunny in July!

We went to Mike and John's on Sunday for dinner. They are here until September, I think. Mike had done curry. He swore he had no idea S hates it though I'm sure EVERYONE here must know by now - haha. S said he would be happy with bread and cheese but Mike rustled up gammon, egg and chips for him which I thought impressive, and S said it was very tasty but I apparently smelled of curry so didn't get many kisses from my hubby that night!

A friend of theirs had been maintaining the garden and allotment for them. So much work given the rains we have had as the weeds are shooting up. John, being John, said how it looked like a jungle when they got home - right in front of their

JULY 2014

friend! I'm thinking they may not have a gardener when they go back.

We had a chat with them about having volunteers to help with the Casita. There are a number of different websites apparently. Mike gave me the details, so I will go and have a look.

Plenty of people today at the meeting in Monterroso which was nice. There was a new chap called Dave who is building a yurt (a Mongolian tent) in a field, and a couple staying with friends who live in a cave - sadly I didn't get to speak with them so no more on that story for now!

Everyone was excited about our news and looking forward to seeing you here permanently.

Thursday am: Sunshine!

Thank you for the bank cards. Sorry, this is a bit short but the post office will be shut if I don't go now. It's still sent with all our love

xxxxxxxxxx

Love you!

Renovating the *Casita* was going to be another big job. The house had been empty for twice as long as ours, and clearing the garden alone was a major project.

A number of our friends in Galicia used volunteer helpers. Anne and Simon always seemed to have workers there and Mike and John swore by them. We had avoided using any outside help whilst renovating *A Casa do Campo*: partly from taking a pride in being able to say we had done everything ourselves; partly from a nervousness at allowing

CHESTNUT, CHERRY & KIWI FRUIT SPONGE

total strangers to live in the house; and partly the fact that at the time when we would have needed the most help, the house was only barely liveable for us.

I still recall with a shudder the cave-like attic room in which S' friend Les had to sleep when he came to help with our roof. There was a space some two metres long by less than a metre wide in between teetering stacks of boxes filled with our homeless possessions. Into this space, Les laid his sleeping bag and roll mat. The only light was a tiny piece of glass in the roof above him which was covered when he and S put the new roofing directly across the aperture. We knew of people who had far fewer facilities than us when they had helpers, but I just couldn't do it.

Still nervous at taking the plunge we carried on renovating our Big Barn and emptying the *Casita* of years of accumulated 'stuff'.

Diary Thursday 3rd July Warm and sunny
Into Taboada early. Warm so opened the car windows. They then stuck in the down position! Good job it's such a safe area. Left the windows open while I did the shopping and tried to sort out my bank account in UK. Eventually got through to someone who said my account was now unblocked. Well, thank you so much for bothering to tell me!
S picked, stoned and froze a huge bag of cherries. Good year.
Lunch: Fillet of pork with first yellow courgette, onion, peapods, rice, and yoghurt sauce. Tasty.
Drove to the garage with the car. They need to order a new electric window unit.
S continued putting the plasterboard ceiling above the mezzanine. At least one of us has had a productive day!

I'd had to ring my UK bank a week earlier to authorise a payment. They had a new system in

JULY 2014

place which asked different questions to the usual 'what's your birthdate, mother's maiden name' etc. I was asked what year I opened my account, (answer, no idea – ages ago), what my overdraft limit was (answer, no idea – I don't use it), what my credit card limit was (answer, no idea – I never use it). To cut a long story short, I failed the interview. When I joked that I would need some easier questions like, 'who's the prime minister or something', the lass said, "No, you have failed the questions. Your account is now blocked. You have to bring ID into a branch to unblock it."

How the hell was I going to do that from Galicia? She didn't care. I was on the phone for three hours that day with no resolution. I was furious and terrified in equal measure. I've never been overdrawn in my life and couldn't believe they could just suspend my account.

Eventually I got through to someone who said they would look into it but couldn't promise anything. I put in a complaint and asked that they inform me when the account was unblocked.

They didn't.

Diary Friday 4th July Mainly sunny
Put the washing on. Made cakes, pastries and lunch. S scraped some of the beams in the Big Barn then got the ladders out to look at the Casita roof. He removed a few rows of tiles and had a good peruse of its condition. Reported that it seems sound. Phew!
Unearthed two wooden tables from the 'ironing room' and cleared the bed in the living room-to-be at the Casita.

The heap of clothes, bedding and catheter bags piled on that bed was... interesting, and unsavoury. I didn't even bother to rummage through it to find any bargains but scooped everything up and stuffed it into bin bags. Unfortunately, the village bin was still full (they seemed to empty it far less since we'd started paying a rubbish collection tax) so we stored the bulging bags at the *Casita*.

Monday 7th July. Sun and cloud again.
Dear Mum,
  Think brother is getting the best of the sun down there in the south. Northern and central Spain have storms. At least here it is dry, and cool enough to get things done outside.
  The car window is still not fixed. Apparently, the second-hand motor which arrived was faulty! We have, however, asked for a quote for house windows for the Casita from a new company opened in Monterroso. Can't be slower than our previous ones, eh?
  Tuesday: Some sunshine.
  They have given it nice for the rest of the week so the lad may get started on the roof at the Casita. He has ordered the corrugated sheets (uralitas). We have also sweet-talked Geert into driving his van to the tip with some of the junk, which will save a few trips with the old Escort. We have counted five beds altogether and the numbers of bags of clothing is scary! Plus, there are two falling-to-pieces wardrobes and tons of other erm… 'stuff'.
  We are going to get the floorboards for our Big Barn. Decided to buy the ones for the mezzanine floor so we can get that done, and finish the ceiling in there. We will then

JULY 2014

leave the downstairs for now so we can work on our other project where a lady 'jefa' (boss) with a whip is overseeing the work haha.

Here is a drawing of the Casita. S says if I don't show you, your imagination will be on overtime so this is the 'idea' so far!

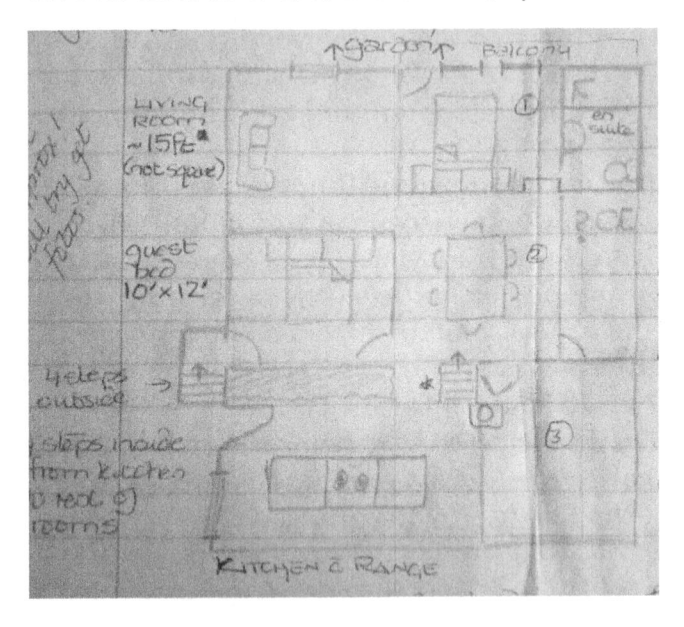

1. Main bed 8ft x12ft plus 'en suite'. Bit small but has a balcony.

2. Central dining room 10ft x12ft plus a long narrow room off, possibly second bathroom-utility.

3. Storeroom-dressing room 10ft square, low ceiling.

Living room 15ft - not square! With good view to the garden and across the fields.

CHESTNUT, CHERRY & KIWI FRUIT SPONGE

Guest bedroom 10ft x12ft with a small balcony and steps outside.
*Kitchen with a range cooker like ours, *4 steps up to rest of the house (see pic).*
Hope you can understand some of this!
Happy birthday! Would send you a key but we don't have one!!
Love you tons and tons
xxxxxxxxxx

We'd planned to buy the wood for the flooring at the *Casita,* and our new mezzanine in the Big Barn, from the place we bought all our previous floorboards. Although Imoltasa had almost caused a disaster by sending the wrong sized boards when we were laying the hallway floor at *A Casa do Campo*, their prices were good and delivery included.

We arrived at the huge warehouse on the outskirts of Lugo to find the place locked and bolted. A helpful passer-by told us they had closed four years previously. Not long, in fact, after we bought our last lot of floorboards from them. We struggled to find any other suitable woodyards selling chestnut flooring nearby. Thankfully Leo came to our rescue, suggesting a woodyard they'd used near Céa.

We set off to Céa early the next morning. The woodyard was a vast place full of planks, beams and everything wood-related. The noise from the giant cutting machines was almost unbearable to my sensitive ears. Everyone was busy whizzing round moving wood from one area to another.

Pedro, when he arrived, was tall and rather good looking. He was full of bonhomie and exuded a love of all things wood-related. He bounced around the place pointing out different woods; pine, red pine, sweet chestnut, imported mahogany, teak... my head was spinning. Then he dragged us up to another vast warehouse of laminated flooring.

The best laminate was the same price as solid wood or as the Spanish call it, *madera madera* (wood wood). The laminate initially appeared to offer a quick and easy way to lay the new flooring at the *Casita*. We were laying over the existing floorboards and could just 'click' it in position. Then Pedro explained that the subfloor has to be completely level and smooth for the 'click-clack' to work. That ended that discussion. Our old floorboards were lumpy, bumpy, and uneven. Anyway, we reasoned, solid wood is much more durable and we know it looks beautiful when finished.

Diary Wednesday 9th July Warm pm, windy
Not a good day to move great sheets of corrugated fibreboard. José turned up this morning with the first lot of uralitas for the Casita. Luckily S had already jemmied the kitchen door open so they stacked them all in there. Another full room!

We couldn't open the kitchen door the conventional way because, as I told Mum, there was no key. Pepe had no idea where it was, and as the bedroom door was unlocked it didn't really matter too much at first. But access to the house at road level was going to be essential so S eventually angle ground (or grinded, I'm never sure) the hinges off and we prised out the solid, and weighty, wooden door. It was quite a magnificent door, albeit painted a hideous blue: a blue which we, and especially Mum, would come to loathe well before the *Casita* was finished.

Diary Monday 14th July Hot
S set off early to collect the floorboards for the mezzanine from the woodyard in Céa. They are

CHESTNUT, CHERRY & KIWI FRUIT SPONGE

narrow boards but good quality and thick as they will not have any subflooring up there.
Lunch: Stirfry with first French beans and carrots, onion and walnuts
Both moved the floorboards into the Big Barn. S counted and collated them all. Took ages!

As a postscript, we actually discovered the key to the kitchen door some five years later. It was hanging innocuously on a nail in the barn behind the house. Of course it was! I love the innocence of a place where an open door doesn't invite squatters, and a key can hang undisturbed for 25 years.

Tuesday 15th July. V v hot and sticky.
Dear Mum,
  I hope you enjoyed your washing and ironing birthday. Strange woman!
  We chose a rather hot day to do our run to the tip. One van full and one car full but that has pretty much cleared the big items of junk now. The guy at the tip even helped unload, and gleefully went off with the huge old TV from the kitchen (I'd forgotten just how bulky, and heavy, they used to be). The kitchen looks much bigger without that and the old gas cooker.
  Geert enjoyed his lunch (swineherd pie with cheese and potato topping). He has been oiling his roof beams with 3-5 coats of linseed oil on each beam. I thought S was a perfectionist until I met Geert.
  Aunty Jan has contacted me asking about photos. I have put an album on Facebook called 'La Casita' so she can show you next

time you visit. The cottage looks better now it's had the junk cleared out, and we've removed the mummified moles from the kitchen. They must've been brought in by the cats. I think that house has been a cat playground for years.

Tomorrow we are off to Monforte to try and get the electric sorted so we have some power. Concha said we can go round behind their barn to cut the ivy off the wall and to access the roof - it is much lower and therefore easier on that side.

Weds: Even hotter and stickier.

A perfect day for Monforte really! We've had a fun day trying to sort out the electrics, with a typically Galician solution. The problem is that as there has not been any electric at the property for so long the meter is obsolete and the wiring needs renewing (unlike ours where the electric was still connected and being paid for when we moved in). Unfortunately, the electricity company, Fenosa, has a long backlog for visits and they say it could take up to three months for us to get an appointment - which is no good as we need power now. The solution? The electrician from the local Fenosa office comes and renews the meter and external wiring and puts temporary sockets inside so S has power. We then buy and fit a fuse box ourselves, which he kindly pointed out he couldn't legally connect to - but would! Then when Fenosa cuts us off,

CHESTNUT, CHERRY & KIWI FRUIT SPONGE

because we are illegal, obviously, he comes back and reconnects us. This carries on until we get to the top of the list and are issued with a CUPS number (don't know what this is... a meter number I think) to make us legal. Simple really. I do love this place!

We had a nice lunch with Mike and John and their helper, in Pantón. We have decided that we are going to join this Workaway thing and try and get some enthusiastic helpers to get the house (and garden) sorted. It seems a good system.

We also visited the big castle keep tower in Monforte. I wanted to look at their staircase as it is how I would like S to make the one for the Big Barn - open with no rail and no boxing in below, so we can still see the wall.

All in all, an interesting and fairly productive day. Back to work tomorrow!

Love you so much. Enjoy your holiday. Hope the sun shines.

xxxxxx

There were so many options for this volunteer thing, I was overwhelmed. There was Help Exchange (HelpEx), Wwoof (originally worldwide opportunities on organic farms, but now apparently just another of life's acronyms), and there was Workaway.

Mike and John's helper was a young American lad who had volunteered with a number of different organisations. He liked the Workaway site best. He said it was clear and easy to use. Mike added that it was also free for hosts, so that clinched the deal. I just had to create a profile for us, add some suitable

JULY 2014

photos, a description of what we expected from workers, and what we offered them, and Bob's your brother (well, S' brother anyway).

Our profile was headed 'Help Renovate a Stone Cottage in Galicia'. We offered three meals a day with plenty of cakes, a comfortable attic bedroom, and trips out when we had time to show people the area, in exchange for four hours work daily. I included some photos of the *Casita*, showing the work to be done. I also took photos of the surrounding area and the Workawayers attic room in the hope of attracting helpers.

Diary Saturday 19th July Wet!
Found all the roof leaks at the Casita then! Spent most of the morning positioning buckets strategically and making good use of the old potties, jugs and other water holding items left behind. S busy laying the new floorboards on the mezzanine. Rather slow going as they are only 7cm wide so three rows are the equivalent to one row of the 20cm wide ones (and four rows would be needed to make the width of our old chestnut boards in the attic room). Still, they look really good and will be solid.

Our attic room was now very different to the one in which Les had slept. In the seven years since he first visited, we had transformed it into a very cosy bedroom.

S had replaced the old barrel stave flooring in the tiny room above our storeroom with rescued 30-centimetre wide, sweet chestnut floorboards from elsewhere in the house. This space we then turned into a bed alcove. The new, slated bed frame which S built fitted perfectly into the space below a skylight window. The original, open doorway to the landing next to the stairs was blocked in with shelving and we fitted an opening window onto the

CHESTNUT, CHERRY & KIWI FRUIT SPONGE

landing. The wall between the newly created alcove and the original small attic room was demolished, leaving an archway through to the bed area. This freed up the main room as a sitting and studying area with an easy chair, desk, wardrobe, and a large wooden box full of novels from my 'library' collection. Above was another skylight which let in much needed sunshine. With the use of our sitting areas also being offered to Workawayers, I felt it was a winner.

Tuesday 22nd July 9.30pm. V v v hot!
Dear Mum,

It does seem odd not texting you - I meant to send one Sunday night but forgot, and of course you had gone by the time I got up on Monday!

Mind you we were well 'bused' this morning - I was asleep and heard beep beep... cheese lady. 'She's early,' said S. No, it was 10 past 10! I was out of the door first but couldn't see what I was buying of course as I didn't have my glasses on. I think buying cheese can be one of your jobs. I'm sure you will be up in time haha. She must have a good laugh at us!

Really must get a new pen, this one doesn't write properly if there is a spot of grease on the paper, and of course I've just moisturised my hands!

It is very hot again now, after some welcome rain at the weekend. I hope it's nice for you on your holiday. The fruit is looking good here. Plums just starting to ripen, have had loads of raspberries and

JULY 2014

gooseberries, and the cherries were loaded this year. The figs are going to be good too, if the blackbirds don't pinch them all first. Picked our first big tomato yesterday. There doesn't seem to be as many as other years, lots of the flowers are dropping off unpollinated - not sure why. My best year for French beans though... a Spanish variety called 'oxinel', very long, straight and crunchy. Yum!

The lad asked for fish and chips for his birthday dinner and I did a big chocolate cake with just one candle - for safety reasons haha!

Found one of the kittens in the hen run last night. No idea how it got in. The girls weren't happy, though I still had a full house of 7 eggs today other than Buffy who is still looking after her four chicks. They are growing well. The boy, Ebony, is very handsome.

Our resident wild cat, Clarence, is fed up with the heat I think. Found him asleep wrapped round a redcurrant bush this morning. He asked what happened to the nice lady with the treats. I usually give him the oil from the tinned mackerel but it was in olive oil this week and he wouldn't touch it. Will have to remember to check next time. Fussy thing!

Looks like we are getting some help with the Casita. Mike and John helped us to sign up for a volunteer programme called

CHESTNUT, CHERRY & KIWI FRUIT SPONGE

Workaway, on the internet. You say what work you want doing, and in exchange for bed and board people come and help from all over the world. We had one request the first day - a Swiss couple who are coming at the end of August. And an Australian guy contacted us today about coming next week! He is a carpenter and has done roofing he says, so that should be useful. The other two are keen to work outdoors and are excited about chopping down brambles! I'm quite looking forward to it. It seems a very efficient way of getting people together and it will be fun to meet new people.

Tell Aunty Jan she can find our profile on www.workaway.info if she wants to.

Weds pm: Just off to Scala. Still v hot.

CJ called round this a.m. He is very impressed with the Casita for the price we paid. I don't understand why Belle can't find the photo album I put on Facebook. Very odd!

Will pop this in the post so you may get two this week!

Love you tons and tons and tons
xxxxxx

As we drove to Monforte the following Tuesday to collect our first ever Workawayer from the train station, we joked that, being Australian, he would be easy to spot by the surfboard he was carrying. Jarrad had sadly left his surfboard with a mate in Portugal, but he did arrive carrying his skateboard and a huge backpack.

JULY 2014

Jarrad was, in every possible way, the perfect first Workawayer. An easy going 26-year-old, he exuded confidence and helpfulness. He was happy to work whatever hours we decided and always started drying the pots after dinner without my having to say a word. Anything I asked was, "no worries".

We were soon to find that Australians and New Zealanders are great Workawayers. Self-sufficient, easy-going, hard-working and any other positive hyphenated word you can think of. Jarrad fitted right in and started work straightaway.

Wednesday 30th July. Very hot.
Dear Mum,

Lying by the outdoor pool at Taboada with our Aussie helper, Jarrad, who deserves some R&R after a busy day.

They have had a productive day stripping part of the roof and putting the uralitas (corrugated sheets) on. It must have been the hottest day we've had so far - S was dripping, though of course our Australian loved the heat. We thought it would be nice to have a relax at the pool so S dropped us off in Taboada and we walked here. Quite a walk in the heat but worth it for a cold dip. S has had to go to his Spanish class as he bunked off yesterday when we went to collect Jarrad. He will meet us in Bar Scala afterwards.

It is 7.30pm now and still very hot. May have to go for another swim in a minute. My English students have all cancelled (3 of them) this week, which I don't mind at all. In theory I have lessons five afternoons a

CHESTNUT, CHERRY & KIWI FRUIT SPONGE

week but I think the sun is too big a lure. One of them cried off ill today and I'm positive I can spy her over on the grass a little way off.

The electrician was supposed to come this morning to connect the Casita but he didn't arrive. I hope he comes tomorrow as the lads need power to cut the uralitas and it's too long an extension run from our house.

I haven't been entirely lazy. I've been sanding down the mezzanine floor ready for varnishing. Think it will look very nice - the boards have some lovely swirls and patterns in them. I've also started jam/ketchup making. Jarrad picked some plums for me this morning before starting on the roof so I have pots of plum jam and bottles of plum ketchup cooling in the storeroom.

Jarrad is here two weeks so they should get a good start on the roof. It makes a big difference having someone who can lift the sheets up to S - I'm hopeless. And it's nice for him to have someone to work with and discuss things.

We all have a few days off over the weekend. It's Monterroso market on Friday, then Davina and her girlfriend arrive on Saturday for a few days.

Our next lot of helpers arrive on the 20th August, then Rob and Keith come in September for a week which will be a nice relax for us. Then it will be our big holiday *in Costa Rica (24*th *November to 7*th *December - please send my birthday cards early haha) and then, we have a very important Christmas visitor. Phew, that's the year gone!*

I have a pressie request. Can you ask in the toy shops in Ashby if they do a walkie-talkie set? Doesn't need to be fancy but would be great for calling the boys for tea. Today I gave S an alarm, set for 2pm, but he didn't hear it so I had to leave dinner boiling over while I went to find him.

Well, don't seem to have much to report, though we have been busy! I wonder where last week's letter got to? I posted it in the box on Weds evening. Will put this one in the box at the post office itself just to be sure. Sorry for the writing - difficult lying down, leaning on my book… such a hard life!

Love you tons and tons and tons

xxxxxx

PS I'm sure someone can find the Facebook pics for you!

The locals were bemused and fascinated in equal measure by our young helper: especially when he skateboarded his way around our tiny market town filming himself on his Go-Pro. We don't have many strangers in Taboada so Jarrad stuck out like a very good-looking sore thumb.

AUGUST 2014
Sleeping Beauty

Diary Friday 1st August Cloudy
Day off. Took Jarrad to the market at Monterroso. 12 for lunch. Mike and John were there with their latest helper who was monosyllabic to the point of muteness. We really did strike lucky with our first timer.

Jarrad's help on the roof had already proved invaluable and the two boys were marching along nicely. He and S had to remove each pantile carefully, scrape it clean of moss and the rather pretty sedum which grows on all the clay tiles around here, then stack the reusable tiles further along the roof before cleaning all the beams below and finally lifting the heavy corrugated '*uralitas*' on to the roof. These then had to be fixed in place and sometimes cut to shape. It all took time and the temperatures on the roof were in the high 30s Celsius. Jarrad deserved his weekend break while our friends were here.

Tuesday 5th August. Very warm.
Dear Mum,
  Well, the girls went home this morning. They said they had a good time. Luisa was very taken with Davina. Big hugs and kisses. They got on well with our helper

AUGUST 2014

Jarrad too, exchanging Facebook details and stuff. Davina's girlfriend is over 6 foot tall so she needed a hard hat for most of our doorways.

It was raining on Saturday when we collected them, though it cleared later. Sunday also started off wet so we decided to go to the hot springs in Ourense. By the time we got to Os Peares (where the three rivers meet) it was hot and sunny. We had a lovely meal there... entrecôte steak, and a huge kitty bag from the kitchen for Clarence.

We met Mike and their almost silent helper at the thermals... a Scottish lad who no one can get two words out of. Not even Jarrad could get him talking.

Yesterday I did 'Sunday' lunch while the girls and Jarrad walked to the market in town (and bought up half the stalls I think). In the afternoon we all went to the outdoor pool for a (very cold) swim.

We dropped the girls off for their flight this morning then the three of us went into Santiago. Lots of pilgrims. We had another good meal at Dezaseis (Number 16). It was 'rabo de toro' (oxtail). Not exactly a summer dish but very tasty. I'm still full.

Wednesday: Got your letter today - that was quick, wasn't it? If you have to change your glasses again when the other cataract is done, do you have to pay each time? Still, it will be worth it. Can't wait to see the new look you (and you will be able to see us haha).

The lads have had a full day on the roof today. We had a laugh the other day - as you can imagine, everyone in the village has been giving us helpful advice about the Casita. Anyway, we were having tea one morning when I heard shouting. Then Concha and Sonia appeared yelling something about the roof. Thinking all sorts of disasters, we ran round there.

"Look," she said. "The uralitas overhang the wall." (This with lots of hand gestures).

"Yes, we have to cut them level," I replied. (The house wall is very wobbly that side so we have to cut them all afterwards to fit the wobbliness. They were sticking out a good metre in places.)

"No, just push them up," she says, demonstrating how to 'push' a half dozen large sheets of fibreboard up the roof.

Then she says; "You need to cut this (ivy), it goes into the roof."

We had noticed and we are going to do so before the next bit of roof goes on. I'm unsure if they think we are really stupid or just plain daft. They probably mean well. And, of course, when we do cut the ivy it will be because they advised us to!

It's our fiesta in Taboada this weekend. We will have to pop in for at least one evening to show Jarrad what he has been missing.

AUGUST 2014

I'm sure he's never seen anything like our 'orchestras'.

Forgot to say, you remember the house next to Bar Scala that Luis owns? (The roof had fallen in if you recall). They have turned it into an outdoor terrace for the bar (no roof). Pointed the walls, concreted the floor and put in a fish pond. It looks really good and just in time for the crowds. Clever lad.

Love you tons and tons. Hope this arrives quicker.

xxxxxxxx

Mum had had cataracts for a while. She'd had her right eye operated on the previous month and was enjoying her improved vision. Last time she'd visited I'd been shocked that on our walk home from the bar, on a clear night with a full moon to light our way, she'd been unable to see the edge of the road.

"But it's so bright with the moon! The road's the dark strip in the middle," I'd joked.

In the end we'd had to walk either side of her to keep her on the straight and narrow. For once we couldn't blame the drink as we weaved back and forth across the road. I hoped next time Mum visited, she'd be able to see the stars with us.

Diary Thursday 7th August Sun and cloud
Ordered more uralitas as the boys have fitted the first load of 24 on the roof. They are really working hard. It's brilliant when you have a good team.
I finished sanding the new floorboards on the mezzanine ready for varnishing.
Lunch: Chickpea stew, Greek salad, pitta breads (homemade). Egg custards with roast plums.
Bathnight but the car battery was flat so we abandoned the idea and walked into town instead.

CHESTNUT, CHERRY & KIWI FRUIT SPONGE

Luis at Bar Scala was experimenting with cocktails. Had a delicious daiquiri which he refused to charge me for.

Our town festival started the following day. For anyone who hasn't seen a Galician '*orchestra*' it really is a fascinating treat.

In most countries, if one wants to see a live band you go to a club or concert hall. Here in Galicia, where amenities tend to be few and far between, the bands come to you. Every town and virtually every miniscule village has a fiesta for its patron saint. And that fiesta will include three basics of Galician life; food, drink, and music.

The fun starts at around 6pm when an articulated truck appears through the streets. This is especially diverting when the fiesta is in one of the tiny narrow-laned villages where manoeuvring can take some time. Once in place, the trailer opens out into a stage. Depending on the venue and the size of the '*orchestra*' as the bands are called, this can be anything from a tiny two metre square platform to a theatre-quality stage with full lighting and laser show.

These travelling shows spend the summer months going from town to town playing to crowds varying from six to six thousand or more. They are the life blood of Galicia.

Tuesday 12th August Dull and un-August like!

Dear Mum,

I think an early night is in order. We are exhausted! NOT from working too hard (though the boys have done a great job on the roof). No, it has been Taboada fiesta this weekend and we thought Jarrad ought to

AUGUST 2014

experience the big bands at least once. We managed to keep going until almost 3am on Saturday with a siesta beforehand, though we all gave up before midnight last night. No staying power... and the band was rubbish - too much talking!

We took Jarrad to the train station this morning. We will miss him; he was so helpful and really no trouble at all. The front of the roof is all covered. S is planning to put some skylights in the back as there are no windows on that side, so that will need thinking about. Jarrad's room was immaculate when he left and he seemed to enjoy any food I put in front of him. We sent him off with cheese butties, half a jar of pickle and half a block of his favourite local cheese.

Don't think the locals quite knew what to make of Jarrad - not too many surfing dude Aussies in Taboada, especially such good looking ones! He will be a difficult act to follow.

Sergio (who 'stole' our other chariot and helped us change the electric bills over) turned up this pm for an impromptu visit. He thought our house was wonderful and that we are 'artists'! Of course we are, haha.

Forgot to say, yesterday evening when we went into town they had folk dancing on in the square. Carmen's daughter and son-in-law were in the Galician dance troop. Very good. There was also a children's Galician

CHESTNUT, CHERRY & KIWI FRUIT SPONGE

dance troop and an excellent Russian Cossack troop.

On Saturday we are having a Celtic festival in town. There are Celtic games apparently, and food of course. Should be fun.

That reminds me, the photos of the Casita should be visible now. I had them on some sort of privacy setting... twit! I will try and add some of the boys on the roof (and of them knocking some of the kitchen wall down... in a good cause, honest!)

Weds am: Some sun so the washing is out and I am hopeful it will dry. I've done the first coat of varnish on the mezzanine in the Big Barn. The floorboards look very nice.

Will post this on the way to lunch at Luisa's. We are meeting Jorge and Kath and showing them the Casita afterwards. You will have to have a ticket system like Buckingham Palace haha.

Love you tons and tons and tons.

xxxxxxxxxx

On the Sunday before Jarrad left us, the lads had decided to have some demolition fun in the kitchen at the *Casita* – knocking out the old open fireplace in the corner. They'd had to abandon the roof, not because of the fickle Galician weather but because of bees. Moving the old tiles had obviously disturbed a honey bee swarm which plagued the boys until they left them to it and moved indoors. Luckily the swarm moved on.

There are many beehives around us and most years one or other of them swarms. One year, a local beekeeper asked if we had a ladder they could borrow as her bees had swarmed, settling on a high tree branch. They needed a longer ladder than the one they had brought to access it. We happily provided the ladder and stood photographing the scene as they carefully sawed off the branch and lowered the bees into a box brought for the occasion. They then gave us a huge jar of honey for our help. I told S they could borrow the ladders every day if they wished!

Diary Friday 15th August, Asunción Hot but breezy S knocked out the rest of the old lareira in the kitchen. It has made a big space in that corner. Seems a bit of an overkill having a wood-burning range cooker and an open fire in the room, not to mention the fire pit upstairs too. Though I guess the latter was used more for chorizo smoking. In fact, I think the whole house was a pork production factory.

I wasn't far out in my assumption. In addition to the two open fires used for smoking *chorizos* and *jamón*, there was a large, concrete-floored room off the outside barn for hanging the pig carcasses. Hanging above the balcony was a further mesh cage for hams and indoors another 'ham' cupboard. An invaluable animal, the pig.

Saturday 16th August 10pm. Hot.
Dear Mum,
 You will be pleased to know that we have had a pleasant lazy day! After tidying up in the kitchen and bedroom at the Casita we put on our 'Celtic' potato sacks and 'Celtic' sandals and went into town. We had a look at the stalls and an excellent hawk demonstration then had a picnic lunch by

CHESTNUT, CHERRY & KIWI FRUIT SPONGE

the outdoor pool. Your brave daughter went for a swim. I only started to get frostbite and earache after four lengths. It has been hot during the day but down to 7°C at night so the pool water hasn't stayed warm. Coward that he is, S stayed on the grass. I think I ought to have gone back in as I've burnt my belly... mad dogs and Englishwomen!

In the afternoon they had team games at the fiesta. We got roped in with another couple to make a team. One game was eating a pear without using your hands. The pear was on a piece of string and I was paired (haha) with another Galego woman. We won easily as Luis had given us instructions beforehand about holding it for the other person using your teeth (and I love pears haha). The youngsters were more bothered about their lips accidently touching to really put the effort in. There was a skipping game (which I'm hopeless at, but S was pretty good). The youngsters won that one! We thought our team had a chance at the tug of war as one chap was a huge bear of a fellow, but Luis' 'professional' team beat us. Think they had been training - plus we had slippery 'Celtic' sandals on and they had very un-Celtic trainers.

S did a turn around the market square on some stilts. He was very impressive as everyone else was falling off (I didn't even attempt it as I can't stay upright on solid ground) and he did some rather professional juggling too. Clever hubby!

Back in later to listen to the bands.

Glad you saw the photos I put on Facebook at last. The little painted pot is a wooden salt pot. It was hanging on the wall near the old cocina. Unfortunately, the design is painted on and I think it will come off if I attempt to clean it.

Tuesday: Very hot, and lots of flies outside while I was watering - they buzz around the hosepipe. The tomatoes are starting to ripen in bulk now for sauce making so I'm busy again. Our new helpers arrive tomorrow so we may make some jam (they asked if they could learn how), as well as clearing the brambles from the Casita garden. S has managed to get the alpendre door open and make a slight gap to squeeze through, so they can at least see what there is to tackle. Hope they don't turn and run haha.

We are all off to Leo and Margaret's on Friday. They are doing a BBQ and have invited Jorge and Kath, and Mike and John and their helper too.

I was looking up thyroid problems and see watercress is a good source of iodine - so eat more of that. I also made a lovely cake today which uses sunflower oil instead of butter, and honey... thought of you so here's the recipe...

4 eggs, 4oz sugar and 1½oz brown sugar whisked together until pale.

CHESTNUT, CHERRY & KIWI FRUIT SPONGE

4oz honey and 4floz sunflower oil, mixed and added to the egg mixture along with the grated zest of a lemon, 10oz plain flour, 1½ tsp baking powder, 1tsp bicarb, 1tsp mixed spice and a pinch of salt.

I added a layer of caramelised pears cooked in honey and poured the remainder of the honey syrup over the cake after it had cooled. Yum!

Bake at 160-170°C for 30-40 minutes in a 9" round cake tin. Loose bottomed one best.
Let me know if you like it
Love you tons and tons and tons
XXXXXXXXXX

Our new helpers, Tara and Rupert, arrived on the bus from Santiago airport to Palas de Rei on the Wednesday afternoon. I spotted Tara first, a stunningly attractive dark-skinned girl of my height, and so slender I thought she would not be able to clear a twig. Rupert was tall and blond, and looked perfectly capable of hacking the brambles to pieces single-handedly. They both wore big smiles and seemed excited to be working as bramble clearers.

The following morning, they set about clearing the ridiculously over-grown garden with a passion. Why I worried about Tara being too slender to help I have no idea. She got stuck in like a whirlwind. They both slashed and chopped and pulled all day.

The garden at *A Casita* had last seen daylight some 20 years earlier. The brambles began just beyond the set of outside steps to the bedroom, virtually obscuring the barn door below, and were part of the reason we had thought the house was small. They continued as far as next door's walled vegetable garden. The entrance to that *finca* had been kept clear but the rest was a bramble jungle.

AUGUST 2014

The brambles had taken over a good two metres width of the track alongside the house and the entire garden was one huge bramble patch from ground level to upper floor roof level. There were brambles through the roof tiles and through the upper storey living-room-to-be window (conveniently left open). Where there weren't brambles there was ivy and grapevines. The only bare patch was inside the large slat-fronted barn or *alpendre*.

The huge three-metre-high doors to that barn were welded closed with more brambles. The only access to the *alpendre* at that time was from the upstairs back room, down some interestingly dangerous stairs which hid obstacles such as moving treads and man-trap holes. It was from here that S had managed to hack away enough brambles to tug open the door and provide a small, man and woman sized, hole into the garden.

The garden below the brambles and vines was dark and cool. It looked like a fantasy world waiting for a prince to liberate Sleeping Beauty after the 100 years had passed.

By midday our two helpers were sweltering as the suntrap garden saw daylight for the first time in years. Without the overhead canopy of brambles to protect them, the sun shone down mercilessly.

Tara remained cool, zipped up in her borrowed blue overalls – preferring the relative protection of the material against the angry bramble thorns. Rupert had succumbed to the heat and was working bare-chested until I peered out of the newly cleared living room window upstairs to take a photograph. He was quickly apologetic for taking his shirt off and asked politely if I minded. I assured him I minded not a jot what he took off.

By the end of their first full day bramble clearing, half of the garden was visible, together with a brick-built chicken coop and a dog kennel.

CHESTNUT, CHERRY & KIWI FRUIT SPONGE

Diary Friday 22nd August Cool in Melide
Our helpers really deserved their day off today. Set off early for Leo and Margaret's house so we could stop off at A Fervenza with its spectacular waterfall. The tiny house sitting below the falls, which we viewed back in 2006 on one of our first house hunting forays, looks to have been bought. Someone has tidied the frontage up with big signs saying 'no entry'. Tara and Rupert enjoyed wandering about inside and we showed them the huge grinding wheels below the 'living room' floor. I think it would make a wonderful honeymoon cottage. Except for all the tourists wandering about and ignoring the no entry signs of course...

Tuesday 26th August 9pm. Wet!
Dear Mum,

We have been to Lugo today... a nice soggy day for it! Better than roofing in the rain though! We ate at the little man's café, Recatelo, and I told his wife about the house. She was very pleased you will be moving here permanently.

We have had a busy week. Tara and Rupert, our new helpers, have done a sterling job clearing all the brambles. Even Concha was impressed! You now have a lovely courtyard garden, about 5 yards by 4 yards, and a very fine view from the living room window. I've put some more photos on Facebook for you.

We've had enquiries from more helpers wanting to come in October so everything is going to plan, so far.

I've painted the walls in our Big Barn a

AUGUST 2014

lovely pale yellow colour, and S has promised to relocate the remaining plasterboard elsewhere (not yet sure where) so I can finally move my storeroom around how I want it without tripping over the things.

I am now busy bottling tomatoes and we picked lots of blackberries from number three before they got chopped up with the brambles. There may be some pots of 'Casita bramble jelly' this year.

We had a lovely meal at Leo and Margaret's on Friday. She had over-catered as usual and the weather was dreadful! They are high up and the wind was blowing ferociously. Leo had bought bags of ice cubes for the drinks but of course no one wanted them. But Leo said we had to as he couldn't take the ice back.

Weds eve: Hot. Just off to Taboada for a well-earned drink.

S and Rupert have stripped the next bit of roof and Tara (with hardly any help from me) has barrowed a huge pile of bramble clippings to the dead hedge on the allotment. Carmen came round to see what they had been doing (Tara speaks Spanish so had been chatting to the neighbours). She was very impressed and said it was a long time since she had seen the garden clear. Judging by the height and spread of brambles I can well believe it!

I had a phone call from the bank today.

CHESTNUT, CHERRY & KIWI FRUIT SPONGE

They have 'investigated' my complaint and were very (but not sufficiently) apologetic. They are crediting me with £75 for distress and £180! for the 3 hours of phone calls I made. I said that was very nice but instead of having to waste customers' money paying compensation they should get it right first time. (Still accepted the compensation mind!)

Thursday: Thank you for the anniversary card and copper penny! We had a good laugh and are very happy, whatever year it is supposed to be.

Love you lots and lots and lots
xxxxxxxxx

Thursday the 28th of August was our fourth wedding anniversary. Four years since we had managed to beat Spanish bureaucracy and get wed in Galicia. According to Mum that made it our copper anniversary. Mum's copper coin was the source of much amusement, and we celebrated by looking where we could fit some badly-needed windows in the *Casita* roof.

By the middle of the week the garden was completely cleared of brambles. Our amazing helpers were covered in scratches and must have been dehydrated, as it was the hottest week we'd had that poor and odd summer.

As one walked down the small lane past the *Casita*, beyond the steps to the bedroom, there were now two newly exposed, blue-painted, wooden barn doors leading to two large rooms underneath the house. Beyond that, at the end of the house wall, was a rusty, but perfectly serviceable, double, metal fretwork gate. This opened into a small but manageable courtyard of around 20 square metres.

AUGUST 2014

The garden gates had been lost in the undergrowth for so long that our neighbours didn't remember they were there.

To the right, as you entered the garden, was the back wall of the house with a rather worrying crack down it. That needed looking at. At the first-floor level, I could now see the living room window. Cleared of brambles, this looked out over the garden and fields as far as the little *rio* which meandered its way towards the river Miño.

To the left, was a high stone wall separating the garden from next door's allotment. Atop the wall were four stone pillars, once used for training grapevines across the track. It was a lovely sunny spot and I could imagine Mum's tomato plants growing against that wall. Beyond was an overgrown bay tree blocking what was, in effect, access to the field below. We had been told when we bought the house that we couldn't register this garden. As that access obviously hadn't been used in over 20 years, we weren't unduly worried. How very Spanish we have become in our thinking over the years.

Alongside the 'access path' was an incredibly ugly, brick and concrete built *hórreo,* or grain store, sitting high above the garden. We pondered what to do with this monstrosity for many months. Suggestions included a greenhouse for the tomatoes, a reading room, and my personal favourite, a glassed-in bath house using CJ's miniature bath tub from the garden. Unsurprisingly none of those things happened and the grain store still sits there only partially obscuring the view – mainly because it would be too difficult to remove.

There were a set of steps up to the *hórreo,* and next to these the two brick-built animal pens. I was already formulating an idea for that bit.

Tara and Rupert were leaving us on the Saturday which meant we had time for one more 'hot' job before they went.

CHESTNUT, CHERRY & KIWI FRUIT SPONGE

Not long after attending our wedding in 2010, our German friends, Barbara and Martin, had been kind enough to offer us their old polytunnel. They were getting some super-duper new ones for their plant nursery. It was a homemade affair of poly-piping held together with various joints. A bit Heath Robinson maybe, but it worked wonderfully. I could start off my vegetables much earlier in the tunnel than outside. I had peapods ready by March and potatoes in April. My peppers and melons loved it and we had rigged up a leaky hose to the two beds to provide irrigation.

That first year we had somehow manhandled the poly-piping home in our old Ford Escort after carefully labelling all the parts as we took it to pieces with the help of Barbara and Martin. Rebuilding the thing hadn't been as easy as we'd imagined and it had taken S and I some time to find which part went where despite our labelling. We'd dug out the beds and lined them with plastic to prevent water loss, I'd edged the beds with water-filled plastic bottles as part of my 'reuse' campaign and we'd dug in a goodly amount of our own compost. We'd bought new plastic sheeting for the polytunnel and managed to fit it ourselves on a rather too windy day.

The only problem was that the plastic covering only lasted around three years. The previous year it had ripped spectacularly in a winter storm and though we'd stuck it together with special sticky tape, it needed renewing. The plastic works best if fitted in summer. The heat makes the sheeting more flexible ensuring a good taut fit. The original cover had been put up, out of necessity, in November so was never quite the fit it should have been.

We'd bought the new 10 by 8 metre replacement sheet of plastic in Lugo the previous week but fitting it was far easier with four people.

AUGUST 2014

That Friday was one of the hottest days we'd had. We all dug out the old plastic sheeting and put it to one side for reuse. (We can always find a use for leftovers). To fit the new plastic, we needed to lift the leading edge over the front of the tunnel and slide it along, unravelling it as we went. Rupert's height really helped as Tara and I could barely reach the polytunnel roof almost a metre above our heads. The temperature inside the plastic bubble we had created rose steadily until my thermometer read 50 degrees Celsius. At that point the thermometer broke so I can't say if it rose higher still. I can say with certainty that we deserved our cool swim, ice creams and cold drinks that evening after our early 'sauna'.

We also had another job ticked off.

SEPTEMBER 2014
The ironing room

Tara and Rupert had been magnificent, and such good sports. We were, once more, sorry to see our Workawayers leave. Our next helper, a French girl, wasn't due until mid-October. We had more friends arriving for a visit on the 6th of September, but for the moment we were alone.

Monday 1st September. V V V hot!
Dear Mum,
  They have given it 37°C this week. Not even a breeze up on the roof today. We didn't go up there until 6pm and it was still too hot. I have been tiling part of the front section and S was mortaring next door's adjoining wall to stop the rain filtering down into the Casita.
  Glad you are feeling a bit better, though I'm not sure loads of washing is quite what the doctor ordered. S says the sooner you get over here and we can find you other things to keep you occupied the better.
  Now Rupert and Tara have cleared the garden at the Casita we can think about how best to use the space. When you come

out at Christmas, we can plan it out and look at what plants you want.

Tuesday: even hotter I think. S had to find a non-roof job this pm. It was far too hot up there so he has finally managed to rehome the extra sheets of plasterboard from my storeroom. Now I can re-organise and make it into my special space. I shall turn the table around so I can work at it.

Wednesday: Cloudy but hot. We have a plague of tiny flies. Horrid when you are watering the allotment as they go in your eyes and up your nose. Ugh!

At least it's better weather for roofing today. S is busy fitting a skylight window in the smoke room. I did a bit more mortaring on the back wall of the Casita, with much well-meaning advice from your neighbour… not that I understood most of it of course. I'm sure you two are going to get on swimmingly.

Billie Jean has two lovely chicks (at last!). She insists on running to the far end of the pen each time I visit, so I haven't seen them close up yet. The others (Buff Puff's) are growing, especially the boy, Ebony. May have to be chicken for Christmas dinner.

Forgot to say Carmen's cat has had kittens too, five at least so that's around 20 cats in the village now. And most are Clarence's… they are all cross-eyed anyway!

We have got our 'cheap pensioner holiday' accreditation through. Since S officially

CHESTNUT, CHERRY & KIWI FRUIT SPONGE

became a Jubilado (pensioner) this year we can go on the Spanish OAP holidays. (Don't you love the Spanish word?) Not sure we will be able to find time mind what with helpers, and houses to finish, and BIG birthday holidays, and IMPORTANT visitors coming!!
Love you tons and tons
xxxxxx

The accreditation for our cheap pensioner holiday had been organised for us by our friend Leo. In Spain the government provides subsidised holidays for those over retirement age or with a disability, through an organisation called imserso (*instituto de mayores y servicios sociales*). Various travel agencies tender for the contract each year but the cost to participants remains low at around 250€ for a week's full board and transportation from their home city. And best of all, for me, each participant can take a 'carer'.

Diary Thursday 4th September Cloudy
Made cakes, cookies, and lunch. S continued roofing the back of the Casita and fitting the second of the new skylights. This one in the 'ironing room'.
Lunch: Bean non-chilli sin carne. Couscous and salad. Yoghurt topping.
Had a look at the crack under the living room window of the Casita. It's thankfully not structural but just where the old mortar has come out. Decided to knock off the cement render around it and mortar that piece next anyway.
Saw Billie Jean's babies at last. So cute, and mummy hen looks rather proud.

Billie Jean was the daughter of our cockerel, Buzz Lightyear, and one of our black hens. Sarah, our original broody hen, a tiny Wyandotte, was now enjoying retirement from the mother hen life having decided to pass the baton onto the younger generation.

Billie Jean and her brood-sister Buff Puff (a product of Buzz and a Buff Orpington we inherited from our friend Anne when she moved away) were our new generation broodies. Unfortunately, Buff Puff's mother, Betty Boo, was a spoilt madam who had refused to join the pecking order anywhere but at the top. No matter how we tried we could not get the flock to accept her and, in the end, she went to one of our friends. Before she left us, though, we did get two fluffy, half Buff Orpington chicks from her.

We tried to raise two or three new hens each year to replace older ones which had stopped laying or died. The cockerels we found new homes, or ate for dinner. Our new broodies were not quite in Sarah's league, but tried hard. Billie Jean had sat for five weeks earlier in the season, failing to hatch any eggs. When she went broody again, we got some fertile eggs from our neighbour's hens and let her sit. This time we were lucky as she hatched two sweet fluffy white chicks called Ester and Eliot.

Diary Saturday 6th September Drizzle
Up rather earlier than normal at 7.15am so we could collect Rob and Keith from Santiago airport. Great to see them after so long.

Rob had been a social worker in the same office as me when I worked as a community occupational therapist some 15 years earlier. We hadn't seen each other for a good many years, although we had kept in touch. We spent a lovely day showing the men around Santiago in the drizzle whilst trying (and failing) to find a recommended vegetarian, Lebanese restaurant there. After wandering in and out of so many alleyways my eyes were crossed, we gave up

CHESTNUT, CHERRY & KIWI FRUIT SPONGE

and sat in a pleasant café. The owner welcomed us warmly, and was more than happy to accommodate my vegetarian friend with a selection of *raciones* (or plates to share).

Tuesday 9ᵗʰ September. Sunny and hot pm.
Dear Mum,
  We were all at Ourense yesterday. It was hot in the morning, but by the time we went in the thermal pools in the evening it was raining. Perfect weather for it.
  We ate at that restaurant we went to with you last time. They were very good with our veggie requests for Rob, but we had to pay for his wine as it wasn't a 'menu of the day' (unlike our carnivorous meal).
  We had a fun journey on the little road train at Ourense. We had stopped in Os Peares for coffee on the way and were running a little late again. The train was already in the 'station' at the thermals as we crossed the bridge. We managed to catch it after a bit of jogging. It set off but came to a halt just down the road as the police had cordoned off the track. We waited ages but as it's too far to walk into the city centre we had no choice. Turns out someone had collapsed on the track, hence the police.
  This morning S discovered that the man had delivered your firewood while we were out (it was dark when we got home so we didn't spot it). Luckily, he had at least dropped it at the right house, though he

had promised to ring beforehand and of course hadn't! Why should I be surprised?

Rob helped us barrow the lot into the barn underneath the house today so we have wood for when we get the cocina going. We thought it best to order it early so it's nice and dry for winter.

The boys seem to be enjoying themselves. They love the area and the food. Keith is practising his Spanish (he used to teach French and Spanish) and Rob is managing to relax and do some writing.

We are going to try Lugo tomorrow (now all your firewood is under cover). Concha said the wood man asked her which house was number three but she didn't know!!! There is only a choice of six houses in the village, and they own one of them! We will try the posh restaurant near the swimming baths in Lugo. They seem to have a varied kitchen.

The Chinese buffet place in Ourense was sadly still closed. But as I say, we had a good meal anyway and a nice soak afterwards. Clarence was sad as we didn't bring him any supper (we had some fish heads left but thought they might have started smelling a bit by evening.)

We are also out to lunch on Saturday, after we drop Rob and Keith off. The couple we bought the Casita from have invited us to a party. If it's late, I'll ring you on Sunday.

CHESTNUT, CHERRY & KIWI FRUIT SPONGE

Just off into Taboada for a drink so will post this in town.
Love you tons and tons and tons
xxxxxxxx

Clarence was our adopted (as in, he adopted us) feral tomcat. He was the scourge of the village and had quite a reputation to live up to. He adored leftovers from our many varied meals out and had made himself quite at home since he appeared two years earlier.

It had taken us eighteen months of regularly putting down food before he began to trust us. One day we were eating our lunch *al fresco* in the outdoor eating area when Clarence appeared. He walked straight over to S and rubbed around his legs, silently. Shocked, we leant over and stroked his thick fur. Still no sound but he seemed to enjoy it and from that day on, Clarence was a fixture at *A Casa do Campo* - unless he had other engagements of course.

Diary Friday 12th September
I spent the morning baking. S spent the morning removing the ivy from the Casita walls. Concha will be pleased he has taken her advice at last!
Lunch: Trout, cauliflower cake (which I made as an experiment for Rob and was surprisingly delicious). Mixed stirfry veg. Chocolate truffle cake with quince ice cream.
Electric off at the Casita. S reported someone sneaking away in a van.
Rang the electricity place in Monforte. They said not to worry and dispatched a friendly young man called David who had it back on in no time. He told us to call him next time Fenosa cut us off!

SEPTEMBER 2014

This bizarre way around Spanish bureaucracy and red tape tickled me no end. As predicted, Fenosa, the electricity company, would come and cut off the electric on a regular basis as we did not yet have our CUPS number so were not legal. On an equally regular basis, David would come along and reconnect us. He never charged us for this 'service' and eventually we received our CUPS number and could use the electric legally. I love Spain.

Tuesday 16th September. Rather April showery in autumn!
Dear Mum,

Well, it was lovely seeing Rob and Keith again. They were very generous and helped with the work. Keith insisted on doing all the washing up too, so he can definitely come again!

They said how much they enjoyed it. They did seem to spend an awful lot of time in the bathroom, though. They wanted to go to the airport early for their flight home but we refused to leave before 8am. Rob was pleased he had managed to have a shower and a shave in the hour before leaving!

Good job we didn't leave too early anyway as their flight was delayed over two hours so it would have been a really long wait. We abandoned them at the airport, clutching a meal voucher from the airline, and did some shopping at the retail park nearby. S bought some holiday stuff (sandals and trunks) with his birthday money so he is all set for November.

We then drove back to Palas for the meal

CHESTNUT, CHERRY & KIWI FRUIT SPONGE

with Mercedes and Pepe. It was very swish. They hadn't told us it was their 50th Wedding Anniversary! Luckily, we had bought a big box of chocolates for them so didn't feel too bad. When we arrived, only slightly late, there was a huge room full of guests waiting, I did feel embarrassed.

We kept the menu for you to see.

After dinner, the family had created a slide show including a photo of the happy couple sitting on the steps of the Casita which was lovely to see.

I've invited Pepe and Mercedes over for lunch after Christmas and to meet you of course. All the family seemed happy we had bought the house and I made them laugh by saying we only needed one more to own half the village.

We have a young French Workawayer coming mid-October and had a request today from a chap for early October so we progress!

Wednesday: More 'April' storms. Hope your weather is better than this on your holiday. I spent most of the day hanging washing out and bringing it in again. Gave up in the end!

Just had a message from CJ. He had his op yesterday. Will give him your love and the exercise instructions.

Love you tons and tons.

Sorry for the writing, I blame the pen

xxxxxxxxx

SEPTEMBER 2014

There was so much food at Pepe and Mercedes' anniversary meal that it made our wedding meal seem light. There were tuna pies (*empanadas*), *croquetas* with cod filling, squid, octopus, and stuffed peppers (with seafood) to start. Then a seafood salad, which I love, and clams in a sauce. Finally, great platters of goat, roasted in the oven came round. Dessert was a layer slice called *milhojas* (one thousand leaves) and chocolate ice creams. The waiters kept walking around the tables offering seconds, thirds and fourths of each course and there were lots and lots of wines, champagnes and liqueurs on the tables. We sat next to our friend Pepe (whose family owned *A Casa do Campo*) who kept trying to top my glass up.

I was distressed there was so much food going back to the kitchens, and bottles of wine with only a glass out (including a very nice albariño I suggested S slip under his jacket when we left - he didn't). Someone asked if I wanted cava and of course I said yes, but no one else had any so the whole bottle was opened for my one glass. It did seem an awful waste. I hoped it wasn't all thrown away and that the kitchen staff had a good party afterwards.

Diary Wednesday 17th September Storms
Decided to put the washing on (despite the weather) then bottled apples, made courgette soup and courgette cake. When will I learn to plant less of the things?
S was over at the Casita cutting a light well in the middle room (dining room) for the next skylight. It's looking so much brighter in there already.
I spent the afternoon clearing out the 'ironing room'.

Windows were an issue for us at the *Casita*. At the back, the house overlooked our neighbour's yard so there were no windows that side. To the west, it was

CHESTNUT, CHERRY & KIWI FRUIT SPONGE

attached to another small house. To the north, there were the two 'front' doors, both with glass in, and a small window in the kitchen. Eastwards, there was the living room window overlooking the garden, and ancient, broken sash windows in the second bedroom, opening into the *alpendre* or open-sided barn. This all meant the house was dimmer than we would like. S, who had installed a number of skylight windows at our house, decided to do likewise at the *Casita*.

Our roof windows in the attic bedroom and in the Big Barn let in plenty of light, and make the spaces feel more airy than before. In the end, the *Casita* would have no less than six skylight windows, bringing in both the sunshine and the daylight. S had started to fit a skylight in the dining room, having already fitted one in the old smoke room and one in the 'ironing room'.

The ironing room, as we dubbed it, was the oddest of the odd rooms at the *Casita*. Running the length of the dining room on the south side, it was just one and a half metres wide but almost four metres long and built into the slope of the roof so one long side was over two metres high whilst the other was barely a metre and a quarter.

When we bought the *Casita*, this room had been dark and squalid with a collapsed floor, sodden, mouldy roof beams, and ivy thrusting through the unfinished walls. Peering into the gloom we'd spotted a couple of decent looking wooden tables at the far end, canted at an impossible angle. Carefully picking our way over to them across strange looking floorboards, we found out the reason for the odd angle – they had both fallen half way through the rotten floorboards and were lodged, stuck fast. Luckily the fall had saved the tables from severe water damage as most of the rain coming through that sodden roof had simply poured off into the barn below. A mixture of pushing and pulling, twisting and brute strength (from S) ensured we got our treasures out. One is two metres long and a heavy-duty dining table. The second we cut down to make a lovely outside coffee table in the *alpendre* seating area.

Nearer to the doorway, we spied a slit in the wall at ankle height. Peering through the thatch of ivy showed the aperture to be at head height outside and probably one of the cats' entry routes into the abandoned house. Just 30 centimetres high by 15 centimetres wide, the slit was the perfect place for a couple of glass bricks. The 70-centimetre-deep recess is now plastered and has a marble shelf along the sill, made from a piece of our old kitchen worktop.

Along the left-hand wall of the ironing room were what looked like bowls of mouldering foodstuffs. Once I got the bowls into the light, I found they contained old dried beans for planting, now somewhat beyond their best. The bowls themselves were my top find of the house. The brown, shallow clay dishes and larger, deep, black casseroles are a traditional Galician pottery made in Gundívos near Sober. Much of it is known as black pottery due to the firing process which leaves the surface of the pots blackened from oxidation. They are sought after and beautiful, and a bit of Galician history. They now sit on my display platform next to the attic room here at *A Casa do Campo*.

The odd floorboards we inched our way across in the ironing room were barrel staves. As in our house, these curved wooden lengths of wood had been called into service as a makeshift floor. And, as at *A Casa do Campo*, they weren't exactly secure.

Directly in front of the doorway was my favourite part of this room and the reason for its nickname. An ancient, woodworm riddled, folding ironing board sat propped against the wall. Next to it was an equally ancient electrical socket sitting proud of the

CHESTNUT, CHERRY & KIWI FRUIT SPONGE

wall with twisted wires trailing from it, and next to that, sharing a wooden backboard, was a water tap.

Handy for dampening the linen but not exactly health and safety conscious.

Outside, being used as a door prop and sadly rusted beyond rescue, we found the original old iron. A huge heavy metal thing made of iron (hence the name); it would have been filled with burning coals from the fire before being used to press the washing. Life was so much harder in those days - though since I never iron a thing, I guess it wouldn't have affected me much.

Friday 19th September Still wet
What a soggy week! S dispatched the last two rabbits. We both cleaned and prepared the carcasses. Off to Carballiño to the swimming pool as we still have 6 goes left on our 'abono' ticket from spring. Arrived at 12pm to find it closed! Back to Chantada. Arrived at the pool at 12.30pm for a super quick swim and shower as it closes at 1pm and we needed to be back on the road for our fiesta tonight.
Excellent show from Panorama. This year's show is dubbed the 'space tour', complete with acrobats in revolving spheres hanging from way above the stage. Brilliant.

Panorama were our favourite of the big bands or *orchestras* which toured Galicia in the summer months. Ever since we had seen them in Taboada in 2009, we had followed the band around. Each year was a different show and each year was spectacular.

Tuesday 23rd September. No rain!
Dear Mum,
I even managed to dry some washing at last! I think this is by far the worst summer

since we arrived and of course it would be when we have a roof to strip! Poor lad takes a bit off then has to cover it up again.

Thankfully, they have given it better next week. We have another Australian lad coming on Tuesday. Hope he is as good as Jarrad was. Then our French girl for a fortnight. All go, isn't it?

Just spent 15 minutes looking for a pen. Could only find red ones... S said it could be a red-letter day, haha, groan.

Forgot to say we found a great museum in Lugo when we went with Rob and Keith. It was near the cathedral and is an excavation of a Roman manor house with lots of artefacts and a good interactive display and - we found out when Rob pushed a hidden button - an English version information film! It was so funny as a Spanish group were happily listening to the commentary when Rob inadvertently swapped it to English. He said the button had a union flag on it and he wondered what it did! Will take you if you promise not to pilfer any Roman stones.

See, still lots to discover in Galicia.

Wednesday pm: Sunshine!

Sitting on the terrace. Clarence says hello... at least he's rubbing round my legs trying to miaow so it's that or he's hungry (again)! Bought some different dried biscuits for him this time and he can't get enough of them!

CHESTNUT, CHERRY & KIWI FRUIT SPONGE

The chickens are enjoying themselves - I can hear the blackbird pecking the grapes off the vines and of course the hens (oh, give up... I'll use a pencil) get the ones that drop off. There was a kerfuffle earlier - a sparrowhawk had got stuck in the pen and was flapping madly. The chickens didn't like that so much. We think he had chased a sparrow inside and got stuck in the fencing. We let it out unharmed.

All the rain has finished off my tomatoes early this year. They have late blight. 24 jars of sauce, less than last year, and only two jars of sun-dried ones. Good job I have some left but there won't be any fresh ones for my birthday this year. Oh, I won't be here so it doesn't matter haha! There are some advantages to being 50! And the storeroom is still full of produce.

S has just finished cementing next door's adjoining wall so it doesn't rain down and into the Casita kitchen. Quite tricky as it's much higher than the Casita and difficult to prop the ladders up on our sloping roof. I did tell him to be careful for you! And we have three skylight windows in place now, so progress.

Clarence is now trying to climb onto my knee. Carmen was shouting at him yesterday because he was fighting. She said he was killing the young one. Daft woman. Clarence tells me he was just teaching the youngster a lesson.

SEPTEMBER 2014

Think we will venture into Taboada for a beverage tonight. I have another fun job tomorrow.

Love you tons and tons and tons, wish you were here too.

xxxxxxxxxxxx

One of the other things I wanted to do was to find the septic tank for the house. Pepe, the ex-owner, assured me there was one. Given the size of the outside space, the only possible place it could be was inside the large *alpendre* or open-sided barn. Jarrad and I had spent a fun afternoon going through the teetering pile of junk in one corner looking for the tank. We had found many interesting items – including a mattress, lengths of wood, bed springs, pottery shards, and a long dead cat, but no septic tank.

I spent another drizzly morning that last week in September looking for the tank but we came to the inevitable conclusion that there wasn't one. Instead, we assumed that, like our house before, the pipe which protruded from the *alpendre* wall into our neighbour's tall, healthy fruit trees had once served a higher purpose and we would have to fit our own tank.

At least we had another Workawayer due, and now we had a hole for him to dig.

Gabriel arrived by bus on the final day of September. We were already waiting in Palas when the coach arrived, but no one got off. Eventually there was movement inside. Our new Workawayer clambered awkwardly off the coach, dragging his fleece and his bulging, unzipped rucksack, hair tangled and mussed. Items were spilling out of the top of the rucksack onto the pavement as he pulled it down the steps.

CHESTNUT, CHERRY & KIWI FRUIT SPONGE

Gabriel crouched by the side of the bus, organising his luggage whilst explaining he had been asleep and the driver had not warned him of the stop as he had asked.

Then he stood up.

OCTOBER 2014
Digging to Australia

Gabriel was six foot five inches tall or just shy of two metres. From my vantage point of five foot two he seemed enormous. He quickly stuffed his possessions into his bulging bag and loped behind us to the car.

I started our conversation, as I tend to, by talking food.

"You said you don't eat meat, so I thought I'd do fish for lunch," I said.

"Oh no! I don't eat any flesh," came the horrified reply.

"Ah. You only stated you didn't eat meat in your email, is there anything else you don't eat?" I asked.

"Um, milk and cheese."

"Oh! So, are you vegan?"

I have to say here that I have no problem whatsoever with vegetarians, vegans, dairy, gluten, or anything else free, visitors – so long as I know in advance. I do find it the height of rudeness not to mention any special diet before arriving. Maybe that's just me though.

"I'm not vegan, I just don't eat meat," Gabriel replied.

"Or fish, or dairy…"

"Fish is meat."

I was getting pedantic now but I couldn't help myself. "Strictly speaking, no it isn't. Meat is the flesh of a mammal or a bird. Fish is fish. And dairy

CHESTNUT, CHERRY & KIWI FRUIT SPONGE

is any milk product produced from a mammal's mammary glands but isn't meat either. What about eggs?"

"Oh, I didn't know that. No, I don't eat eggs either."

"So, you are vegan then?"

"Am I?"

It turned out that Gabriel had only just become a non-flesh eater, which partly accounted for the confusion. From what I gathered, he had overindulged some time previously and decided to cleanse his body by abstaining from all animal products and from alcohol. A vegan plus then! Luckily, as readers may know, I was vegan myself for five years so cooking for our new friend was not a problem.

Wednesday 1ˢᵗ October. Hot and sunny.
Dear Mum,

We have our new helper. Gabriel is 6'5" tall, an ex-rugby player... and vegan. Probably unique in that respect.

Luisa was very taken with him last night when we went out for a drink (he is teetotal too... did I mention that?). She made him a lovely tortilla today (no, not exactly vegan but it was the best she could do and he enjoyed it!). She then insisted on having her photo taken with him. You can imagine the height difference.

Poor lad is getting used to ducking under every doorway in the place (and some ceilings). I told brother we won't need his special machine for plasterboarding ceilings after all as Gabriel will be able to reach.

OCTOBER 2014

Brother had been in touch to say they are struggling to manage to come over half term as flights have doubled in price (I did suggest booking early). And they forgot about the dog!! I suggested if they are busy, they may be better coming in spring.

The window man came today. He says they have the kitchen window, kitchen door and bedroom stable-door ready. We've ordered a window for the living room too. They are the same as ours, walnut colour uPVC, but with shutters so you can close the 'curtains'. It means the house might even have some keys by Christmas, haha.

Oh, Leo has booked our Spanish pensioner holiday. We all go to Benidorm in March. He had difficulty getting us all on a holiday together as they live in a different province and the travel dates tend to be different. Very odd. Anyway, the agent managed to get this one for the same week, but we are in different hotels.

It should be fun and we can get a job translating for the Spanish: Pepe said when he went to Benidorm the menus were all in English!

Guess we had better get a move on with our project and get our new helper working. Can't promise windowsills for your knick knacks but S says he can make shelves a plenty.

Love you tons and tons.

Xxxxxxxxx

CHESTNUT, CHERRY & KIWI FRUIT SPONGE

Luckily, Gabriel's visit improved after our first encounter. He was a helpful lad, if a little awkward - his height and breadth made him appear to dominate any room. But he worked hard and seemed to enjoy our meals.

Diary Friday 3rd October Hot
S took Gabriel on to the roof to help carry and fix the uralitas. S says he is willing and eager but not as graceful as our previous helpers. I think he's worried the lad might fall through the exposed bits. Postman arrived with a letter needing a signature. It was a letter from the tax office. Apparently, we should have registered the Casita with the hacienda within 30 days. Went up to the registro in Chantada but they couldn't help so we need to go into Lugo. Don't recall having to do that for ours!
Lunch: Paella with chickpeas and peppers. Apple charlotte.
S fiddled on the roof trying to straighten out the rather obvious dip in it. I continued barrowing soil from the alpendre to the allotment. Nice, well-rotted compost!
Bathnight and then on to the café Cantón in Chantada. Very good tapas - we all had (probably not vegan) cakes, which were rather good!

Catering for Gabriel at home was no problem, as I said. I even enjoyed creating tasty meals for our new vegan convert. Eating out was another story entirely - as we found out the following week when we visited Lugo to sort out our tax issue.

Diary Monday 6th October Wet
Day off for all! Decided to go into Lugo as it was too wet to be on the roof. Dropped Gabriel off to explore then went to the hacienda to register the Casita. Apparently, we will be fined for 'non-presentation'. Oops!

OCTOBER 2014

Difficult to think where to eat at lunchtime so ended up at the new eco-pizzeria in As Termas shopping centre. Never again!
Nice enough place but so complicated. The menu choice is salad or soup to start: you can choose 5 items for your salad from a huge long list (in Spanish obviously). Main course is pizza or pasta, again with a choice of 5 items from a different long list. I had to translate each one to Gabriel then 'discuss' the relative merits of each vegetable item endlessly before telling the waiter our choices. As my little brain cannot remember 30 different items without exploding, I wrote it all on their placemat. The waiter was not impressed!

Eating out apart, I was happy to provide for Gabriel's vegan diet and to answer his questions. He had obviously not researched his new diet in any depth: his question as to whether there was more 'goodness' in mushrooms or peppers rather floored me. I wanted to say, 'how long do you have' but instead handed over a couple of my vegan nutrition books and left him to buy his jars of chickpeas from the supermarket daily. These he seemed to devour cold, straight from the jar, late every night. That his room didn't have a certain aroma on his departure was a miracle.

Tuesday 7th October. Wet.
Dear Mum,
 Oh well, the sun was nice while it lasted. NOT good roofing weather at the moment but the majority of the actual house is covered and weatherproof. The rest of the roof (as much again) is over the alpendre.
 We went into Lugo yesterday. I bought a new camera with my birthday money

CHESTNUT, CHERRY & KIWI FRUIT SPONGE

(thank you so much xx) so I can take lots of photos on our holidays.

We also booked the hotel in Lugo for Christmas. The lady was very pleased you are moving over. We booked three rooms this year as Debs and Al are stopping over too. They stayed in the 'posh' hotel in town last year but were rather more impressed with our 'cheap' hostal.

Then, after we had booked everything, we happened to walk past the Chinese restaurant... and it's gone! Closed! No more! Kaput! So now we have to find somewhere else open on Christmas day for our lunch. Debs suggested a picnic on the Roman walls, I thought a midday dorm feast in the biggest room and S proposed the restaurant at the hospital (which will be open and is pretty good value!).

Wednesday: Very wet! We took Gabriel to his next hosts today. Boy is that a project and a half! 20 acres with falling down buildings, and no water or electric. Don't envy them at all.

Gabriel was a nice lad but a bit dilatory. He managed to leave his brand new, two-day old camera on the bus and realised a few days later he had also left his winter ski jacket on there. We went to the bus station in Lugo to see if the lost property had found anything but sadly neither had turned up. Our sledgehammer head (which flew off

OCTOBER 2014

during one of his rather over enthusiastic attempts at demolishing the old chicken house at the Casita, and which disappeared into the undergrowth below the trees) hasn't turned up either - despite Gabriel searching for hours.

Hopefully that's his three things and his next Workaway will be smoother. I now have to clean his bedroom before our next helper, Francine, arrives on Friday.

Gabriel certainly made a hit in town - despite having no Spanish. He walked in most nights to chat to Luis and the 'old men' in Scala. He also dug, very quickly, a huge hole for the septic tank. S says it would have taken a few days to do it himself and it was safer than letting Gabriel loose with any more hammers! I think he was digging to Australia!

Your letter had arrived when we got home and was unfortunately sitting in a nice puddle in the bottom of the letter box. As I'd decided to light the Sunroom fire, we have managed to dry everything out including our crosswords.

Your vegetable marrow is probably fine inside... you will need an axe to chop it though (Oops, no! Don't try that at home.)

Love you tons and tons

xxxxxxx

PS Suggest you stop reading the news if it upsets you. Be like us and ignore it!

Xxx

CHESTNUT, CHERRY & KIWI FRUIT SPONGE

PPS What do you mean you are not moving in at Christmas? Who needs furniture… you have a roof! Nearly! Fussy woman!
Love you tons xxx

S had been on the roof when Gabriel had swung the sledgehammer and caused the heavy metal head to shoot off. S said he had shouted twice to our Workawayer to hit the concrete 'lid' of the old chicken house upwards not downwards and to be careful of the hammer head.

Gabriel however had his own ideas and swung the sledgehammer again and again with an incredible force. We were fortunate that the thing flew off away from the house, and our helper, and into next door's undergrowth. Despite numerous scouting parties, that hammer head stayed hidden for the next seven months. Gabriel was however a champion digger.

I had failed to find the septic tank on the property (probably because there wasn't one) and the only place we had to put a new one was in the open barn. The floor however was solidified earth, compacted over many years by feet and by tractors, and full of boulder-sized rocks.

Within four hours Gabriel had dug a two-metre-deep hole, one and a half metres square. And had single-handedly lifted out all the rocks creating a low wall around his work area. I have a wonderful photo of Gabriel down that hole, S standing on the edge above him. It was the only time he looked small.

We were, again, sorry to see our giant Workawayer leave.

Diary Friday 10th October Sun and showers
Had to light the sunroom fire last night, more for the damp than the cold, but milder today. Went into Lugo to try and find an alternative Christmas

restaurant. They all said no when I asked if they were open Christmas day. It might be the hospital after all!
Collected our new helper Francine at the bus station and had lunch at The Wok. It's an Asian buffet restaurant but most of the items seemed to be deep fried in batter and there were no labels. I ended up eating aubergine fritters with chocolate sauce. An interesting combination but not one I'd recommend.

Francine was also vegetarian, but she informed me that she ate fish, and chicken. It seemed that the whole family had been vegetarian for a long time, but her mother had worried about the children getting enough protein so reintroduced fish and then chicken into their diets. Francine didn't however like mushrooms – which was a shame as I had done a mushroom *tortilla* as her first meal.

Wednesday 15th October. Very wet!
Dear Mum,
  Oh well, we had a nice sunny day yesterday so can't complain, though it was a damp day to show Francine around Monforte today - we mainly hid in the shops.
  We had to go to Monforte to get the electrics legalised. Fenosa cut us off yesterday (again) and when he came out, David said the papers were ready to sign at the office. Another tick!
  Glad you went to the doctor's on Monday. Have you chased the hospital about your appointment? Keep at them. Tell them you need two good eyes to view your new house

CHESTNUT, CHERRY & KIWI FRUIT SPONGE

(though it may look better with cataracts at the moment!)

I must put some more photos on Facebook this week. Myself and Francine have been knocking off the old plaster on the back wall and mortaring the stonework. S got rained off the roof so he's pulled the old, mouldy kitchen ceiling down instead - destructive lad!

Thursday: Even wetter! Jayne and Richard came for lunch today to go over Jayne's roster for November while we are on holiday (She is house sitting for us) and to see the Casita.

Not a great day for doing anything else to be honest. S did clear some rubble out from above the kitchen ceiling (plenty of that as you can imagine).

Got your letter today. No idea where mine has got to. Your dinner sounded very nice. We had a vegetable stew with baked potatoes and a ginger and lemon cheesecake.

First the cocina was really slow this morning and I thought the stew wouldn't cook, then it got breezy out and the oven temperature shot up to 200°C. We had to have the windows open in the kitchen while we ate!

Do you mean to dig flower bulbs up and put them in a pot to bring, or to buy some and pot them up? You would also have to be here to water them but that's good too! We

OCTOBER 2014

could really use our 'tweeny' at the moment (tea making would be good!).

Concha poked her head into the kitchen today, as we were in there working, to ask if the cocina was lit (not yet) and if there was water in the well (yes)...!

Off to Monterroso to chase some windows tomorrow (sound familiar?). I'll post this on the way.

Love you tons and tons
xxxxxxxx

Although the window place had told us they had the windows and doors made, they didn't seem to be in any hurry to fit them. I thought a gentle nudge might help.

It didn't.

Diary Friday 17th October Very wet
Took Francine into Taboada, shopping, as too damp to do any work outside. She then cracked a huge pile of walnuts while I made lunch. Fish van arrived so we chose our lunch fish together. A type of bream and very tasty.
S continued making a lovely mess in the kitchen at the Casita knocking out the kitchen ceiling and collecting all the dust and accumulated junk from above. Brings back fond memories of doing ours. Happy days!!

The following day the erratic Galician weather switched once more.

Monday 20th October. Very Hot!
Dear Mum,
Our helper was cold when she arrived from

CHESTNUT, CHERRY & KIWI FRUIT SPONGE

Granada - now she's too hot! She was chestnut picking this morning (it's that time again) but I don't think she enjoyed it - ½ a bucket in the time Carmen's daughter had filled a sack, haha. She is good at knocking cement off the outside wall though, and very friendly and chatty (though sadly had never heard of John Wayne!!).

We went to Ourense yesterday - the Chinese place there has definitely closed down too, as it is to let now! It's a conspiracy. We caught the little road train as usual into town but it was the most hair-raising ride ever. It was a new, young lad and I think he wanted to be a rally driver. Foot to the boards and weaving about so much we were getting whiplash on the rear coach. You can tell, as he knocked 15 minutes off the journey time. He was grinding gears and jolting his foot on and off the accelerator all the time. There was an American family on board looking terrified. I did tell them it wasn't normally like that. It was the same driver on the way back but I think someone had told on him as he went so very, very slowly this time - except for a couple of times when he roused himself and floored the accelerator, shooting forward before slowing right down again. I hope he either gets another job or takes a driving test.

S is cracking on with the roof at the back. He is currently looking at where the fifth

OCTOBER 2014

skylight can go, this one in the en suite (to the back bedroom). They have given it nice all week (26°C today). Francine and I have been mortaring the back house wall. The granite stones look nice and I need to get it done before we sort out the garden as I make rather a mess below. I've also demolished half the chicken house (that Gabriel started before he lost our sledgehammer head). Now it's a bit lower, I thought it would make a nice raised flower bed/rockery garden.

Tuesday: Very hot. So glad that both letters arrived - I was starting to think I'd imagined posting it! Very odd that they should both come together, makes you wonder if one was sitting on a shelf somewhere when someone spotted the second one and said 'Oh, we'll send that on'. Still not had your postcard from holiday, mind.

Weds: Just back from Taboada. Hope you are practising for your language competition with Luisa. S taught her the word 'tomorrow'... he pointed at her nose and said tu morro (your nose/snout in Spanish). She thought that hilarious. She was asking how long it was since we first went in her bar. It was well before we moved in so we reckon 8 years ago. Mencia is now as tall as me - she would've been four when we first met!

Love you tons and tons and tons
xxxxxxxx

CHESTNUT, CHERRY & KIWI FRUIT SPONGE

Francine turned out to be a lovely and enthusiastic Workawayer, despite not knowing the most famous actor in the Western world! She was French and found our pronunciation of her language bizarre. We would often engage helpers in doing the Telegraph crossword after lunch. Rupert had been a demon at the cryptic crossword despite English being his second language.

On this occasion we were doing the general knowledge crossword.

"I think therefore I am."

"Oh, Descartes," said S.

"Who?" asked Francine.

"You know, French bloke, philosopher, Descartes." I was pronouncing his name the 'English' way as des-'cart-ez.

"Ah!" she said. "De-'car."

"That's what I said, des-'cart-ez."

Leg pulling aside, Francine fit in well. She helped me to chisel off the old and dusty render from the back wall of the *Casita*. She had tried re-mortaring a section but was not happy with her own efforts so decided to continue to chisel off while I re-mortared. When the weather was wet, she cracked walnuts, picked chestnuts and helped in the kitchen. Francine left on the 24th. I was sorry to see her go.

Francine was our final helper of 2014 but we were keen to continue with our Workawayers next year. For now, we had lots to do before our first holiday of the season, including getting those windows fitted.

Sunday 26th October. VERY HOT again!

Dear Mum,

We are definitely having an Indian summer. It's been nicer the last week or so than it was in August. Good for getting the roof done, and mortaring the outside wall.

OCTOBER 2014

We had the morning off to go into Monterroso as they had a cheese and chestnut fair on (odd mix!). A few interesting cheeses and lots of different chestnut products - like chestnut biscuits, marrons glacé and chestnut empanadas. We wandered about getting free tastings which was rather nice! Pity Francine went back on Friday, she would've enjoyed it (although the tasty chestnut pie I tried did also have big chunks of ham in it... obviously!) We also chased the windows again! They have promised to fit the ones they have if the others are not ready by the end of November. We really wanted the two doors fitted before we go on holiday so we can at least lock up the house.

Forgot to tell you that the café has reopened at the swimming baths. Friendly chap called José. The first week we went with Francine and had (huge) baguettes and free wine as he wanted us to try it - he makes his own and it is really very good. Last week we just had wine but he brought over olives and two slices of baguette each with grilled ham on so we didn't need a butty! The cost? 1.40€ for two wines and two butties. Very nice but he won't be making much profit. Angela had refused to tender for the new contract as she said she couldn't make a profit with what the council were asking in rent... and she had run the café for 10 years!

CHESTNUT, CHERRY & KIWI FRUIT SPONGE

Monday: Still hot. I have been helping to hump the corrugated sheets (uralitas) onto the roof today. Wish brother could have made it - they are so heavy, and with this weather too it would've been perfect.

Tuesday: Also hot! Heard from both brother and Belle today! Have you been telling people what I said about no one volunteering to help? Haha. Brother says he will definitely be over next year. Belle will be over for demolition work asap!

I got your postcard today... 'rerouted due to insufficient postage' - first class stamp rather than EU stamp. I would love to know what the alternative carrier is which takes so long. S says it was just our usual postie not a man on a donkey, so who knows!

Weds: Still hot and dry. I am still watering the allotment - at the end of October! We had Concha and Granny (her mum) advising us today. They are getting better and not shouting so much, but they couldn't believe you weren't having chickens. They told me off for demolishing the chicken shed! I said you would have eggs from me but they weren't impressed. They asked if you were growing lettuces (not yet!). And Granny said we should get the roof finished before winter... S said he will bear that in mind! Not long 'til our hols now so had better get a wriggle on!

Off to Scala, will post this on the way.
Love you tons and tons and tons xxxxx

OCTOBER 2014

We hadn't had any holidays, other than our annual two-day breaks visiting the local area and biennial trips to the UK to visit Mum, since we had moved to Galicia seven years ago. But my 50th birthday was coming up in December and S had turned 65 that summer, so it was a good excuse for a proper holiday.

Costa Rica had been on my must-see list for a long time. We bought a made-to-measure trip at a good price from an online company and were all set. This, of course, was all organised before we bought another renovation project. But we deserved a break and I was looking forward to some winter sun, though at that moment we had plenty of winter sun of our own.

NOVEMBER 2014
Windows on the world

Our Indian summer lasted up to the 2nd of November that year.

Then the rains began.

We were told, when we first arrived, that Galician weather goes in two-week cycles. This is often true. We can often have two weeks of wall-to-wall sunshine, followed by two weeks of solid rain. What no-one told us, is that sometimes the consecutive two-week cycles may be of the same weather.

Tuesday 4th November. Wet wet wet
Dear Mum,

Oh well, couldn't expect the sunshine to last forever, but it has gone awfully cold in comparison! Good job S managed to get the house part of the roof covered - at least that's dry! We have moved indoors to work for the moment.

Did well for the big market for Todos Santos at Monterroso, weatherwise. It actually didn't rain and was quite mild. Debs and Al came with us. Think Debs enjoyed herself, she came back to the café loaded up!

NOVEMBER 2014

It was very busy in the market so we didn't look round that much... me and crowds. Every time I spotted an opening in the mass of bodies and aimed for it, someone would come and fill the space. In the end we just went back to the hotel.

We had decided to go to Luisa's for lunch as Monterroso is always busy on All Souls' Day and the restaurants put their prices up because of the special market. There were 20 of us in the end. Luckily, I'd warned her there may be a few.

We finally met the Dutch couple who bought Anne and Simon's place. They said they hadn't been before as Anne told them the meeting was for 'English only' - sounds like Anne, haha. They didn't seem to have two heads or anything, though they have got rid of all the animals as they were 'too much trouble' (despite buying a working smallholding). They also no longer believe the world is ending... so that's a relief then!

Ironically, there were 12 Dutch at the 'English only' meal and only 5 English.

Weds: Wet. Geert kindly came over today to help S lower the new septic tank into the hole Gabriel dug. Much better than me trying to help! He stayed for lunch so we got the afternoon off.

Hope you have a lovely party. I will ring you when you let me know you are home.

Love you tons and tons

xxxxxxxxxxxxx

CHESTNUT, CHERRY & KIWI FRUIT SPONGE

It continued to rain off and on all that week. S spent his time in the kitchen, fixing new ceiling beams and cementing the many gaps in the wall. I polished some of the old wooden bedboards we had found in the *Casita* and had fun pulling hundreds of nails out of the sweet chestnut beams in preparation for cleaning them. In between showers we did our annual mushroom hunt and I was rather pleased to find four huge horse mushrooms in a nearby field. It was a shame Gabriel had left; he would have enjoyed our treasures.

We also paid our non-presentation fine for the Casita which arrived in the post on the Thursday.

"150€! That's a bit steep," I said. "We'll have to be more careful next time."

"What next time?" asked S, suspiciously.

"Well, I thought number four is empty and it would make a good..."

"No."

"I would do anything for love," I smiled.

"But I won't do that!" retorted S.

The subject was closed – for now.

Diary Friday 7th November Still wet
Made my Christmas cake so it has plenty of time to mature! S removed the wooden slatted sides from the large cupboard in the living room. Much more space without it even if the concrete plinth looks ugly. And some useful wood to reuse.
Lunch: Paella with cod and prawns. Lemon tart.
Booked ferry for 5th Feb returning on 22nd Feb. Three out, two back!

In addition to our Costa Rican holiday that winter, we were off to England in February. It was Mum's year for Christmas here in Galicia, my brothers and I taking turns to invite her. Unbeknownst to Mum we planned for her to stay a bit longer and return to England with us on the ferry from Santander in

NOVEMBER 2014

Northern Spain. It would be a mini-cruise and hopefully a fun Christmas present, as Mum had never been on such a long ferry ride before.

Tuesday 11th November. Rather soggy.
Dear Mum,
 All go today. The window people said they were coming (after I chased them up again yesterday) and two very nice lads arrived at about 10am. Not the weather for being outdoors but they worked very efficiently and soon had the kitchen door and window in, then the bedroom stable-door and the living room window. They all look very smart. S says Concha came to pass her opinion and check out the shutters - which are to stop nosey people peering in haha.
 While S was busy levelling the septic tank, I had another hunt for the missing sledgehammer head. No luck. Gabriel should have been entered into the Olympics - he would've been good at hammer throwing! Goodness knows how far it's gone.
 This pm, during yet another downpour, José turned up with the wood for the kitchen ceiling and the chipboard for the new sub-floor in the bedroom. Of course, it was soaked by the time they had got it off the open-backed lorry and into the kitchen so S had to blow dry it all!
 Now he's kindly doing a spot of sewing for me - good job one of us can, eh?
 We got all our documents for our holiday yesterday and I've organised the parking at

CHESTNUT, CHERRY & KIWI FRUIT SPONGE

the airport. Jayne is coming for lunch again next week so we can run through any last-minute things, though she is pretty au fait with most of the house's quirks by now. She also agreed to housesit when we come back to the UK in spring. So, we've booked the ferry.

Weds eve: Still soggy! Please tell Aunty Jean that I hope she would like some kiwi fruit in Feb. I have never seen so many. We have taken 300 off (you have to store them over winter) and it doesn't look like we've touched them. Must be 500 or more still on. Think we will have to bring a sack with us and stand in front of the market hall in Ashby.

I've also got quite a lot of persimmons (Sharon fruit) on this year. The branches are touching the ground with the weight. As they store well too, we will have plenty of fruit for winter.

Friday: I've started to sort clothes for our holiday. I think the weather can be quite variable from the lowlands to the mountains in Costa Rica. It seems to be a big pile.

I assume you still have your list for what clothes you have here? I don't think you took too much back. We will have to start stockpiling stuff this end now, ready for your big move.

The window chaps came back today to fit a new threshold on our barn door. They spent

ages levelling the doors. We are hopeful it will keep out the rain. They also fitted a new handle we can open from outside.
 Love you tons and tons.
 xxxxxxxx

Our original Big Barn door had been yet another window company disaster. It never fit the way it should: it had a handle on the inside only, which meant it was virtually impossible to pull closed from outside; and water poured in when the rain came hammering from the west. Sadly, the new threshold on our Big Barn door didn't prevent the rain coming in either. It's a problem we still haven't one hundred percent solved.

Although the doors and windows for the *Casita* were fitted quickly (relatively speaking), and efficiently, we did have some inevitable problems with them too.

I had requested a proper threshold with the kitchen door. Most standard doors no longer come with one due to wheelchair access requirements, but because of the problems with water coming into our Big Barn, and as the kitchen door to the *Casita* is at the bottom of a slope, we thought it better to be safe. Unfortunately, the window people seemed unable to provide a multi-locking door with a threshold. At least that's what I assumed – as they actually fitted a window.

I only realised when I went to open the door the first time. If the handle was pulled up whilst opening the door, it fell towards you on a tilt mechanism. Quite terrifying! The handle had to be horizontal to open or close the door then pushed down to lock it. As most people depress a door handle automatically as they pass through, the door was in a locked position as it was closing so the mortise bolts were continually being bashed and dented. It was a

CHESTNUT, CHERRY & KIWI FRUIT SPONGE

ridiculous design, and I spent many woman-hours trying to get it changed.

The original bedroom door had been a stable door: that is, a door with an upper and lower leaf which can be opened separately. As this room opened onto a small platform at the top of the steps leading down to the road, I thought it would be a nice feature to keep. I can only assume that the window manufacturers had never seen a stable door. Yes, the door was in two halves but the top half had to be opened first in order to release the mortise bolts on the lower half. Not ideal for an emergency escape. Also, the two halves could not be secured together in the open position, so flapped about annoyingly. We gave up trying to change that one. We really don't do well with window companies, do we?

Diary Tuesday 18th November Dry
Spent most of the day moving the chickens. We wanted to get them onto the allotment field while we are away. It's more secure down there with the wire covering, and now the leaves have fallen off the trees at the top they are a bit exposed.
Picked another 600 kiwis.
Cleaned the house thoroughly for Jayne (don't want her to think we are slobs) and popped into the town hall to re-register that we are still living here. You are supposed to do it every five years apparently. We wouldn't have known if we hadn't called in about the Casita. Only took two minutes anyway and two years late, we are 'legal' again!

We were due to fly to San José, the capital of Costa Rica, the following Monday. Our original flight from Santiago had been for 9.15am, giving us a leisurely start and plenty of time to find the parking and check in for the hop to Madrid. Unfortunately, our onward flight to San José was changed at the last minute meaning a new 6.45am flight from Santiago.

Monday 24th November Dark!
Up at 3.30am. Left the house at 3.50am for a very quiet and lonely drive to the airport. Arrived 5.10am. Went to the parking booth as indicated on my booking for the off-site parking. The chap there said they had problems with the barriers off-site so we should leave the car in the main underground carpark at the airport. He assured me the price would be the same. As we had allowed time for walking back from the off-site, this meant we were ridiculously early! Had a tea and twiddled our thumbs until called.

Our short hop flight was perfectly on time and when we arrived in Madrid an hour later, I was ready for my breakfast. This ended up being in an airport MacDonalds. Most of the airport cafés were ridiculously overpriced, so big MacDs it was. Not being a burger fan, I had never used the new (to me) computerised ordering system but after a few attempts and some mutterings we managed to order, pay for, and even collect our breakfast successfully.

Our onward flight was not until 11.40am so despite taking as long as possible eating our breakfast (how long can a MacMuffin last after all) and a truly lengthy walk to terminal T4S we still had hours to kill.

Our flight was with Iberia, simply because it was the cheapest and only direct flight to Costa Rica from Spain. When I had been booking the holiday, our travel agent had suggested a flight via Frankfurt as the best option. Being me, I ran a check of my own and found the Iberia flight was not only half as long, but half as expensive. The agent apparently had no idea the flight existed, though she did manage to

CHESTNUT, CHERRY & KIWI FRUIT SPONGE

secure our short Santiago-Madrid flights with the same carrier for no extra cost.

Of course, a cheap price can come with a downside, and Iberia don't feature on the 'World's best airline' list.

The crew on our flight were helpful and friendly – they were an older crew and seemed relaxed and happy, but the plane was elderly and the two feature films were shown on a tiny screen halfway down the aisle. Then there was the food.

I'd booked vegetarian meals for the flight as I've seen Arthur Hailey's *Terror in the Sky* once too often to trust the meaty options on board. (It's the one where everyone who had the chicken got food poisoning including the two pilots, and Doug McClure has to take over).

I remember saying to S how impressed I was with the choice of cuisines one could book on Iberia. There were 27 options – including vegan, kosher, dairy-free, gluten-free and vegetarian. What I couldn't have known were that they were all the same option.

Our meals were free from everything: dairy, gluten, meat, and flavour. Our main meal consisted of a frozen salad (very cold and crunchy tomatoes) and a foil tray of plain rice with a packet of olive oil dressing to add. We didn't even get the chocolate pudding, which S was most upset about. Having an aisle seat did mean I could accost the steward each time he passed with bread rolls, as our 'free-from' rice cakes tasted remarkably like cardboard. Luckily, I had come prepared with homemade cheese pies and cereal bars to keep us going.

At 'tea time' there were sandwiches. By the time the crew reached our row, near the back of the plane, the only option left was ham and cheese.

"I'm a vegetarian," complained the woman in front of us. "I can't eat that."

NOVEMBER 2014

The steward shrugged, eloquently. "It's all that's left."

"I booked a vegetarian meal," the woman said, "that is unacceptable."

"The front of the plane chose all the vegetarian options. This is all we have left," repeated the steward.

The woman humphed and complained, and went hungry.

As ham and cheese on white sliced bread ticks pretty much every box for not being 'free-from', I did wonder what the other 'special' passengers were eating. The sandwiches were probably the best meal we had on that plane and I've never gone the vegetarian route on a flight since.

Conversely, I was impressed with Costa Rica the moment we touched down. Our driver for the hour-long journey to our first hotel was a chatty fellow on whom I practised my South American Spanish, asking him about his country. He was knowledgeable, political, and proud of the eco-credentials of Costa Rica.

At that time Costa Rica were one of the top recyclers in the world, and a few years later became the first country to commit to a climate change strategy to become carbon neutral. Between 1986 and 2006 Costa Rica increased its forest cover from 21 percent to 51 percent. Quite an achievement.

Our room at the Radisson in San José was the single biggest I have ever been in. It had a table to seat six; two, three-seater sofas; a 60-inch TV and a bed so vast I never did find S all night. The bathroom would have been suitable for a visiting football team to shower in and the whole room was the size of a decent apartment in Spain.

Sadly, by that point jet lag had caught up with me. I fell asleep halfway through *Harry Potter and the Philosopher's Stone*, lying diagonally across the huge bed.

CHESTNUT, CHERRY & KIWI FRUIT SPONGE

Tuesday 25th November Drizzly
Up at 6am refreshed and raring to go. Had another shower, just because it was so good! The most amazing buffet breakfast consisting of cereals, eggs, rice and beans, too many fruits to count, juices, pastries and cakes. Loaded up for the journey.

One of the things I loved about Costa Rica was the Interbus service; basically, a door-to-door minibus service between resorts, it was eco-friendly and fun!

That first trip set the scene for many more over the next 12 days. We were collected in front of the hotel by a comfortable minibus at 8.30am and driven along roads which can only be kindly described as rutted. Some of the holes were deep enough to lose a small child in and this was the main highway. Our well-deserved halfway stop was a roadside café. After four hours of bouncing about and enjoying the scenery we arrived at the Hotel Arenal Montechiari, our stop for the next three nights, close to the Arenal volcano and La Fortuna.

The town of La Fortuna, was renamed 'the fortunate one' following its miraculous escape in 1968, when the dormant (and many believed, extinct) Arenal volcano suddenly erupted, destroying three other much less fortunate villages and claiming many lives.

Our accommodation was a small, basic wooden cabin comprising a decent sized but dark bedroom (due to the inefficient eco-lights, dark wood ceilings, and wooden walls) and a bathroom at the rear. I didn't care that the room was dark because it opened onto a tiny deck at the front from where we could watch any amount of glorious wildlife without having to move a toe.

We also had a perfect view of the volcano from the walkway in front of our cabin – if the mist ever lifted enough to see the top.

NOVEMBER 2014

That first day we relaxed in the small pool, just a few steps from our cabin, cooling off from the intense humidity and watched a humming bird hovering at one of the magnificent plants which grew throughout the gardens. The vibrant foliage all around us was alive with birds, insects, and lizards. I was mesmerised by it all.

Later, we walked into the town of La Fortuna to find some food. As we were perusing the various cafés and restaurants in the main square we were gently accosted by an elderly man, sweeping brush in hand.

"You want good food?" he asked. "You come here. Tico open 24 hour. Very good price. I show you."

With that he guided us into the café which was open to the street on three sides, except for a low wall. Along one side was a long glass-fronted counter full of cooked meat, fish, beans, salads, plantains, rice dishes and sweet potato.

"Seven dollar," said Tico man. "One main, one side, one salad, drink natural juice."

"Looks good," I said, my stomach agreeing with me.

I gazed around at the spotlessly clean café, then at my husband. A nod was enough. I was off asking about the ingredients and the choices. We later found that this sort of menu was common in Costa Rica and was called a *'casada'* or a marriage – being a large mixed plate, usually accompanied by watermelon juice (*sandia*) or occasionally cola.

Tico's became our home from home in La Fortuna. We ate there each of the three days we stayed in the town. Each time there was something different on the menu. Often we saw a man carrying in chickens, or another loaded with fish still dangling from his line.

That first day we wandered the hotel gardens in the humid dark of a tropical evening, listening to the cicadas and sounds of the night. Unable to resist, we

CHESTNUT, CHERRY & KIWI FRUIT SPONGE

took torches and hunted for the croaking frogs which we found in a large but unfinished pool in another section of the complex. It was magical.

Wednesday 26th November
Awoke to the noise of a tropical dawn chorus interspersed with sounds of home (heavy rain and cock crowing). Up for breakfast at 7am. Interesting mix of rice, eggs, fruit and pancakes, though the staff seemed a little disorganised and just brought heaving mixed plates to the table. Couldn't help thinking a buffet would be easier!

Our first excursion of the holiday was a half-day trip to Caño Negro Wildlife Refuge, with a boat trip along the Frio river and lunch included.

Caño Negro is a seasonal lake some 800 hectares in area and three metres deep. The refuge is made up of lakes and swampland formed by alluvial sediments and is on the Ramsar list of wetlands of international importance.

We were the last pick-ups on the bus. There was already a lively American group on board who were loudly joshing each other. Debbie, Terry, Bobby and Jim were from Oklahoma. Jim had a desert-dry sense of humour. While we were boarding Jim was trying to persuade Terry, or maybe Bobby, I never did get the androgynous names of that couple straight, to sit on his lap. Terry or Bobby, was a six-foot cowboy wearing a ten-gallon hat and was steadfastly refusing to sit on his mate's knees.

"You'll pinch ma ass," he said, sitting determinedly on the minibus floor.

"It's a swell ass," replied Jim.

"Where y'all from?" asked Debbie, handing me a business card.

"Spain," I replied.

"Great, we'll come visit y'all one day."

NOVEMBER 2014

"She will an' all," muttered Jim. "Best keep ya doors locked."

On the way to the Caño Negro we stopped to see a group of huge green iguanas reclining at the very tops of the trees. The males had orange frills and were completely oblivious to the hordes of tourists clicking cameras at them. I was beginning to appreciate just how much wildlife there was in Costa Rica.

This small country, with a landmass the size of West Virginia or Denmark, claims to have over 500,000 species of animals, making it one of the most bio-diverse countries in the world.

Our boat trip was in a low-slung, canopied, motorised ketch, captained by Dani, an able pilot and an eagle-eyed wildlife spotter.

We would all be peering into the trees festooned with lianas, growing out over the water when Dani would suddenly shout, "sloth!" We would drift closer to shore, still unable to see a thing in the thick green canopy until abruptly, the outline of a lazy bear-like mammal would emerge from the greenery.

We saw kingfishers and herons, spoonbills, howler monkeys, 'Jesus' lizards, and tiny bats clustered on the trunk of a tree – indistinct to us until within touching distance, but clear to Dani from mid-stream.

It was a fabulous day and the rain held off until dusk when it returned in force, accompanied by a 'lights out' for a couple of hours. We enjoyed wandering the quiet, half-completed complex of cabins in our little jungle paradise before turning in for the night, lulled by the unfamiliar tropical sounds.

The following evening saw us standing on a Costa Rican road in a warm drizzle with another couple. It was pitch black. The only illumination was an occasional passing car and a single, feeble torch beam. We were wearing bathing costumes and our

CHESTNUT, CHERRY & KIWI FRUIT SPONGE

minibus had just left with all our belongings on board.

Our adventure today had been billed as a day trip to the Arenal Volcano National Park. We had seen many companies offering similar trips but we'd spotted one that looked somewhat different and was half the price of the rest. Unable to resist a bargain, we booked.

Our minibus when it arrived that morning, was ancient and rickety. The seats wobbled alarmingly, had long since lost all vestiges of stuffing and sported exposed springs ready to impale the unwary. We were the last ones on board. I perched carefully on the edge of my seat. There were no seat belts.

José, our knowledgeable guide, more than made up for our lack of transportational comfort. By turn raconteur, botanist, and medicine man, he told us endless anecdotes; persuaded us all to try herbal remedies taught to him by his grandfather and managed to find elusive red-eyed frogs for us to see, hiding beneath a massive leaf, as we spent the day hiking through the park.

As darkness fell, we'd made our rickety way in the minibus towards the 'highlight' of the trip, a thermal pool. I had seen photographs in some of the travel agents' windows showing people reclining in beautifully manicured surroundings, drinks in hand. Our experience was going to be different, promised José. The minibus stopped and we were told to leave everything behind: shoes, towels, mobiles, cash.

"There are no changing rooms," José explained, giving us a flickering torch and pointing off into the gloom "That way. I will see you soon."

Then they were gone and the darkness surrounded us.

Having little choice, we made our way down the dark track at the edge of the black road. The mud oozed between our naked toes and bushes scratched our bare legs. The wavering and rapidly dimming light of the torch helped not a jot. I was pondering how to explain to our insurance company the loss of our possessions when we heard noises ahead: laughter and the growling, roaring of water.

A steep step; a wade through cool water, the current insistently tugging at our ankles; over a small waterfall and we sank into the blissful warmth of a bath-like pool. Candles lit the riverbanks in a gentle glow like a fairy kingdom. A plastic cup appeared at my elbow, next to it the smiling face of José.

"We had forgotten to bring the drinks. *Salud*!"

Diary Saturday 29th November Wet
Off to our next stop. As before, we were collected by minibus for the long and very damp journey. The trip to Monteverde includes a half hour journey by boat across Lake Arenal.

We were looking forward to that boat trip.

Lake Arenal is the largest artificial lake in Costa Rica, man-made in 1974 to provide hydroelectric energy for the country. The views of the Arenal Volcano are said to be spectacular – on a clear day.

Unfortunately, the rain and the mist conspired to obscure any chance of a view. The journey across the lake on an open boat was cold and miserable. Unlike the other Interbus rides, our driver on the far side of the lake was uncommunicative. The weather closed in until we were bumping through puddles the size of small lakes and getting colder by the minute in our damp clothes.

It was then, in an unfortunate frame of mind that I arrived at the Monteverde Country Inn: cold, wet and thoroughly miserable. It was also more than a little windy. Lisa is a fractious girl when cold and wet, and hates the wind. She was also hungry and that is never a good thing. Our room, on the ground

CHESTNUT, CHERRY & KIWI FRUIT SPONGE

floor of a two-storey block, was large and comfortable. Our only neighbour, on the floor above, was a vampire elephant who insisted on furniture removals at four in the morning but never seemed to appear during daylight hours.

Abandoning our room, we walked into the nearby town of Santa Elena, stopping at a tiny roadside stall which was advertising *empanadas* for a dollar each. I spied a kettle behind the friendly and chatty lady and wondered if we could have tea with our pies. Our host happily produced a couple of teabags and two huge, mainly clean, mugs. We sat on the kerbside, eating flaky crisp pastry and guzzling builders' tea as debris blew around us and the wind tangled my hair beyond rescue.

A howling gale blew up that evening causing all the power to fail again. This was apparently a common occurrence in Costa Rica and not any cause for alarm, but the damp cold had me wishing for my nice cosy wood-burning stove in my nice cosy home, eight thousand kilometres away in Galicia.

Luckily, the following day brought some welcome sunshine for our first trip to the cloud forest park itself.

The term 'cloud forest' is used for a rainforest with exceptionally high humidity. In Monteverde Cloud Forest Park this reaches virtually 100 percent causing almost permanent cloud cover. This in turn allows the growth of humidity-loving species such as bromeliads, ferns, and mosses in addition to the unique animal species of the rainforest.

The company, Sky Adventures, runs guided walks along the 'Sky Walks' - suspension bridges at tree top level and tracks through the forest, and the 'Sky Tram' - a cable car which rises 1600 metres above sea level to the continental divide. They also run zip-lining trips but we wanted to experience walking amongst and above the forest, rather than zipping through it at speed.

NOVEMBER 2014

I loved the peaceful setting and the myriad wildlife. Our guide along the Sky Walk was a friendly young chap who had plenty of enthusiasm, if not the experience of José.

We enjoyed spotting the sometimes shy wildlife, including a small snake which seemed to live in a hollow pipe. The coati which nuzzled S' camera back at the cafeteria was certainly not shy however.

The cable car ride to the top of the mountain was hair-raising as the wind swung us from side to side, and my baseball cap attempted suicide by flying over the side of the car. At the top we stood looking at the Pacific Ocean on one side of us and the Atlantic on the other. The wind howled on the Pacific side but all was surprisingly calm just a few steps away, peering out at the Atlantic and the rainforest below.

A cheap and filling taco lunch, at the aptly named café Taco Taco, revived my spirits even more. Stray dogs, roaming the street outside the café, were quick to grab my last few tacos as a vicious gust of wind blew the paper tray from the tiny table. I was happy to see them enjoy it.

DECEMBER 2014
Catastrophe at the *catastro*

Our final day at Monteverde was a leisure day. We deliberately didn't book any tours, instead walking a forest trail called Bajo del Tigre. In the trees there was a troop of white-faced monkeys which called to us and followed along, swinging easily through the branches, probably hoping for a snack. Metallic-blue morpho butterflies flitted in and out of the shade and innumerable brightly coloured tropical birds alighted on nearby branches. As I looked at the forest floor, a parade of leaf-cutter ants marched by, each carrying a large oval section of leaf above its head.

We stopped for an expensive, and frankly poor, hot chocolate on the way back. I suppose we are spoilt with the *chocolate caliente* in Galicia where one can stand a spoon up in the cup and requires the said spoon to scoop out the thick gloopy mix. As we sat on the balcony of the café, the clouds once more descended and the rain returned.

The storm was brief and the sun hot when it reappeared. We spent the rest of the afternoon relaxing by the pool and collecting the flowers from its surface. I have a lovely photo of S modelling a pink gardenia in his hair.

My memories list of Monteverde included: cable cars; a local microbrewery with delicious, if top-price, beers; and howling relentless wind!

DECEMBER 2014

Diary Tuesday 2nd December Sunshine
Awoke at 4am as the elephant above us dragged their heavy-wheeled suitcase across the floor and bumped it down the outside steps. No more chance of sleep so I woke S and opened my cards. S had made me a huge badge 'Yo Soy 50' it says, ungrammatically. At least I shall be noticed!

My 50th birthday was also transfer day.

Our last stop on this holiday was to be Manuel Antonio on the Pacific coast. The five-hour journey along potholed and dusty roads was now predictable and I wore my birthday badge with pride the whole way, pinned to my baseball cap.

Cabinas Playa Espadilla were single storey bungalows set in parkland. And our bungalow, again, opened onto the swimming pool area. Only a two-minute walk from the Pacific Ocean in one direction and a backpackers' hostel serving great value *casadas* in the other, I couldn't fault the place.

The first thing I saw as we walked to our cabin was a huge iguana sunbathing next to the pool. He was a good two feet long (S says three, but is prone to wild exaggeration), and had no intention of moving. Iggy became our constant companion as we lazed by the pool or wandered the landscaped grounds.

My birthday dinner was a typical *casada* meal of chicken, rice and beans, and salad plus a couple of daiquiris at the popular backpackers' hostel. We relaxed at a high wooden table and listened to the squirrel monkeys overhead, scooting along the electricity cables, and a toucan in the trees nearby.

Diary Wednesday 3rd December Sunshine
Dreadful night. The pillows are really bricks disguised to look soft. A very poor disguise I may add! Ended up rolling up the duvet and using that as a pillow.

CHESTNUT, CHERRY & KIWI FRUIT SPONGE

Rock hard pillows aside, I adored Espadilla and would have happily stayed much longer (as in, never left). Breakfast was at its sister hotel, across the dirt road behind, and more than made up for an uncomfortable night. I sat and watched the chef cooking eggs to order and went back and forward collecting tropical fruits, pancakes, cakes, and the ubiquitous rice and beans. I even made myself a one-eyed Texan stack of pancakes, bacon, and fried eggs, dripping with maple syrup as S looked on with horror.

A bus had been booked to take us to the national park that morning for a walking tour. It duly arrived, collected us outside our hotel, and deposited us at the park entrance one hundred metres along the road. We hadn't even had chance to sit down.

Manuel Antonio National Park was opened in 1972 and includes 1980 terrestrial hectares plus 55000 marine hectares: comprising rainforest, beaches and coral reefs. It is the smallest of Costa Rica's national parks but has a remarkable diversity of wildlife.

Our guide, Andrés, was another eagle-eyes, helping us to spot fruit bats, red-eyed frogs, lizards and monkeys. He let us photograph some of these incredible wonders through his telescope. Andrés was a biologist and his speciality was sloths. Over the course of our walk, we learned more about the mating, eating and sleeping habits of that fascinating creature than I believed possible. We also saw far more of the shy mammals than any other group, having soon been left behind by the speedier but less observant tour guides.

We had taken a picnic lunch with us and were to spend the afternoon on the beach within the park before walking back to our cabin.

"Just be careful of the racoons," said our guide as he left us. "They are far too tame. Do not feed them or leave any food out."

DECEMBER 2014

I was reminded of *The Gremlins* film: 'And don't get them wet', I wanted to add.

We lay happily in the shade of a huge tree on the beach watching the Pacific Ocean calmly burbling along a few feet away.

Suddenly, I heard a warning cry. Looking up I saw a racoon deftly unfastening our rucksack clips, not two feet away. Another shout had us scanning the beach. A second gang of racoons was trying the same trick on some fellow bathers a little way along the beach. As the tourist jumped up to shoo the first racoon away, his fellow thieves dived in and grabbed her picnic lunch. The lady screeched at the bandits in their striped masks and received a bare-toothed growl in reply. Deciding to forgo her lunch for a full complement of fingers she let the merry band of racoons make good their escape. It was a fun end to a delightful day.

Interestingly, while researching this chapter, I found that the park has now banned food from being brought in to protect the environment and, no doubt, discourage the racoons. Probably a sensible move, though I thoroughly enjoyed our picnic on the beach and our racoon encounters.

The rest of our holiday at Manuel Antonio was spent walking on the beach, dipping in the Pacific Ocean or swimming in the pool, watched by Iggy the Iguana.

Our final day, the 5th of December, dawned drizzly. We set off to walk the length of the beach wearing just our bathing suits. It was a typically warm and humid day and a perfect stroll. Even on the beach there was wildlife to see. Herons fished in small rills, monkeys ran in and out of the trees bordering the beach, and iguanas sat on driftwood, gazing out to sea. S juggled coconuts and I wore my fancy frilled bikini and decided that being 50 wasn't really so bad.

CHESTNUT, CHERRY & KIWI FRUIT SPONGE

Diary Sunday December 7th So cold!
Arrived at Madrid at 11am. Long wait for our evening flight to Santiago so we caught the metro into the city. Found a nice-looking restaurant called Terramundo which turned out to be owned by a Galego. It's so good to be home!

After two full days of travelling, we arrived at *A Casa do Campo* at 9pm on the Sunday to a blazing fire left in by our kindly house-sitter. We fell into bed and slept straight through to 9am the following morning. Then we got back to work. We had just three days to tidy round and get organised before *La Jefa* (the boss lady) arrived for her Christmas holiday.

My first task was to put the washing machine on, my second to check on the chickens. Sadly, Jayne had to report the loss of one of our young hens. A buzzard had somehow got into the outside pen, through the wire mesh top, and killed Daffodil. Jayne was most upset but had had the forethought to clean and gut poor Daffy and pop her in the freezer for us.

It wasn't Jayne's fault at all, but we did need to sort out the buzzard situation. S decided more over-engineering was necessary as we added another layer of chicken wire to the top of the outer run. The pen began to resemble a high security arena.

Diary Wednesday 10th December Cloudy
Not cold but boy does it feel it after two weeks of tropical heat!
Up late again to the sound of the cheese lady hooting outside.
S continued over-wiring the chicken run. Need yet more wire! I'm thinking buying eggs would be much cheaper, if not as tasty.
Planted out peapods in the polytunnel and weeded the rather overgrown allotment. Chickens spooked

by something. They were all hiding in a corner chuntering. Shut them inside.
Changed the bedding and got ready for our VIP visitor by finding the Christmas decorations in the loft and wrapping her presents.

Mum was due the following afternoon. I spent Thursday morning cleaning round the *Casita* and trying to make the best of what we had achieved so far. I hoped she wasn't going to scream and run the other way at the first sight of her new home-to-be.

Silly idea. Mum loved her little cottage, especially the views across the fields from her newly fitted window in the upstairs living room. She also had ideas of what she wanted in her tiny courtyard garden and in her kitchen-to-be.

The kitchen at the *Casita* is built in the same configuration as ours. It is an almost rectangular shape with a three metre long, low working area in the centre of the room into which is set the *cocina* or wood-burning range cooker. Set into the surround on either side of the range are drawers and open cupboards. Mum's surround is mainly built of brick like ours, but on one side is a huge granite stone. I have no idea why just the one, although it is a good three feet long, two feet high and 12 inches thick. Perhaps it was already there and no one could move it. As ever it is a bit of history and remains.

The worktop and surround tiles were beautiful: old quarry tiles in a yellow, blue and terracotta Aztec-inspired design. I desperately wanted to keep them but many were cracked or had been replaced with mismatched newer, glazed tiles. We decided it would be more hygienic to fit granite worktops like ours around the range cooker, sourced from the local marble workshop.

As you enter the kitchen door at ground floor level, the *cocina* is to the right, running along the centre of the room. Next to the door was an old,

CHESTNUT, CHERRY & KIWI FRUIT SPONGE

shallow stone sink below the only window in the room. To the left, when we bought the house, there was a small table housing a huge old-fashioned TV and two mummified moles. The TV, and the moles, had long since been disposed of, the table was in the barn waiting to be cleaned and repurposed.

Behind the *cocina* was a long wooden bench. As in our house, this makes a lovely cosy spot to sit and eat in the foulest of weathers. The heat from the range radiates behind it and keeps diners warm and cosy. Unfortunately, there had been more than a little water ingress over the previous 25 years. As I lifted the bench to move it, the thing fell neatly in half where it had rotted through.

In the far right-hand corner of the kitchen had been an open fireplace or *lareira* which S and Jarrad, our first Workawayer, had enjoyed demolishing back in August. Now there was an empty, sooty space which would one day house a fridge-freezer. Next to this space and beyond the end of the *cocina* worktop was a stone-built structure with a solid wooden door at waist height. This was the *Casita's* well.

Unlike our well, which is in the garden and already had an electric pump connected to it when we bought the house, this one was a traditional well: an open circular hole, one metre in diameter and disappearing into the depths below, housed in a stone cupboard. One of our many jobs was to fit an electric pump so water could eventually be piped around the house.

I had already started to clean the whitewash and underlying blue paint from the front of the stone housing and to clean the door. It was sweet chestnut beneath the years of whitewash and looked beautiful. The back and top of the well housing extended into the room behind and above the kitchen; which was one day to be Mum's dressing room.

DECEMBER 2014

In the far left-hand corner of the kitchen were four wooden steps up to the main living accommodation. Again, like our house, the *Casita* is built into a slope so the upper story is only a half-level above the lower one. Very handy for an 83-and-a-half-year-old. Next to these steps was an old-fashioned glass-fronted built-in cupboard containing some ancient tins of mushrooms, jars of honey (which actually turned out to be full of pig fat), pretty thumb glasses, and crockery.

Mum loved the place and we spent many happy hours discussing what would go where and what colour granite worktop she wanted. Mum also wanted to buy a brand new *cocina*.

To be fair there was not much left of the existing range cooker after so many years of neglect. Rain and damp had left their mark: the top was brown with rust and great flakes came off inside the oven when the door was opened. We decided it was time for a visit our local ironmongers, known to us affectionately as 'Arkwright's' after the Ronnie Barker comedy show, *Open All Hours*.

Diary Saturday 13th December Wet, heavy overnight
All into town to view cocinas for the kitchen. Mum liked one the same model as ours, a Lacunza number 9. We also bought another roll of chicken wire for covering the pen on the allotment.
Lunch: Pasta, leek, mustard, bacon and cabbage, with a cheese sauce. Good stodgy grub and just what I needed as I've got a cold. Must be the change in temperature!
Spent the evening writing out my list of 'things to bring from the UK' for Mum.
First egg from Emmeline.

The idea was for us to go back to England in February to help Mum put her house up for sale and,

CHESTNUT, CHERRY & KIWI FRUIT SPONGE

in expectation of a quick sale, for her to move over permanently in the summer. This gave us chance to get more work done on the *Casita* in the meantime.

Of course, we weren't to know then the problems we would have selling Mum's house.

Diary Sunday 14th December Cloudy but dry
Eggs a bit hard. Think the chef is out of practice!
Made lunch (chicken stew with mushrooms, carrots and pumpkin) and popped it in the cocina to cook while we had a trip over to the Christmas fair.

The Christmas fair was organised by Barbara and Martin, our German friends who had provided such a lovely touch of greenery to our wedding all those years earlier and who had donated the polytunnel frame to us. Barbara ran a plant nursery and each Christmas they held a fair in one of their barns.

With fairy lights strung in the rafters, straw on the floor, glühwein to drink and German bratwurst hot dogs to eat, the atmosphere was convivial and seasonal. We inevitably met many of our friends there and chatted until early afternoon. Dinner was cooked perfectly by the time we arrived home and poor Daffodil was very tasty, even if her life had been shorter than it ought to have been.

Over the next few days, we continued wiring over the chicken pen roof: a long and slow job which we sincerely hoped would prevent the buzzard attacks.

It wasn't always buzzards which attacked the chickens. Just the previous December I had gone down to the allotment, where we now kept the chickens overwinter, to shut them in. Flapping madly around the inside pen was a goshawk. In one corner I could see the remains of one of my youngsters, Danni. The hawk was black and white barred and had a wingspan of over three feet. How it had managed to get into a pen with only a six-inch square 'door' to it I have no idea. My best guess was that Danni had struggled and tried to get back to safety, dragging the goshawk with her. The remaining flock were hiding outside, huddled terrified in a corner. I had the problem of a large and angry hawk with, I noticed, a vicious set of talons and a sharp hooked beak to deal with. I did what I always do in these type of circumstances – I called for S.

Goshawks are protected species, for good reason, but what does one do with three feet of snarling scratching hawk in a tight spot. Three feet of snarling bird which, by the way, knows exactly where to find dinner for the next fourteen days? What would you do?

Diary Tuesday 16th December Sunshine and very mild
Off to Monterroso. Did some shopping. Mum bought a doormat for her new home and some new shoes. Back at home she then created a lovely Christmas wreath for the door while I made lunch (Trout with home-made pesto, chips and French beans. Lemon curd tart)
S still reinforcing the chicken pen. I treated the new ceiling boards for the kitchen with woodworm killer or 'carcoma-killer' ready for S to renew the ceiling which he pulled down before our holidays.
Mum and I emptied the glass-fronted cupboard in the kitchen and sorted and washed the glassware and crockery. One can never have too many glasses and some are so cute, less than the size of my fingernail, but we didn't keep the quarter century old pig fat.

The sunny weather meant that Mum was eager to go walking.

Our village is perfect for walking, ending as it does, just past our gate. Beyond are chestnut woods and tractor tracks for miles. Mum began exploring

CHESTNUT, CHERRY & KIWI FRUIT SPONGE

these tracks and enjoyed the freedom of walking safely and peacefully around the place.

Diary Sunday 21st December Mist then sunshine
Perfect boiled eggs and soldiers today. The chef is regaining his badge!
Mum helped me make lunch. Our nine-day cured ham with mash, butternut squash, parsnips, brussels and Romanesco broccoli all out of the garden. Cherry parkin pie with ice cream.
Did our annual photo-shoot in front of the Casita by propping the camera on next door's wall. Hopefully next year it will look smarter! In the evening Mum and I decorated the tree.

The following day was our annual *matanza*. Mum opted to stay home and prepare the tubs for my sweet cure hams and black pudding rather than attend the slaughter.

The pig, from our friend, was 83 kilogrammes of delicious meat. Mum helped me make sausages and hams; to cook the head for chawl, or head cheese; and generally package up and freeze our year's worth of pork. Unable to face cooking with all the piggy stuff going on we ended the day with a tasty, non-piggy pizza in our nearby pizzeria.

We were still making sausages when Debs and Al arrived on Christmas Eve. Luckily our friends are not the squeamish type and happily tucked into our home-cured ham, head cheese, and pickles before a nice long walk around the area, leaving Mum in charge of our oxtail stew for dinner. Debs' delicious cherry and apple crumble for dessert ensured we had a most enjoyable *Noche Buena.*

Debs and Al were staying overnight on Christmas Eve so we could go to our traditional Christmas day Chinese in Lugo in convoy that year – after our scrambled eggs and smoked salmon brunch of course.

DECEMBER 2014

With luck, our scouring of the city had discovered a second Chinese restaurant, near to the Roman walls and an easy walk from our *pensión*. The Restaurant Shanghai was open on Christmas day and is now our new Christmas home from home in Lugo with excellent food and friendly service. I look forward to being able to return there this year.

As ever we had a fabulous Christmas. The weather was kind and the company convivial. On the way out in the evening we found a set of weighing scales in the road. With no obvious home or owner, we decided to make use of this unexpected gift by speaking people's weight to passers-by. The youngsters off out for a drink loved the impromptu display and the novelty of having their weight read out in English.

Mum, having had her cataracts operated on not long previously was still having problems with one eye. There was quite a to-do about it later, but for now she was wearing her dark glasses that night as we bar crawled around Lugo.

The bars were heaving and there was standing room only. In the first bar I asked a large group if we could have one of their chairs for Mum. They quickly acquiesced, being Spanish and thoughtful. We had just settled Mum on her throne when we noticed the bar had cleared. We all grabbed seats, of which there were now far too many, drank our wine and ate our double tapas.

This incredible Lugo speciality cannot be iterated too often. One gets, with each drink one has, a free tapa from a circulating tray and a free tapa cooked to order from the kitchen. It is beyond wonderful!

Anyhow, back to our bar crawl. The next bar was again heaving but within minutes of our arrival it had emptied. This happened in the next bar, and the next. By this time, we were sniffing our armpits and wondering if our breath smelt of garlic. Then Debs began to laugh.

CHESTNUT, CHERRY & KIWI FRUIT SPONGE

"Look at mother," she chuckled.

I looked, then looked again. Then I began to laugh too.

"It's the bloody mafia," said Debs.

Mum, with her dark glasses, long grey overcoat and her attentive aides, was the spitting image of a Mafioso 'godmother'. No wonder everyone cleared the bars when we entered. It was a handy trick and we told Mum to be sure to bring her dark glasses in the future.

The following day after a breakfast of *chocolate* and *churros* in the nearby Café Azul, we wandered the streets of Lugo, buying cheeses from the sadly now defunct cheese shop, in which I could happily spend hours looking and tasting and sniffing. Thinking about it, maybe that's why he closed – too many tasters. Then we left Mum in a café whilst we headed for the *catastro* or land tax office.

We'd had problems a couple of years earlier when our neighbour's small barn was suddenly and inexplicably transferred to us to pay the land tax on. A complicated series of events had seen us paying the tax then claiming it back from the *catastro* on the basis that we would otherwise be fined for late payment. As the money was refunded with a very decent rate of interest a year later, we assumed the case was closed.

But, of course, the wonder that is Spanish bureaucracy could not let it end there. We had returned home from Costa Rica to find a bill from the *catastro* for outstanding back taxes for – you've guessed it – our neighbour's barn. Our helpful local office had been unable to sort out the mess this time and suggested we needed to visit the main office in Lugo. An office which our friends had described as '*fatal*'.

Leaving Mum to enjoy her coffee, we made our way to yet another flag-bedecked government building. The armed guard at the entrance checked my mobile phone and car keys then, smiling, let us through to a vast hall and showed us how to use the ticket machine.

As always seems to be the case in government buildings, the huge room was devoid of any features. There were worktables along one wall and a single office behind glass windows. In the centre of the floor were lines of bolted down orange plastic chairs.

"We're number 86," I said, peering short-sightedly at the screen above our heads.

"It's on 42," said S, helpfully.

Eventually, having exhausted I spy, What's My Line, and 'guess who gets to use the fancy office', then deciding I wanted the smiling, overweight young man at table one to serve us, our number came up. I couldn't see the corresponding table number but the smiling young man pointed to the office.

"Oo, we get the fancy boss's office," I said admiringly.

I'd practised for hours to get my speech right for this encounter so I started straight off in my best *castellano*, explaining our problem to the bored looking, bearded chap behind a large desk overflowing with papers.

"We have a bill for this property but it does not belong to us."

I showed him the bills and the refunded money from two years earlier. He read the bill sourly then booted up his computer. After a few minutes of random searching, he showed me a screen.

"Here, this is the tax you must pay."

I peered at the screen of numbers and the reference numbers. "Yes," I said, pointing. "These are ours but this one is not. It is a neighbour's property."

His expression became more sour.

"Wait!" he said imperiously. He got up and left the office.

I shrugged at S, but a few minutes later *el jefe* was back, smiling.

"*Si*, as I thought this bill is for 2012 that is why you must pay."

"But we didn't own the building in 2012," I said, confused.

"Yes, you did, here is the bill."

"No, we were repaid for that, we didn't own it."

"Ah, but you owned it before you sold it to the current owners."

"No, we didn't, we have never owned…"

He cut me off. "I have given my answer, you may leave."

"I'm not paying it," I said, angry now.

"Then don't pay. It is not important to me. Now leave."

"I'm not leaving until you listen to me," I replied.

To this he got up and opened the door. I folded my arms. He walked out.

"Now what?" asked S.

"Dunno, but we're not paying, are we?"

"Of course not…"

The boss returned. Behind him was the friendly security guard. He was no longer smiling.

"You have to leave," he said.

I stared at the beard. "You are kidding?" I said, in English. He ignored me.

"Please," said the security man.

"But he hasn't explained…" I started.

The guard twitched. I saw his gun move slightly and decided that the better part of valour and all that. We stood.

"An English speaking colleague?" I asked, in desperation.

No, obviously not. The beard folded his arms and turned away as the security guard kindly but firmly escorted us to the exit and onto the street.

DECEMBER 2014

"Well, that went well," I said.

S looked at me and started to grin. By the time we got back to Mum, patiently waiting at the café, we were both helpless with laughter.

"We were thrown out," I tried to explain to a bemused mother. "Escorted off the premises."

"At gunpoint!" added S, miming a gun in my back.

"It was a catastrophe at the *catastro*," I quipped, giggling even harder.

The legend grew. We told the tale to our local office, who said the *catastro* were *loco*. Everyone agreed the beard was a menace. And everyone loved our story. It was almost worth being thrown out for.

Oh, and yes we did eventually get the barn ownership sorted and to date have not had another bill...

Diary Saturday 27th December Sun and cloud
Up early and better rested in my own bed! L and Mum continued doing piggy things... rendering the fat, cooking the bones, turning the hams, and tidying the storeroom. Sent Mum up to the supermarket for lemons as she is enjoying her walks so much.

Mum was staying with us for another month and a half so this was a real test of the 'new normal' when she moved over. Previous holidays had been about visiting places of interest together, and time off for us. This time there were more day-to-day jobs and less travelling, but that didn't stop us visiting nearby places, fiestas, and friends.

We had been invited to a party at CJ's on the Sunday and a birthday party on New Year's Eve. We even had some down time in between, enjoying our home-produced food.

The end of the month suddenly turned frosty with temperatures hitting a low of minus six Celsius and my poorly covered geraniums on the terrace

CHESTNUT, CHERRY & KIWI FRUIT SPONGE

getting frostbite. Our carefully tended avocado tree bit the dust but the persimmon fruit survived, looking like huge orange Christmas baubles on the now bare branched tree.

Mum made marmalade and persimmon jam, S continued with the never-ending task of reroofing the whole chicken pen (some 100 square metres) in tiny mesh and I tidied my allotment ready for the spring. Our threesome was working well.

JANUARY 2015
Living Life to the full

Mum is my inspiration. I think most of you who have read my previous books will know of my playful banter and gentle teasing of my mother within their pages, but the reality is much deeper.

Born in 1931, the elder of two sisters, Mum's formative years were spent under the cloud of the Second World War. At 14, Mum started work, gas mask always at hand, in the drapery department of the local Co-operative store. Do drapery departments even exist now? What a world of changes Mum has seen.

Her entertainment in those days was the 'pictures' and local dances. There was no internet, no Facebook, no mobile phones, no TV. There was rationing, and refugees.

Mum was clever and artistic, beautiful and feisty. She still is all of those things. At 14 she won a scholarship to art college, but instead she left school and began work. In 1950 she met my father at one of those local dances. Mum tells me that she was impressed with his lighting of two cigarettes together (very film star, very flash in those days) but thought him arrogant on their first meeting as he had his foot on a stool blocking her way and teased her.

Whatever her first impressions, Mum was soon stepping out with this older man, not long back from the war . In 1951 they married and once my eldest

CHESTNUT, CHERRY & KIWI FRUIT SPONGE

brother arrived Mum became a housewife or, as it is now called, a homemaker. She settled into her new role, learning to cook and to keep home with her weekly 'allowance'.

Mum was a born mother. She would always have a home-cooked meal ready for us and would read bedtime stories from her own fertile imagination. One of my earliest memories is listening to the adventures of 'Squiggy Squirrel' and friends. I wish Mum had written her stories down. I often think she ought to have been the author, her imagination is much wilder than mine.

I always felt home to be a place of safety, knowing Mum was there. She didn't take any nonsense from us but was loving, kind, and protective.

When I was 13, I was bullied. Mum quickly discovered the reason I no longer wanted to go to school. She followed me to the bus stop one morning and when the much bigger and stronger girl started to attack me, Mum appeared. Although my nemesis towered over Mum too, she stood looking ashamed as Mum wagged her fingers and explained a few home truths. The bullying stopped after that day and Mum says that many years later the bully still used to speak deferentially to her whenever they met.

Diary Thursday 1ˢᵗ January 2015 Frosty overnight L and Mum in the kitchen all morning making kaki jam... the persimmons have a high pectin content but quite a tannic aftertaste. Either need to be riper or maybe they are better suited for chutney.
Lunch: Whole salmon trout with 'new' potatoes, French beans and hollandaise sauce. Last of Debs' crumble from Christmas with toffee sauce.

Mum was sadly widowed at the age of 55 when Dad left us far too early. Although devastated, she threw herself into life. She learnt to drive; "because Dad had only just bought the car and it's a waste". The first solo drive Mum ever made was to visit me in London. She says my brother paralleled her as she joined the motorway for the very first time, worrying she would be okay.

He had no need to worry. Mum made that journey numerous times, once telling me she had 'done a ton' to see what it was like. When I asked what she would have done had she been pulled over at 100 miles an hour she replied; "told them it was my wedding anniversary."

That first time, Mum had made it safely to my home in Muswell Hill but chickened out of driving the few miles more to Friern Barnet Psychiatric Hospital where I worked. She walked instead, arriving just in time for a massive hug from my nursing colleague, 'Mary', a six-foot two cross-dresser who his colleagues and all the patients adored despite management's misgivings as to his suitability for psychiatric nursing.

That trip was a baptism of fire for Mum but she never wavered in her belief that she could do things if she wanted to badly enough.

Diary Friday 2nd January Sunny during day, -3°C overnight
S continued fitting the new kitchen ceiling at the Casita.
Mum made some fat balls for the birds while I prepared lunch, then we tried some kaki chutney. The soft persimmons definitely have a better flavour but have lost their bright orange colour after the frosts.
Lunch: Ham and cheese quiche with leaf salad, sun dried plums, blue cheese and walnuts. Kiwi roulade with chestnut flour. Very good!
Bathnight. Mum is up to 6 lengths at the pool. I told her that's not bad for a soon to be 84-year-old! She had a couple of José's excellent vinos to celebrate... as did we.

CHESTNUT, CHERRY & KIWI FRUIT SPONGE

For Mum's 60th birthday I'd bought her a glider lesson. My family and friends were stunned as Mum hates flying, but I knew she would love the peaceful silent soaring. She did, and the pilot flew her further and for longer than anyone else that day. Mum is nothing if not adventurous.

She had been visiting us in Galicia for longer and longer periods of time since her first 'solo' Ryanair flight back in April 2008. That spring she had arrived alone and suffering with pneumonia but happy to have made it safely. Since then, her enthusiasm knew no bounds and I was delighted when she finally said 'yes' to living here.

I suppose moving to Galicia at the grand old age of 83 and eleven months was an extension of Mum's determination and desire to be living life to the full which still shines through, some six years later at the grand old age of 89 and eleven months.

Diary Tuesday 6th January Warm pm
Mum did her ironing! I tried to persuade her that it wasn't necessary to iron her undies but she is happy. S has almost finished the kitchen ceiling in the Casita. The boards have been a real pain to fit as they bend all over the place, being thinner than ours. But they look good and are pre-varnished which should mean less work in the long run.
Lunch: Mum 'took' us to the grill at Baiuca. Holiday menu for three kings. Excellent.
Started to knock the plaster off the end wall in the living room-to-be. I like having one feature stone wall in a room and as that wall is an internal one it won't need the insulation provided by the plaster. Mum wants to put a new wood-burning stove there so it will be a nice feature.

The living room-to-be was, like most of the rooms at the *Casita*, an interesting shape.

JANUARY 2015

The easiest way to imagine our little cottage is to draw a rhomboid or diamond then to place a square in the centre of it. The square is the central dining room. This leaves the six rooms off it most peculiar and unique shapes. The living room, in the upper eastern corner of the house, has two walls which form a 30° angle and another two which form a dog-leg. It is really quite original.

Shape apart, the living room was a large space. When we bought the *Casita*, that room was being used as a bedroom. There was a large wooden-framed bed just inside the doorway taking up a considerable proportion of the room and piled high with clothes, blankets and other items I didn't wish to investigate. The cats and the mice had been living on and in it for some time.

The part of the floor not protected by the bed had rotted from the rainwater which continually dripped through the roof and old ceiling. It was quite a feat to attempt to negotiate the floor as far as the window. Pepe, the owner, had carefully thrown a dining chair across a two-foot square hole the first time we viewed the house, and our friend Leo had managed to add to the general disrepair by putting his foot through another section.

At the far end of the room, beyond the bed, was a large floor-to-ceiling wooden cupboard some two metres long and a metre deep. This was made of very nicely finished sweet chestnut and I had initially assumed it was a wardrobe. Closer inspection showed the door to have a wire mesh grill in it. There was a six-inch square hole in the outside stone wall, also with a mesh grill over it, and inside the cupboard there was a wooden bench, a poured concrete floor and a large tub of *unto* or pig fat. It was evidently a ham cupboard, nicely aired for storing the *jamones*. Of course!

Functional and beautiful though it was, the ham cupboard had no place in our new living room-to-be.

CHESTNUT, CHERRY & KIWI FRUIT SPONGE

It took up just too much space and had to go. And therein lay our next dilemma. S had removed the sides already, but the wooden bench inside the cupboard actually fulfilled a purpose beyond that of a place to store *unto*. It seemed that the floor in the living room was lower than the top of the doors leading to the barns underneath the house. The bench was a raised portion of floor to allow the barn doors to open. Ingenious and another interesting problem to solve.

That, though, was a problem for the future. For now, I was concentrating on the stone wall opposite the cupboard. It was going to be my feature wall and I was looking forward to making it beautiful.

I also wanted to make the *Casita* presentable as I had invited the former owners to lunch on the Saturday and I was anxious they would like what we were doing to their family home.

Diary Saturday 10th January Hot. Frosty overnight
Mum and L spent the morning preparing lunch.
Roast pork, roast veg (potatoes, carrots, pumpkin, parsnips all from the garden)
Cherry cheesecake, Apple and gooseberry pie and custard.

Leo and Margaret also came to lunch. It was lovely to have a mixture of Spanish and English being spoken around the table and Margaret happily helped me translate for Mum. Mercedes had been practising her English which was really sweet. Both she and Pepe thought we were doing a good job of the house.

It is always difficult as 'incomers' not to feel that you are stealing someone's heritage. We have tried with both our houses to retain as much of the character of the original as possible, whilst making it comfortable for 21st century living. I hope we have succeeded.

JANUARY 2015

My beautiful niece, Belle, was due for her annual visit the following week. I always looked forward to her trips: for one we usually had better weather when she arrived and secondly, she was ever cheerful and willing to help out, especially if it meant demolition work.

Diary Thursday 15th January Snow overnight!
That's not supposed to happen when Belle is due!
Off to the airport in the afternoon, calling at Leroy Merlin on the way for an electric water pump for the well and other stuff amounting to more than we ever expect.
Collected Belle and stopped off for bacon butties on the way home.

This was the one time the weather did not cooperate for my niece's visit. The previous Tuesday we had seen the first rain since before Christmas. On Thursday it snowed. On Friday it was cold and icy, reaching a maximum of zero degrees Celsius. On Saturday, Sunday, and Monday it continued snowy and cold. Luckily, Belle was happy to be visiting us and had even come prepared with some winter clothing and no flip-flops.

Belle was eager to help me remove the old, chipped and blown plaster from my feature wall in the living room. S had a bright idea. Rather than have an entire exposed stone wall, he suggested we expose a large half-round section in the centre of the wall, leaving the rest plastered. This would provide an artistic back drop for the stove and keep that acute-angled corner from being too dark. S produced a piece of string and a pencil and proceeded to draw a half-oval using geometry and his makeshift compass. After that it was just a case of Belle and I carefully chiselling off the plaster in the centre part (and me later repairing the plaster around the edges where it hadn't quite come off neatly).

CHESTNUT, CHERRY & KIWI FRUIT SPONGE

My niece and I spent a happy day, chatting and chiselling. Mum was left in charge of lunch which was a rather tasty Portuguese cod dish with one of our many pumpkins roasted alongside it. We enjoyed our demolition but were both in need of our Friday night 'bath' and sauna by the evening.

On the Saturday a party of us met in Ourense. As it was cold and snowing, the thermal pools south of us were a definite draw. One of our friends had recommended an Italian restaurant in the city.

"But be sure to arrive by 1pm or you'll have to queue," he'd said.

Unlikely as that seemed, we were happy to have a slightly early lunch and longer to lounge in the steaming, mineralised waters afterwards.

When we arrived at the restaurant at 1.30pm (we are rather Spanish in our timekeeping), it was to a queue snaking along the pavement in front. There must have been 30 people, with red noses and red hands, stamping their feet and looking thoroughly miserable but determined. What restaurant in Galicia, land of cheap meals and good food, could attract such a crowd? I was to soon find out.

Luckily our friends are more prompt so we bypassed the waiting crowds and entered the restaurant. Kath and Jorge were sitting with Mike and John at a long table eating bread and salad, and drinking wine.

"Sorry we're late," I said, pulling up a chair and divesting myself simultaneously of coat, gloves, jacket, jumper and scarf. I sat down and pulled off my woolly hat. "Don't need those in here!"

"Can you order quickly," asked Mike. "John's hungry."

Indeed John did look hungry, being used to the more English mealtimes the pair normally kept. We grabbed menus and I translated for Mum.

"There aren't many starters as such," I began. "But I think you can mix and match if you want. That couple look like they are having pizza to start." I inclined my head towards the next table.

One of my favourite habits in a crowded restaurant is to look at what everyone else is eating. There were myriad dishes passing us as the black clad waiters raced around and the waiting hordes peered longingly through the fogged-up windows. Everyone seemed to be tucking in happily.

The lasagne looked particularly inviting and at 6.50€ for a portion, a bargain. The waiter suggested that maybe we would want a half portion as it was quite rich. Knowing Galician meal sizes well after seven years of living here, I was happy to defer to his judgement. S and I decided to share a half portion of lasagne to start and ordered salmon and chips for our mains.

That lasagne is imprinted on my brain. It was an eight-inch diameter, deep casserole dish filled with layered pasta and ragu sauce and topped with a cheese sauce so rich my arteries groaned just looking at it. And that was the half portion. Sadly, no one tried the full portion so I can't comment on its extra size, but the taste was divine.

Mike had chosen a *chuletón*. This is supposedly a rib of beef. In Galicia, that is exactly what you get – an entire rib of beef. Overhanging Mike's plate on all sides, the *chuletón* left no room for his accompanying chips.

The waiter brought more platters of salad and we ate our way through a delicious meal with more than a few leftovers for our delighted cat. Coffee was offered to us free of charge, even though it was not a *menú del día* we had eaten, and the salads were also on the house. All this meant we'd had a huge, filling and very tasty meal for 40€ for the four of us. And we would be sure to return many times – but always by 1pm.

I have written before about Ourense's thermal pools but it is worth repeating here how fabulous

CHESTNUT, CHERRY & KIWI FRUIT SPONGE

this free city resource is. Yes, that's correct – these outdoor, beautifully built, stone-lined, hot, mineralised pools set in parkland are free to the public. I am still astounded, after 14 years living in Galicia that this is so, but it is. There are two private spa buildings along the seven kilometre stretch of the river Miño but the other five pools are completely free. I cannot think of a nicer way to spend a winter's evening than to wallow, neck deep, in a soothing hot bath, chatting to friends and watching the steam form a fog above the river before it drifts upwards to obscure the road beyond. It was another lovely day of friends and food here in Galicia.

Mum says that she has never had such a social life as she has here. In England, even before she gave up driving, she would never have gone out in the evenings. It just isn't the done thing for elderly ladies. Here, socialising is everything. Friends meet up for coffee, for *tapas*, for lunch, for drinks and *tapas*, for dinner... are you spotting the trend here? Galegos love to socialise and, I have to admit, love to eat. Old and young, infirm or not, everyone goes to the café-bars many times during the day and in the evening.

In Galicia, there is no real distinction between a café and a bar (or a pub in England) – both sell a range of drinks including coffee, wines, and spirits. Most also serve food; either *tapas*, or *raciones* which are a more substantial snack. There is also no age limit in Spanish café-bars. Far from breeding a race of drunks, it seems to eliminate the novelty of going into a pub in England for the first time at age 16. It also means that from a young age, children interact with people of all generations. Children here seem much more able to have a conversation with an adult and have few qualms about chatting to everyone, young and old alike.

JANUARY 2015

Belle's visit, though cooler than her usual fine weather stays, did include a number of trips to the bars in Taboada and further afield, plenty of fun... and a little hard work.

Diary Sunday 18th January Sleet!
Belle helped S lift the septic tank back out of the hole Gabriel dug. He wants to add a carbon-filled soakaway and get it all a little deeper before connecting everything up. Glad Belle was on hand to help as it's pretty heavy even when empty.
Lunch: Roast chicken (Cleo) who was very tasty once slow roasted in the Le Cruset. Roast potatoes and creamed cabbage. Plum and walnut sponge, and custard.

On the Monday we all took a trip to Lugo. We wanted to get Mum's residency sorted out so she was legally here by the time she moved over. The first task was to get her paperwork together for her Foreigners' National Identity number (NIE, *numero identificación de extranjeros*). We took all her documents with us to the police station plus copies of everything we thought they may need. These needs seem to vary on an hourly basis, or depending on who one sees, so we wanted to be prepared. Unfortunately, we had forgotten to photocopy Mum's passport. The foreigners' office could not, of course, use one of their many photocopiers littering the place and the nearest photocopy shop had closed down, so S tramped for miles looking for one whilst we sat and drank coffee and waited for him.

Paperwork sorted, for the moment, Mum celebrated by spending some of her money on fixtures and fittings for a house which was still at the demolition stage. Still, it made her happy. The following day she continued her spending spree by ordering her brand new *cocina* (wood-burning range) for the kitchen from our local ironmongers 'Arkwright's'.

CHESTNUT, CHERRY & KIWI FRUIT SPONGE

Another task ticked off, we adjourned to the wonderful restaurant Casa Descalzo in Taboada. That cold January day, the tiny dining room was icy except where the Calor gas stove sat. Our kindly waitress sat us so close to this single form of heating that I feared the table cloths (or our scarves) would set alight. It was a kind thought, though in a way it made the side of me without benefit of warmth feel even colder.

The home-made noodle soup and *caldo Galego* warmed our bellies. And the sight of our elderly waitress wobbling along, soup almost pouring over the lip of the dangerously tilted soup bowls, warmed our hearts. The main course of pigs' liver was delicious. I feel that liver has had a bad rap for years due (on my part) to poorly prepared school meals with rubbery overcooked pieces of elderly meat. This was as different from that as caviar from frogspawn. The liver was lightly grilled, brown outside and tender in the middle. It was the best I've tasted. The home-made flan for dessert finished off a meal which, to my amazement, was still only 7€ a head.

We managed to warm ourselves up for a while back at *A Casa do Campo* before setting out to take Belle to the airport for her flight home. It had been lovely to see her as ever and Mum had enjoyed being lady of the manor, even if her 'manor' was a half ruin.

Diary Wednesday 21st January Cold and wet
Belle didn't leave us with any better weather either, then! Paid the holiday balance for our trip to Benidorm in March and looked at opening Mum a bank account here.
Lunch: Mum's favourite: sausage, mash, broad beans. Last of the plum sponge and custard.
Carlos arrived with the new cocina this pm. He was alone as usual. He and S managed to get it out of

JANUARY 2015

the van and into the kitchen. Getting the van safely backed down the narrow lane to the Casita was probably the most difficult part!
I mortared some of the stone wall Belle and I had exposed and left S to ponder the new stove.

Of course, fitting the new *cocina* wasn't just a matter of removing the old rusting one and putting the new one in its place. Oh no! Although the model number was the same, it was made quite differently to the ancient, existing range cooker – as S found out when we offered up the front.

Galician range cookers consist of a cast iron front with three doors; the oven door (with metal oven box behind) on the right and the fire door, where the wood goes, on the left with the ash door below it. The ash door on the new model was a good five inches lower than the old one which meant the new door opened onto a lump of concrete which needed to be chipped out to form the new ash box. This was going to take some time so I carried on mortaring in peace in the living room-to-be.

Thursday 22nd January Milder but still damp
Jayne and Richard arrived bearing gifts... Mum's new fridge-freezer and the second-hand cupboards we bought in the Rastro in Lugo for the kitchen. There seems to be rather a lot of them, now they are unloaded and lined up in the dining room.

The weather finally picked up towards the end of January and Mum took the opportunity to go walking along the track, up to the shop on the road in to town, or to visit one of our friends who lived in the next village and spoke English, having lived there for many years before retiring to her childhood home.

CHESTNUT, CHERRY & KIWI FRUIT SPONGE

We returned to Lugo to collect Mum's NIE and residency card. I had to go for my biennial mammogram so I left Mum and S to sort the residency. It should have been simply a case of collecting the little green card. Unfortunately, they encountered a different person who wanted all the paperwork they had already submitted. S tried to explain, but in the end he gave up and went off to photocopy everything again, leaving Mum in the waiting room.

On returning, he met the assistant we had seen before.

"Why do you have all these photocopies?" she asked. "This is already done."

S, admirably, kept his temper and they emerged with Mum's new tiny green card proclaiming her a foreigner 'resident' in Spain.

I, meanwhile, had been sitting waiting patiently for over an hour for my mammogram appointment. There was never any rush and, as the health authority put on a bus for the appointments, it was a chance for friends and neighbours to have a good chat, sitting in the warmth of the waiting area. Anyway, the service was provided for free to all residents over the age of 50 so there was no need to complain. Instead, I sat and read my book and greeted various *vecinas* as they came and went.

Once Mum's paperwork was sorted, she and S had had a pleasant time visiting an artisan crafts and design museum so well signposted they almost missed it entirely. I was so jealous we had to return at a later date.

On the ground floor was a section showing typical Galician pottery, much of which we had happily found in the *Casita*: brown terracotta with designs around the rim or occasionally black ironstone (*cerámica negra*), it is very beautiful in a rustic way.

JANUARY 2015

In one room was a display of traditional Galician clothing. This comprises heavy underskirts and a thick overskirt, generally in white with embroidery around the hem. An apron, also heavily embroidered, comes atop the skirts. There is a blouse and waistcoat above, a headscarf or sunhat and heavy clogs. The whole ensemble is at once beautiful but practical (in winter at any rate). One year Luisa insisted on dressing Mum in one of the dance troop costumes. She looked great but said it was so heavy she could barely move, let alone dance.

There was a fascinating display of musical instruments through the ages. A chap was working there, recreating ancient instruments depicted in stone carvings found on Santiago cathedral. He was more than happy to chat about his work and to show us the pieces he was making. There was a loom, and carding combs such as we'd found in *A Casa do Campo* – a large block of wood with nails banged in to tease the sheep's wool before spinning. There was an iron, like the one we found being used as a door prop at the *Casita,* and a large four-armed contraption. This latter explained another item we had found at the house. The arms were set vertically on a base and turned by means of a foot pedal to wind the spun wool into hanks. Our one now forms the base of a fabulous ceiling light which S created for our Big Barn.

That idea was still years in the future at this point as we tried to get a rather derelict cottage fit for a rather particular mother to live in. We already knew it wouldn't be ready for the summer but we thought Mum could stay with us at *A Casa do Campo* (and be on site to supervise) until it was. Our six weeks together had proved we were unlikely to kill each other in the meantime and Mum's help in the kitchen, and the sowing and sewing departments, had been invaluable. We had preserves lining the shelves, my tomato plants were in trays in the

CHESTNUT, CHERRY & KIWI FRUIT SPONGE

kitchen, and my jeans were repatched, again. It had been a good trip. I was looking forward to our minicruise back to the UK at the beginning of February to help Mum organise her move and the sale of her house.

FEBRUARY 2015
Snowy weather

We had presented Mum with her ferry ticket at Christmas. She was excited at the thought of a long boat ride and of us accompanying her home, rather than having to fly alone on Ryanair. But her perceptions were about to change.

Diary Monday 2nd February Rain
Text from Brittany Ferries to say the ferry time has changed due to weather conditions. Our new sailing is Friday afternoon at 6pm, landing late Saturday. As we have our appointments made for the opticians on Saturday morning, that is no use. Rang the ferry office and a friendly assistant gave me an alternative sailing of this Wednesday morning (4th) at 10am. Not ideal as it means leaving here silly early in the morning and a fair bit of rushing around to be ready in two days, but no other options. Still, it could be worse.

Oh! It was. It was much, much worse.

We had invited our friend Susana and her husband over for afternoon tea on the Tuesday but I swapped our get-together to brunch so we could pack and get organised for our 3am departure the next morning. Brunch was CJ's home-smoked salmon and our girls' eggs, scrambled, on muffins; homemade blueberry pancakes with almond butter; and kiwi smoothies.

CHESTNUT, CHERRY & KIWI FRUIT SPONGE

In the afternoon we packed the car with some of our haul of kiwi fruits and walnuts for the family, all the remaining eggs, and our picnic lunches to eat on the ferry. Then, confident we were sorted, we had an early night listening to the rain thundering on the roof.

Diary Wednesday 4th February
Woke at 2.30am to a white out. A bright glittering Christmas wonderland. It had been snowing, and heavily by the looks of it. Outdoors the frost sparkled and the car wouldn't budge. The temperature must have dropped overnight and the rain turned to snow. Very pretty but not good when we have a 5-hour drive ahead.

That drive was a journey from hell, or rather from the frozen wastes of Lugo.

We set off at 3am. That is, we were out of the door by 3am. Even with our nice new gravel driveway, our attempts to get the car out of the gate took me back to a similar disastrous journey to Vigo five years earlier when we had been trying to legalise our documents to allow us to marry in Galicia.

On this occasion, after half an hour of pushing and shoving, and the occasional rude word, we man (and woman) handled the car onto the tarmac and set off.

I drove the first section as far as Lugo. The roads were treacherous – unsalted and icy. They glittered in the street lights and the snow pushed against my ineffectual windscreen wipers as I peered through the gloom. I dislike driving in the dark, and I hate driving in snow, so it was with great relief that I handed the wheel to S for the leg up to the coast.

We always drive like this. Taking it in turns for an hour or so each. We find it breaks up the monotony of a long drive, and normally every other changeover is accompanied by a tea break. Not this time.

FEBRUARY 2015

The 45-minute journey to Lugo had taken me well over an hour. As S drove onto the high plains beyond Lugo, the *Terra Cha*, the snow, if it were possible to do so, got worse. It was like the inside of a snow globe agitated too harshly by a small child. The temperature had dropped again causing icy patches. Our average speed was around 50 kilometres an hour.

As we started to descend to the north Lugo coast, the snow thankfully stopped and the roads were clear. I took over at the coast and made up time along the silent and empty A8 which traverses some of the most beautiful of coastlines. Much of the road is on elevated sections giving tantalising views of the sea. Today, that sea was churning menacingly, white horses becoming white mammoths judging by their size.

At 6.30am we pulled into a service station, which was just at the point of opening, for a much-needed break and food. By my calculations, we had made up just enough time to reach the ferry at Santander safely if we didn't stop again. The coast road would of course be free of snow, being at sea level for most of its length, so we could maintain a comfortable 120 kilometres an hour the rest of the way.

The day before I had seen a weather forecast giving the '*cota de nieve*', or snow level, as '0m'. I assumed this was a typo as we never get snow at sea level. You know what they say about assume... it makes an ass out of you and me. Well, it definitely made one out of me that day. As we left the service station, the snow returned. By 8.30am we were still 30 minutes outside of Santander when we came to a grinding halt. The snow was laying thickly across the *Autovia*.

The authorities obviously hadn't believed the meteorological office either as the snow ploughs sat patiently at the side of the road, unused and unloved. The *Guardia Civiles* were out in force

CHESTNUT, CHERRY & KIWI FRUIT SPONGE

though, together with the emergency services, creating chaos by diverting everyone onto one lane – a lane much trampled by heavy wagons, and slick with ice. The other two lanes were thick with pristine white snow.

Heavy lorries were making hard going in the slow lane causing a huge build up behind them. A couple of the more daring car drivers had given up and headed through the snow on the outside lanes. S was driving once more. He looked at me.

"Well, if we want to make the ferry it's our only chance," I replied to his silent question.

S pulled out behind a four-wheel drive and carefully set us in its tyre treads. We made our way cautiously, but with far greater speed than in the 'official' lane, toward our destination.

Our ferry was due to depart at 10am. Last boarding is 45 minutes before. It was 9.58am as we drove through the streets of Santander.

"No chance," I said, pessimistically.

Poor Mum was almost crying in the back seat and I was already wondering what we would do in Santander until the next sailing, the following week. Then I looked across the five lanes of traffic and there it was. The funnels of the *Pont Aven* gleamed in the morning light.

"It's still there!" I yelled excitedly. "Quick! Quick! Cut across here!"

I was almost bouncing on my seat in excitement as S deftly negotiated his way across the road to the port entry.

As we swished through slush to the boarding gate, I noticed another lone English car just ahead of us. He passed through security, and as we came to the booth I asked if we were still okay to board.

"Yes, of course," replied the French Brittany Ferries representative. "We have delayed the sailing for customers to arrive. The snow is bad," she added, unnecessarily.

FEBRUARY 2015

We pulled up on the car deck next to the other Brits.

"That was close," I said. "A five-hour journey took us over seven hours."

"It's taken us ten from Valencia," he replied. "The snow over the mountains was horrendous."

"Still, we are here so it's all plain sailing from now on," I laughed, as we ascended to our cabins.

Oh, how I lived to regret catching that ferry!

The tumultuous sea we had passed on the way to the ferry was nothing to what lay in store during that journey. I have been in worse conditions: we were once on the old P&O ship, *The Pride of Bilbao,* in a gale force 11. That ship was an ex-icebreaker and pretty much unstoppable. Although we rocked around overnight, the only damage was the loss of a flag pole and the breaking of every piece of crockery in the officers' mess, according to Clive, our friendly whale expert. He kindly showed us a video of the waves crashing over the wheelhouse on Deck 11.

The *Pont Aven*, new though it was, was no icebreaker. It was designed to ride the waves rather than to cut through them. This meant the whole ship was moving up and down and side to side alarmingly.

I am never, ever seasick. Apparently, it is to do with having a dreadful sense of balance – my brain never knows which way up I am normally so doesn't worry about it. I'm told NASA chooses astronauts in the same way. I could've gone to the moon in a different life! S, on the other hand, has a wonderful sense of balance and was seasick for all his years in the Merchant Navy. This time we were on an equal footing and I experienced something I never want to experience again. Poor Mum, who like me has no sense of balance, swore blind our lunch was off and had given her food poisoning.

I slept virtually the whole 24 hours, down in our inside cabin, in the dark, and thankfully awoke to

CHESTNUT, CHERRY & KIWI FRUIT SPONGE

clearer skies and calmer seas the next morning. We docked on time and arrived at Mum's house by 3pm to find her neighbour and friend, my godmother Aunty Jean, had kindly lit the fire for us.

The following morning, well rested and happy to no longer be swaying, we offered to take Mum and Aunty Jean shopping.

Now, I hate shopping. Loathe it. I am in and out of the supermarket as quickly as possible, using my trusty list system to ensure I get everything I need in record time. If I know the shop, I even write my list in the order in which I will get to each specific aisle. Mum and Aunty Jean, on the other hand, wander up and down. Every. Single. Aisle. Musing on choices and even, horror of horrors, going back to an aisle they have previously visited. This I can stick for only so long. About 30 minutes usually does it.

In the afternoon we visited the local estate agency and instructed them in the sale of Mum's house. It was really happening. The estate agent thought the house would sell quickly and that being an ex-local authority house wouldn't adversely affect the sale as it was in such a perfect spot.

Diary Saturday 7th February Drizzle
L and S drove to Burton for our eye and ear tests, to do some beer shopping and to buy a new mattress. The idea is to send it with Mum's stuff when she moves over as our existing one is doing my back no good at all.

I'd found that the mattresses in Costa Rica were so much more comfortable than ours at home and I was determined to find one just like them. Most of those mattresses had had a 'topper' on them which sank just enough to cocoon my body and ensure a perfect night's sleep. Of course, one has to test a mattress thoroughly to be sure it's the correct one, after all it is a large investment and should last years.

FEBRUARY 2015

To that end we spent a very happy afternoon in a large furniture emporium called Toons, just a few miles from Mum's house. The jolly assistant agreed that we needed to check the mattresses properly and positively encouraged us to lie on each and every one until we were satisfied. I quite enjoyed the attention we got from other customers as we lay there, shoes off, seemingly snoozing on one bed after another. At the end of an enjoyable and relaxing afternoon, we paid for our new mattress which would be delivered within the month.

My local village was once home to a large coal mine, a clay works, and lime kilns, as well as a working canal. The mine and lime kilns have long since closed down but a cottage industry is thriving in the grounds. The canal has been restored in part, with a barge festival held each year, and the lime kilns' area houses an interesting museum in addition to native woodland walks. On the site of Dad's last workplace, Rawdon Colliery, there is an interactive child/adult learning and adventure centre.

On Sunday morning, while Mum prepared our traditional roast beef dinner, S and I walked the short distance to Sarah's Wood and onto the Railway Arms for a proper pint of Burton Bass bitter. The old boys in the pub thought it hilarious that we had come all the way from Spain for a proper sup of ale.

We had a lovely time exploring old and new haunts, some of which were exactly the same as I remembered them – like the derelict Norris Hall across the fields behind Mum's house, and my favourite village of Boothorpe. Others had changed out of all recognition with new walkways and paths to explore, and acres of mud to negotiate.

One of the things we wanted to do whilst at Mum's was to start the endless task of getting rid of some of the 63 years of accumulated 'stuff' she had in the house. And to empty Aunty Jean's garage of

CHESTNUT, CHERRY & KIWI FRUIT SPONGE

our 'newt collecting gear' which, after five years of not working as ecologists, had probably perished or rotted. We rescued what we could, recycled what was possible, gave away most of the rest to charity shops, and took the dregs to the local tip: a tip which is open daily – except the day we visited with a car stuffed to the roof with old plastic bottles, rotted waders and other junk from Aunty Jean's garage.

Not wanting to return home and unload everything again we went to a local pub for a pint and a think. I used their excellent Wi-Fi to find another tip nearby, so thankfully the day was saved. And the beer was pretty good too.

Our next task was to try out the walkie-talkies which had arrived that morning. I'd had the bright idea that a couple of walkie-talkies would be perfect for summoning S and our Workawayers in for their meals. We could even use them to communicate between the two houses, once Mum moved in. S and I took a long circular hike, leaving one of the radios with Mum and carrying the other with us. We kept calling her, much to Mother's consternation, to give details of our progress.

I decided I was the Gingerbread Kid and Mum was Mother Duck. S stuck with his nickname from his time as a laundrette owner, Captain Bagwash. It was great fun playing with our new toys and constantly admonishing Mum for not saying 'over' or 'out' at the right times.

I took photographs of Mum's house from all angles in the spring sunshine. The estate agent said the sun never shone when they visited for a photo shoot of a property so he was pleased with my efforts. I had to admit that our family home looked pretty good on the shiny estate agent booklet and I was sure Mum would soon have a sale.

On Saturday the 14th of February, we all visited my elder brother in Nottingham. This included a visit to a local soft-play centre with Mum's two great-grandsons. The eldest was insistent that someone joined him on the soft play. It looked fun, climbing up child-sized ladders, across child-sized netting, and down child-sized slides, so the big kid of the family... erm, that'll be me then, volunteered. All went well for the first traverse of the climbing frame, then I got mugged.

I'm not entirely sure what happened but one minute I was play fighting with my great-nephew and the next I was jumped on by around 12 kids, all kicking, rolling around and holding me down. I decided to ham it up for my audience, shouting 'help' in a nicely pathetic voice. Of course, not one of my extended family came to my rescue, despite my lovely great-nephew running as fast as his little legs would carry him to the adults' table where they all sat drinking cola and ignoring my desperate pleas. Eventually, in an amazing act of bravery he returned alone and began to try and pull the pile of kids off his poor aunty. I told him he was my hero that day as I retook my seat as a dishevelled, sweaty and slightly crazy, grinning member of our family.

Diary Monday 16th February
Back from Nottingham 10.30am. L and S repacked the car and drove straight off again. Stopped at Stafford University to drop off a load of my old text books to the library and chat to some of my old lecturers. Lunch in the canteen there with one of my friends. I sometimes struggle to believe everything that has happened since I was a (mature) student only 12 years ago.

Our next trip was to visit friends and family in Rochdale, and to sup a few more beers in convivial company. Although I loved our life in Galicia, I did miss a good pub argument of politics – and beer.

After a further week of relaxing, last minute shopping, and helping Aunty Jean with a few jobs,

CHESTNUT, CHERRY & KIWI FRUIT SPONGE

on Sunday the 22nd of February we once more set off at dawn for the ferry port. Thankfully there was no snowy weather this time, and we arrived in plenty of time for our 10am sailing. Unfortunately, our cabin cleaners were not so prompt, so we had to hang around the communal areas until it was ready.

I'd loved that old P&O icebreaker ship and really missed it. In addition to being the most stable thing on the water, it had a lovely observation lounge with old, squishy sofas and a 180-degree view of the waves. Clive, our whale man, would periodically interrupt the quiet reading going on in the lounge with an announcement:

"A pod of dolphins at 10 o'clock, starboard," he would yell over the Tannoy as 50 people rushed to the right-hand side to peer over the water.

Although the Brittany ferry is quicker, newer, and smarter than the old *Pride of Bilbao*, it can never get into my affections in the same way. Their 'whale person' was a young girl of about 14 years old who knew little more than the fact that there were whales in the Bay of Biscay. Never mind, we were on our way home.

The following morning, we were soon off the ship and on the road. At around 1.30pm we decided it was time to start looking for a lunch stop. We found a likely looking place with a *menú* board outside and went in.

We sat at a large wooden table and ordered our lunch from the options chalked up on the blackboard for the lunchtime *menú del día*. I was gazing through the picture window at the front as a car pulled up. I watched the occupants pile out, stare at the restaurant then, ignoring the front doors, head round to the back entrance.

I was just thinking how odd that was when S said, "I bet they're English."

"Is it a right-hand drive?" I asked.

"I don't know," he replied. "But look."

S nodded to the bar where the man was trying to place an order.

"Ah!"

Only a Brit would approach a bar in Spain. The Spanish always expect to be waited on. Our guess was confirmed as the elderly gent came to the table next to ours where his wife was patiently waiting.

"They've only got cheese and 'am as ah can see, pet. Not much choice."

Sandwiches! In Spain! At lunchtime! No wonder the barman looked bemused. I had to help out a fellow countryman.

Okay, so I'm actually an interfering devil, but I couldn't resist, and it was with the best of intentions, honest.

"Sorry to interrupt, but I couldn't help but overhear. You would do much better with a menu of the day from the board. It's three courses plus bread and a drink for less than your sandwich would cost." I smiled and pointed to the board.

"Oh, thank you," said Mrs Brit. She looked at her husband pointedly.

"I don't know what they are," he admitted, sheepishly.

"Starters are *ensaladilla* - that's Russian salad - mixed vegetables and tuna in mayonnaise. *Sopa* is noodle pasta soup. Or there's mixed salad - that's with tuna too. Mains are tuna steak grilled - that's the *atún*. Or pork in apple sauce. We're having that one," I added.

We were relaxing with our cups of tea after a really rather good meal when I overhead Mr Brit again. He was trying to order dessert.

"D'you 'av yoghurt?" he asked.

There was a pause, I guessed for the waitress to translate his question to herself.

"*¿Flan?*" she queried.

"No, yoghurt."

"*¿Helado, melocotón?*"

CHESTNUT, CHERRY & KIWI FRUIT SPONGE

I couldn't stick this farce. The poor chap sounded red-faced and frustrated, and the waitress was just ploughing through everything on the dessert menu with no consideration for the sound of the word. This is quite normal in our part of Spain, where the gene for guessing games must be very rare. I leaned across the gap.

"*¿Hay yogur?*" I asked, pronouncing it the Spanish way 'yog'oorr'.

"*¡Sí!*" Her face cleared as she bustled away.

"What did ah say, different like?" asked poor Mr Brit.

They told us it was their first time in northern Spain and they were rather shocked that English was not more widely spoken. Still, they were an adventurous pair, heading across the coast towards Asturias and Galicia before returning via León over the course of three weeks. I suggested they visit our local Roman, and World Heritage, city of Lugo and wished them a pleasant trip, whilst keeping my fingers crossed that they would survive the experience.

Wednesday February 25th 2015. Wet and windy.
Dear Mum,
Seems so long since I wrote to you!
How are you surviving the hordes? I didn't realise until I went online today that the estate agency is sending me every viewing request. I had dozens of emails.
Our journey home was marginally better than going – at least we were safely in bed when it started getting bumpy so were just rocked to sleep. Ended up 30 minutes late docking but we were one of the first off as we

FEBRUARY 2015

had arrived at Portsmouth early (for a change).

It poured with rain almost the whole way home which was, as I say, marginally better than snow. Had lunch on the way. Couldn't manage it all. We had forgotten how big Spanish 3 course meals are (though not really any bigger than Mother's two course ones, haha).

We got home about 7pm but boy was it cold. Jayne had kindly lit the cocina but upstairs was only 10°C. Luckily it soon warmed up. Not sure how, but the lever for the damper has broken so we couldn't turn the stove down. It was roaring all night with flames shooting up the chimney.

My tomatoes don't seem to have grown at all. I have put the peppers and aubergines back into the kitchen or they will never grow on. It must've been really cold while we were away.

Clarence was pleased to see us, though he is busy stalking the ladies again and has a lovely chunk out of his tail!

Thurs: Milder and some sun. Keep forgetting what day it is so sorry, this letter will be a bit late.

I've been doing the washing. We'll just about be sorted when it's time to pack again for our OAP holiday to Benidorm!

Tried your steam mop on the hall and kitchen floors today. Seems very good and they look nice and clean. It says it has some

CHESTNUT, CHERRY & KIWI FRUIT SPONGE

hand-held attachments too if you find them. I may try cleaning the stone wall of your well with it as there are still bits of paint on there.

Our first job when we got home was to move firewood, which had arrived in our absence. Why does he always manage to deliver it when we are not here?

CJ has said he's happy to chicken sit in March so that's good. Hopefully he will water the tomatoes too. Leo and Margaret are coming for eggs next week and to discuss our next holiday adventure. We have dozens of eggs if you'd like some. It doesn't look like Jayne ate any... though she swears she did. She even made us some cakes for the freezer (delicious too).

I believe, from the estate agent emails, that you have had at least one second viewing so that's good. I hope all goes well and we will soon have a moving date for you. We are working hard to get things done. We have some lights at last so that's a start haha.

Love you tons and tons and tons.
xxxxxxx

The house sale was not quite as speedy as ourselves, or the estate agent, had hoped in the end but we weren't to know that.

We spent the rest of our first week home tidying up and continuing working on the *Casita* using some of our DIY haul from England. S installed the lights we'd bought, I got busy planting and digging, and enjoying the late February sunshine. It was good to be back home in Galicia.

MARCH 2015
Dressing for the Costa Blanca

We didn't have long to enjoy being home before we were due to fly to Benidorm, on the Costa Blanca. We had an over-abundance of holidays that winter. There had been our 'big' trip to Costa Rica in November, and of course we had just returned from England. Now, in a week's time we had our very first Spanish pensioners' holiday. With all we still had to do on the *Casita*, it was going to be a busy week.

Tuesday 3rd March. Very mild but damp.
Dear Mum,
  We now have electric lights in two rooms at the Casita - the kitchen and the 'dressing room' behind it. Makes quite a difference, especially for seeing with!
  We (or rather you) bought the wood-burning stove you liked for the living room this week. We told Arkwright we didn't need it delivering for a while as the room isn't ready. 'Put it on a piece of wood,' he said... 'But there isn't any floor!' we replied. That confused him! He agreed to keep it in his warehouse until we want it. As he has three or four huge properties around town which

CHESTNUT, CHERRY & KIWI FRUIT SPONGE

he uses as warehousing I don't think storage space will be a problem.

Your neighbours still have the builders in. They were delivering a palletful of cement bags yesterday. S reckons they must be rebuilding the whole house.

Monterroso market was busy again. We all went to Luisa's for lunch. Mencía thanked you for the rug, though I'm not at all sure she appreciated a Spanish bull-fighting scene! We had a good laugh unrolling it in the café. I'd forgotten how large it was. Luisa asked when you were back and why we had left you in the UK rather than bringing you home.

We popped into the bank where we opened your account. The chap there asked when you were back too. I also discovered that he speaks much more English than he let on before. We are moving our account there too as the other bank keeps charging us. The last time it happened we went into the bank to complain and they removed the charges and reimbursed us. Another Galician solution to a problem!

Weds: Sunshine. Very pleasant. I'm dressing for the Costa Blanca, or at any rate packing my carry-on case. Looks like good weather is forecast for next week so I'll take my frilly bikini just in case!

Leo and Margaret may not be coming to Benidorm now. Leo was two days late paying the balance for the trip and imserso cancelled their booking! They are now on a waiting list. Don't take any prisoners, do they? This time next year hopefully you will be on a trip with us.

Could've done with my washer-upper today but even more so my seamstress - I filled 4 old maize sacks with the wool from the old mattresses and thought they would make good outdoor bean bags for summer. Of course, it's taken me half the day to sew up the ends. CJ said they were comfy to sit on anyway.

We are off to Scala. Hope your sightseers are all behaving. Had a quote from one furniture removal company. Seemed a bit steep so we will try some others.

Lots and lots and lots of love
xxxxxxxxx

PS. Thank you for two! letters. The second one arrived this morning with your Spanish bank statement. I wonder where it has been hiding. Your pension is being paid in the bank okay so that's good.

S says he can't remember a suit. Can you describe it (don't tell me…black?) The books in the back bedroom are ones I wanted to keep. We ran out of room in the car when we came home, if you remember.

Fixing the electrics in the 'dressing room', or ex-smoke room, meant we could finally see properly in there, and what a strange room it was.

Behind, and a half level above, the kitchen was a three- metre square room with what looked like a

CHESTNUT, CHERRY & KIWI FRUIT SPONGE

stone firepit in the centre. The ashy remains of burnt logs and the soot encrusted stone walls confirmed the room's use as a smoking area for *chorizos*. It also seemed to be a meeting place for groups of drinkers judging by the empty wine bottles littering the floor beneath rotted wooden benches.

The ceiling was low at one side where the roof sloped and the sky could clearly be seen in between the blackened beams and slipped roof tiles above. On one side of the room there was a large stone structure: the top of the stone well-housing in the kitchen. Although taking up a good proportion of the space, that wasn't going anywhere.

That there was also a heavy metal-framed bed in the ceiling space above the kitchen rather clouded the issue of the room's purpose, but the electric light did clarify one thing: the firepit was not, as we had suspected, a hearth of thin stones laid over the wooden floor but four rectangular granite blocks, each some 60 centimetres long by 30 centimetres wide (24 inches by 12 inches) and 20 centimetres, or eight inches, thick. These were laid into a bed of cement.

An examination by torchlight in the barn below showed the wooden floor beams were bent into a U shape by the weight of cement and granite above, and almost touching the earth floor below. There was no way those blocks were coming out without redoing the entire floor from below. We were reluctant to give ourselves more work at this stage.

Monday 9th March. Very hot.
Dear Mum,
We are all packed for tomorrow. Looks like it's going to be a hot week here in Galicia so hope my plants will be okay. CJ is kindly on watering, chicken, rabbit, and cat duty.

MARCH 2015

S has put up new metal posts for our grapevines next to the terrace (the old wooden ones were rotted) so I took the opportunity to weed the garden path... which is now three times the width! I've also potted on my pelargoniums and sown more flower seeds in the triangular bed beneath the vines. Difficult not to get carried away when it's so hot. I must remember it's only March.

The lad has also started building a wall behind where the fridge-freezer will go. He has knocked out the rest of the old chimney remains in the dressing room behind, and widened the old fireplace in the kitchen, so you have room for your wine store too.

Weds: Sunshine in Benidorm, but breezy. I will be as fat as last year's piggy after 8 days! We arrived at the hotel last evening in time for dinner. (Nearly missed it as I thought the chap said dinner started at 9pm... Spanish mealtimes, but he actually said until 9pm... very English haha). It's a huge hotel with an iconic tower spire, 44 floors and a viewpoint at the very top. Must go up one day.

Lots of Brits (you can tell them by the shaved, white heads at breakfast and shaved, red, sunburnt heads at dinner and by the fact that they were all on their sunbeds by the pool in trunks and bikinis with a pint of lager at 10am). The arrival of

CHESTNUT, CHERRY & KIWI FRUIT SPONGE

3 parties of 'Mundo Senior' (us lot) has balanced up the nationalities a bit.

The Galegos were also on the sunbeds this morning... sitting primly upright, fully dressed in trousers or skirts, woolly jumpers and jackets! I wish I had taken a comparative photo!

This morning after breakfast we had an introductory talk where the rep tells you about the trips available and tries to sell face cream! There were people from Lugo, Pontevedra, Santander, and Toulouse in France.

After lazing about the pool for an hour (but definitely not swimming as it was freezing), it was time for lunch. We are on full board, which consists of a huge buffet breakfast, lunch, and dinner. The latter two meals include a bottle of wine between us so we are not spending much!

This afternoon we walked two miles to the 'old' town to walk off lunch. I've now had a bath before more food! I'm just watching 'Midlands Today'. How bizarre to have your local English news programme on in Benidorm. Your weather tomorrow is apparently dry and 12°C. Ours is 14°C now (8pm). It was warmer and quite pleasant this afternoon. Benidorm itself doesn't seem as 'Britified' as I expected. Very clean, lovely beach, and excellent flat, paved promenade all the way along the front. A few too many

people in hired disability scooters but otherwise...
Will post this tomorrow and see if it is quicker or slower from the south!
Love you tons and tons and tons
xxxxxxxx

The Government sponsored Spanish pensioner holidays are a great idea. Participants don't even have to live in Spain as there are trips organised from France, the UK and other foreign climes where Spaniards are resident. They are also open to foreigners over retirement age and resident in Spain.

The idea is that pensioners get a cheap holiday out of season in hotels which may otherwise have to lay off staff during their quiet time. The Government doesn't have to pay unemployment benefit, businesses get revenue, and we get some sunshine. There are trips organised to all the Spanish mainland *costas* and to the islands, including the Canaries, as well as cultural trips and spa days. All are extremely well-run and very good value.

Being Spain, food is a big part of any holiday experience. The huge meals and free wine meant we really didn't spend anything on food, though we found the optional tours were worth paying for.

Unfortunately for me, I had toothache on the first day which slowly got worse over the course of the holiday. I visited the dentist twice but they could only give me antibiotics and painkillers until the swelling subsided. Luckily the huge buffet choice meant I could live on soft foods for the week.

Friday 13th March Sunny and windy on the Costa Blanca
Tramadol from the dentist helped overnight as did the extra scrambled eggs at breakfast (without toast!). Walked to a small beach called Finistrat and

CHESTNUT, CHERRY & KIWI FRUIT SPONGE

read in a sheltered spot. Who knew Benidorm was so windy! After lunch, we walked to the old town again and had a proper cuppa in Scooby's. Their advert (in verse) said 'real builder's tea, in a mug and made with boiling water from a kettle'. How could we resist?!! They also have a book exchange and fabulous homemade cakes.

On Sunday we went on one of the optional trips to a village called Guadalest, up in the mountains. The village was completely geared up to tourism but very pretty with great views from the castle walls, sitting high on a pinnacle above the town.

One of the highlights was the doll's house museum. The tiny settings behind glass were exquisite, the workmanship incredible. There was a butcher's shop, a barber's, entire dolls' houses in a table top cabinet, and complete rooms smaller than my thumb. We were sadly hustled through rather too quickly, to make room for the next group of bewildered tourists, and then disgorged back onto the roadside where yet more tourists queued. We didn't feel our second visit, to a micro museum, was worth the entrance fee; especially as the advertised performing fleas seemed to have been to the taxidermist. The stairs set into a huge conch shell were pretty cool though.

Even though this was only a half day trip, the coach stopped on the way back for refreshments and the opportunity to buy some muscatel wine. The latter was very tasty and, I felt, extremely good for toothache.

Diary Monday 16th March Very windy on the Costa Walked into the old town again (not very old generally though there is an interesting part overlooking the sea on a bluff). We wanted to do a bit of shopping. I'd promised CJ a stick of seaside rock. I don't think it says Benidorm all the way *through it but there was rock! So British. Also bought him a spoon holder which says 'we went to Benidorm and remembered you'. I'm sure he will appreciate it!*

We needed to keep walking to alleviate some of the over-eating, especially as the outdoor (unheated) pool at the hotel was far too cold for swimming, even for me. The area round the pool was surprisingly draughty too. I suppose guests need to cool down in the summer.

On the Monday afternoon we finally took the glass lift up to the 44th floor *mirador* or hotel viewpoint. The views across Benidorm and as far as the mountains behind were stunning, though it seemed such an artificial place compared to our beloved Galicia.

Around each towering hotel or apartment block there were banks of flowering shrubs and palm trees but beyond each carefully tended lawn was... nothing: an expanse of bare sandy rubble with a few scrubby bits of grey coloured grass filled the spaces between the villas and hotels. It looked like a film set – the brown bits off screen, unimportant and desolate.

Even the food was getting repetitive. There was plenty of variety but it was the same variety every day. I was longing for our Galician farmhouse and our home-grown food, our chickens and our big beautiful cat.

Diary Tuesday 17th March Sunny but very windy
Spent the morning reading by the pool and getting the final top-up on our suntans. Left the hotel at 6pm (breakfast and lunch were included on the last day and we were given a picnic supper to take away... in case we should starve on the way home). As we went to get on the airport coach, the company rep explained the bus was 'only for

CHESTNUT, CHERRY & KIWI FRUIT SPONGE

Spanish people', in rather condescending English. I countered that it was actually for imserso customers of whatever nationality, in probably dreadful Spanish. Think I made my point. Landed at Santiago at 11pm. Arrived in Lugo at 12.30am on the provided coach. Home 1.15am. Bed.

It was hot, green, and considerably less windy at home. The first thing I noticed when I woke up the next morning was how colourful everywhere was. The fruit trees were blossoming, the grass grew lushly, and the sky was a bright, unpolluted blue.

Oddly, it had been as hot and dry in Galicia the week we were away as on the Costa Blanca. The chickens had drunk every bit of water, though it was only a couple of days since CJ had visited. It was breezy at home too but we have plenty of shelter in the *horno* eating area so it felt much warmer than sitting by the hotel pool.

CJ told us Clarence was there waiting for dinner each time he visited and our adopted moggy was very pleased to see us when we arrived home trailing left over ham sandwiches. He kept popping back to check we were still here. He also gave S a nip, as a warning not to try running off again.

Diary Wednesday 18th March Sunshine and no wind
Made an appointment with our dentist. He says I have very healthy teeth. Which is no help at all.
Lunch: Omelette 'fines herbes' with a salad of walnut, blue cheese, left-over imserso picnic oranges and sun-dried plums. Natural yoghurt with honey. None of that weird sugared yoghurt they had on holiday.

My toothache had not abated at all in the eight days we were away and the aeroplane trip back seemed to have made it worse. My dentist reluctantly agreed to grind down a couple of teeth as he felt one of my wisdom teeth may have grown too much.

Meanwhile, we were ready to get stuck into working on the *Casita* again after our break. We had a Spanish Workawayer coming at the weekend. He was called Ramón; said he didn't like cold water and was not very strong. It wasn't the most positive profile description I'd ever read but it made me smile, and Ramón was happy to volunteer all weekend. He lived just an hour from us and worked during the week. For some reason he wanted to spend his time off helping us. That was fine by me!

Diary Friday 20th March Sunshine
Ramón arrived in time for morning tea and cake. Seems a really friendly chap and speaks excellent English. He works in an office during the week so wants to do some physical work during his time off. Lunch: Cod, chips and peas (very English) and queen of puddings. Not sure Ramón had ever seen a pudding of eggs, jam and meringue, but he ate it all.
S showed Ramón his work for the afternoon... more hole digging! L continued mortaring the house wall.
Bathnight. Discovered the swimming baths were closed for Father's Day (San José... which was actually yesterday bizarrely). To Bar Scala for drinks instead. Picked up my emails... dozens from the estate agent again!

The estate agency were sending a steady stream of house hunters to Mum's home. I felt a bit guilty leaving her to cope with them all alone, though Mum seemed to quite enjoy showing people round and had already chosen who she would like to sell the house to. One couple had put in an offer for the full asking price and were just awaiting their mortgage

CHESTNUT, CHERRY & KIWI FRUIT SPONGE

confirmation. Everything seemed to be going well for an early summer move to Galicia.

Tuesday 22nd March 2015.
Dear Mum,

S is back at classes this week so I have a treat...Seven Brides for Seven Brothers on DVD! I can even sing loudly along with Howard Keel.

Sorry the sale fell through. Never count your chickens I suppose. I rang the estate agency to see what happened. It seems the buyers needed a mortgage but the bank refused to lend on a timber framed building. I guess British banks aren't used to that sort of construction. They should have gone to a Norwegian or Canadian bank, haha. Anyway, the estate agent said they would make sure the next buyer has a mortgage offer in place before proceeding. They think it will still sell quickly so don't unpack just yet!

I have been carrying on mortaring the wall at the Casita while S is not using the long ladders, and clearing the soil and weeds from the stone threshing floor by the barn doors. I think it will look very nice.

Our Spanish helper Ramón (I like hot water and I'm not very strong) was an excellent worker. He coped admirably with the cold water and declared it was good for him! He dug and dug for the carbon filter soakaway from the septic tank, which S is

MARCH 2015

now connecting up. He (Ramón) also cleared lots of brambles from my fruit trees and even helped with knocking off some of the old plaster from the house wall. He came Friday (Bank Holiday here) and though he said he had things to do on Sunday, he stayed until after 6pm and worked solidly in between. Very good 'value', and he may not think he was very strong but he got a heck of a lot done. He said he enjoyed himself and may come back with a friend... we are making a to-do list in anticipation.

S has built a very neat wall behind where your fridge-freezer is going in the kitchen (where the old open fireplace was) and has skimmed the slightly raised floor ready for me tiling it. Then we can move the big lump (the fridge-freezer, not S) out of the way.

Forgot to say on Saturday, did you see that Terry Pratchett had died? It was on TV in Benidorm while we were there. Very sad and no more Discworld stories.

Wednesday: Sunny. Got your letter today... that was quick. Don't throw away the books in the back bedroom! They are classic Ladybird books and Beatrix Potter which I want to keep and my old Enid Blyton ones. I will find a space for them somewhere.

Hope your renewed viewings are going well.

Love you tons. Hurry over.
XXXXXXXX

CHESTNUT, CHERRY & KIWI FRUIT SPONGE

PS Sad to report one of my new Millets expensive socks has a hole in the heel already.
PPS We are working hard to sort out your Casita, worry not. Looking forward to you being here soon.
Hope you find a kettle you like for the cocina hob. Cream sounds very sophisticated!

Our helper, Ramón, has turned into a very good friend over the years. We meet for lunch together and he has visited us numerous times; sometimes bringing a friend to work, at others helping at Mum's garden parties at the *Casita*. He always brings a smile and his cheerful, can-do attitude and I still rib him for that profile description.

Diary Thursday 26th March Sunny but cool
Plastered (very slowly) around the 'arch' in the living room that me and Belle created. S built a brick wall in the soakaway hole which Ramón dug – it all looks very technical!
Lunch: Fried trout, mash, watercress and parsley sauce. Lemon curd tart
S cut the floor tiles for the fridge-freezer alcove. L laid the tiles while S went off to sort out our solar water. Then both looked at possible positions for a sink in the Casita kitchen. Bit of a dilemma!

The original kitchen sink at the *Casita* was a shallow stone affair, similar to ours at *A Casa do Campo*. It had no waste, just a hole through the stone wall to the outside and was tiled around in the same pretty tiles as the *cocina* surround.

MARCH 2015

Our dilemma was that we wanted to fit a proper waste and U-bend at the *Casita*. At our house we never throw anything down the sink, instead carrying the waste water to the compost heap for recycling. It's something we have got used to and saves water. We couldn't expect an almost 84-year-old to do the same. Unfortunately, the solid 70-centimetre-thick stone wall was causing a headache in the waste fitting department and it took us some time to figure out a fittingly quirky solution.

Monday 30th March. Very warm
Dear Mum,
 Good news about the house.
 We are trying our best with the Casita! I've been taking advantage of the good weather to point up the outside wall. It looks very nice.
 I was outside yesterday when granny came out of her finca with an armful of ivy she had been cutting. 'Are you putting flowers in there?' she asked pointing at the bed I'd made. I was just going to say yes when she held out the ivy and said; 'you can have some of this, it will climb.' Granny making a joke - whatever next!
 Clarence is making himself at home at the Casita, mainly by spraying on the gate post, though he did have a good inspection of what we had been doing inside too. The ladies are finally off heat (and no doubt pregnant) so Clarence is doing a lot of resting up.
 Our first house martins have returned and the bullfinches are back eating our plum

CHESTNUT, CHERRY & KIWI FRUIT SPONGE

buds. All the fruit trees are in flower though some things seem late. We haven't heard the cuckoo yet and my tomato plants are still tiny. I was potting them on this time last year. Hope they get going soon, I have a lady asking for a couple of plants for her new garden haha.

Wednesday 1st April. Hot. Busy Monterroso market day. Being so warm and sunny, there were lots of plant sellers. I had great fun looking at plants while S was enjoying himself in the hardware shop. I bought some tomato and pepper plants since mine are so poor.

Lots of people at the meeting again including a new couple from north of Lugo who came over with her 94-year-old mother (gosh, you are such a youngster.) Eleven of us at Luisa's for lunch. Would have been lovely if we could have set up the table on the pavement outside in the sunshine - inside the restaurant it was icy!

Glad the house is going through this time. Hope it progresses smoothly so you can join us for some sunshine soon.

Love you tons and tons and tons
xxxxxxx

PS Millets say they will replace the socks if you have the receipt but I don't suppose...?

PPS I will come over, once we have a date, to help with packing so please don't do any more on your own! I'll never find anything!!
Xxxxxxx

MARCH 2015

Once more a sale had been agreed on Mum's house for the full asking price. This time they were cash buyers and had no property to sell, so there were no mortgage issues. All that was needed was a buyers' survey. We were optimistic that this time it would go through successfully.

Mum had only bought her council house after Dad died. There was one of those rumours circulating about moving single occupiers of three bedroomed council houses out in favour of families, and she had panicked. To be fair it was also a fabulous deal though I don't agree with the selling of local authority housing stock in general.

Dad had thought about buying a house once, Mum told me. They had seen a property in a nearby village for £600. My godparents next door had considered buying the adjoining property, but Dad worried about paying the mortgage if he was injured down the mine and unable to work, so it didn't happen. I didn't mind, I loved our old council house and especially the garden.

APRIL 2015
A working man

If Mum is my inspiration in life, then Dad is my guide.

I was just shy of my 21st birthday when he died, and he of his 65th. We would have shared my majority, and his retirement just four weeks apart had he lived. But I still feel him beside me, every step of the way: whether it was deciding to move to a foreign country, holding my hand as I walked down the 'aisle' when I married S here in Galicia, or, most often, in the garden, helping me dig and plan and plant.

Spring is a time when I especially think of Dad. He was in his element in the garden with his flowers and his vegetables for the table. Maybe spending his life down a dark coal mine made him appreciate the outdoors more. I don't know, but love it he did.

It was Dad who told me that the souls of gardeners live on in the humble robin. Certainly, our local robins would watch me closely whilst I dug and sowed my seeds, often helping out by snatching a juicy caterpillar or cricket from under my nose before hopping back onto my spade. In the polytunnel I would often disturb one, sitting on the abandoned fork, just examining my work to date. And I would think, 'there's Dad, keeping an eye on me'.

Dad was a demon digger. Up and down his perfectly straight rows he would go, earthing up his spuds or making trenches for his runner beans. I know he would have approved of our life here, and I'm sure he would have made the move Mum was planning, years earlier.

Monday 6th April 2015. Still hot
Dear Mum,
Re. buying a new bed for the back bedroom from England, S suggests leaving it for now. We can look here once that room is done (which may be a while) and you can see what will fit where. Sorry!

I am getting on with the gardening. I have the usual problem with the mice or moles digging everything up and nibbling the roots. The polytunnel is doing well though, and no mice in there. Think I'll just cover the whole allotment in tunnels!

Tuesday: Still very hot. They've given rain on Thursday - maybe. We went swimming last night. It was shut last Thursday and Friday for Easter so it had been a while since our last bathnight haha. We thought about having a second glass of vino but without the old woman to lead us astray we decided to come back for a cup of tea instead.

Had your letter today, thank you. I assume you 'found' the gift voucher while sorting? It's a kind thought but it expired last year on 31st March 2014...

I love your description of your pastry overload! Have you thought about freezing your cake in slices? It would be a lot less

CHESTNUT, CHERRY & KIWI FRUIT SPONGE

wasteful, though I'm sure the birds appreciate it. Just an idea. Jam tarts freeze well too.

Please leave the books. If I'm coming over to collect you, I can help you pack and take any spares to the charity shop or something. We could even have a garage sale haha. Anyway, soon as you have a moving date, I'll book a flight and we can sort everything out together. Don't panic! (And please don't keep packing.)

Employing a builder is not a problem but getting them to do what we want in the Casita may be, if our neighbour's experiences are anything to go by. We will stick with our willing helpers for now and see how it goes. You can stay here until it's ready you know. And if you think we are too slow when you arrive, we will let you decide if we get someone in!

First asparagus spears up this morning. I know a 'customer' who would be queuing for those!

Weds: Still hot, but drizzle this evening (as the roof isn't entirely covered over the alpendre of course.) Our asparagus was delicious with a rabbit liver and blue cheese salad.

Got your text. Hope you manage to get the sewerage issue solved. It really is time the council sorted it properly. Fly over here and leave them to it. There's fresh asparagus for lunch again...

APRIL 2015

I have been sowing cabbages today. Had a lovely pot of basil going in the cold frame - looked today and it has gone. Disappeared. It is no more. One single twig and 6 slugs in the pot. What use are slugs really - other than as chicken food of course!
Love you tons and tons and tons
xxxxxxx
PS home-smoked mackerel delivery from CJ tomorrow (maybe lunch with asparagus!)

Mum was, maybe understandably, anxious about our getting the *Casita* finished. We aren't the fastest workers in the world but we are particular. I think I get that from my dad too.

Dad was always a conscientious worker and a perfectionist in everything he did. He would happily turn his hand to any DIY project, though woe betide it if it didn't work out as he wanted. Like his daughter, Dad did not allow for not doing one's best.

I can still see Dad's face after he had retiled the bathroom only to find that one of his wall tiles had been inadvertently put on upside down. It was only Mum's gentle persuasion which prevented him from ripping them all off again to get to the defective tile. I used to look at that tile, glaring at me from just above the washbasin, each time I visited Mum, and the memory used to make me smile.

I spent many happy hours helping Dad with one or other of his projects, especially after his enforced retirement which happened when I was just 15. It probably stood me in good stead for all the building work we have done in Galicia.

Diary Monday 6th March Sunshine
S laying bricks for his soakaway 'box' down in the septic tank hole and moving tiles on the roof. L

CHESTNUT, CHERRY & KIWI FRUIT SPONGE

filling the holes in the next bit of wall with stones before mortaring.
Popped into Monforte to see the medieval fair. Really busy but great fun.

The medieval fair in Monforte, the second and only other city in Lugo province, is held yearly in April. That day it seemed everyone in Monforte had dressed up in medieval costume, or someone's idea of medieval costume. Knight's Templars, fair maidens, and medieval pages vied with Roman togas, iron age Celts and Spidermen.

In one square there was a demonstration of birds of prey. It was a hot day and the poor things looked miserable, especially the owls, blinking in the unaccustomed sunshine. There was an archery competition running, and stalls winding up the streets of the old town. In the Plaza de España, was a demonstration of chain mail making which was fascinating to watch, though I'd hate to have to wear it – knight's horses were by necessity hefty beasts, similar to a shire horse, not the Arab thoroughbreds often portrayed in films.

As we ascended the hill to the old town there was a cry from above and two men on stilts came hurtling down the slope, a page running in front clearing the throng. I dived to one side as they sped past, both over ten feet tall, heading downhill in what appeared to be a rather suicidal race to the bottom. I didn't want to think about the consequences of a fall from that height onto cobblestones.

In the square near the Roman bridge was a children's fairground, complete with wooden, hand-turned fairground rides. The 'big' wheel was a wonder of engineering and I was sorry I wasn't even smaller, though S said I'd probably get away with pretending to be seven years old. Huh!

APRIL 2015

On that occasion we didn't stay long, but we have visited the fair many times since and there is always something new to see. The jousting on the school playing fields is an unmissable event. Although a rehearsed piece, the action when we visited was absorbing even as the heat beat down on our unprotected heads. There were boos and cheers, good guys and villains, an unsportsmanlike stab in the back and falls from the horses. Great stuff!

Sunday 12th April. Still hot
Dear Mum,
   What a lovely day again. We just went for a walk down the track. Everything is blossoming - the gorse and heather are beautiful and it is still so warm. It really has been a very dry spring. Good for roofing, though S says he's too hot up there already!
   I've sown some peas and French beans in the garden. Pity the tomatoes are still so small. We may end up with a sauce shortage this year. I potted up some self-seeded tomato plants yesterday (they grow rather well in our compost heap). They are already as big as the carefully hand-sown ones from February.
   Monday 11pm: We watered the new hazel trees this afternoon so of course it is now raining very hard to the accompaniment of thunder and lightning. Good job S secured the roof at the Casita. (Update 11.30pm... stopped!)
   Wednesday: Got your letter today but realised it is this week's letter (Sat. the 11th newspaper) so we are still missing the Easter

CHESTNUT, CHERRY & KIWI FRUIT SPONGE

week letter! Please tell me you didn't put money or an Easter egg in it?!

Oh well, you will soon be posting letters in the other direction, eh? I'm glad you are happy to come back with me in the summer as you would only be sitting around at brother's waiting for the sale to go through, and we can use your help here. The estate agent said they would talk to the buyers' solicitor and let me know how they are getting on with the searches etc., then I can book a flight over.

Brother says they are away at the beginning of June, and I don't want to leave S with all the summer watering in July, so I will sort something in between maybe. I shall have to find S a nice female Workawayer to look after him while I'm away haha.

Just been egg collecting. Nine... that's everyone, even Sarah. I wonder what the record is for the oldest laying hen? She must be at least 7 now.

Funny you should mention plants. I had been looking at Monterroso. They had very good prices on camellias, nearly as cheap as Dad paid for yours all those years ago. My book says the cuttings need bottom heat and to take in June/July so we can give it a go when I come over. Could dig up some bulbs too if you wanted. Label them now before they disappear.

Love you tons and tons and tons xxxxxx

APRIL 2015

Dad left school at 13. A skinny kid of five foot and a bit, he got a job at the local pipe works. Those clay pipes are huge; used for sewerage systems, they weigh more than my dad must have done in those days, and stand as tall. After a failed attempt to gain a pay rise – I can just see my diminutive father standing up to the corpulent figure of his boss and asking 'please sir, can I have some more?' – he went to work in the local pit.

Countless generations of Dad's family had worked in those coal mines, including his father and grandfather. Wrights had been mining coal in the area for over 200 years, and Dad was the last. Except for the war years, when he joined the RAF and spent much of his time as ground crew in South Africa, Dad spent the next 45 years in the dark of a coal mine.

Dad's garden was his escape. With fair skin and auburn hair, he burned easily but once he was forced into early retirement, after one too many heart attacks, he developed a golden-brown suntan from his hours in the sunshine, hoeing and digging. Dad grew beautiful auriculas, those camellias he bought for Mum, tiny bonsais from ordinary oaks and sycamores, and delicious vegetables from next door's garden which he tended.

On days when he couldn't get into the garden, Dad would occupy himself with his other hobbies of marquetry, woodwork, and decoupage.

His marquetry pictures, created from minute pieces of thin wood veneer, were incredibly detailed. He would collect old calendars of Welsh hillsides or country houses and use these as guides. I still have one of his pictures on the wall here: it is a Welsh cottage in shades of brown, looking like a sepia photograph. Even the clouds are of a different wood. Dad would choose from his dozens of veneers to get the effect he wanted . Sky was often from large

CHESTNUT, CHERRY & KIWI FRUIT SPONGE

pieces with wavy lines or knots in, looking for all the world like cirrus clouds. Brickwork would be red pine or cedar, and doors might be a piece of spalted walnut giving the appearance of an ancient knotted wood. He used artificially coloured pieces sparingly, mainly keeping to the variety found in natural shades – from white birch to dark ebony. It was a work of love.

Or, he and I would make place mats with decoupage. I would carefully cut out fiddly pictures of birds or animals from wrapping paper. Dad would glue these to the wooden mats he had made before covering them with 20 layers of hard-wearing varnish. I think at one point the whole extended family had some of our place mats. Mine are still in daily use, and looking good, some 40 years later.

Dad was also a social creature and a good talker. He was invited to the local Women's Institute to give a talk about his marquetry and was soon doing the rounds, his notes in his hand and his specially made display pieces in his bag.

Dad taught me to aim high and to go for what I wanted out of life, and to never hold back for fear of failure. That I ever moved to Galicia is probably due to Dad's influence.

Diary Friday 17th April Drizzly
Booked my flight to the UK for 9th June. Mum is coming back with me on the 18th. Booked hire car category B as I feel I will need the space. She says the sewage problem is still not sorted. Wish I could go and smack someone!
S is moving tiles about on the roof in the drizzle. Asked Carmen if I can use her water for jetwashing the living room wall as the hose won't reach from our house.
Lunch: Smoked mackerel tart with asparagus and leeks. Orange sponge.

APRIL 2015

Moved Billie Jean and her eggs up to the top chicken pen and shut her in – at which point she went off being broody and left the eggs!
Fiddled with jetwasher, which is playing up, then cleaned the newly exposed living room 'arch', and the well in the kitchen.

Mum had had problems with the sewerage from her house ever since they were first built. The sewer was elderly now and it ran through a small copse. Inevitably, every few years there would be problems with tree roots cracking the pipes in their quest for water. Every time this happened Mum's house was the first to back up, causing foul-smelling problems. That it happened this time whilst she was trying to sell the house was unwelcome. That it happened on the very day the buyers' surveyor arrived, was bad luck in the extreme.

Tuesday 21st April. Thunder
Dear Mum,
I timed that badly. I'd just finished plastering, whilst listening to the thunder, and as I walked back home the heavens opened. I took shelter on the terrace but by then the rain was coming horizontally. The entire terrace including the 'key hat', cushions, chairs, and me were soaked. Then it stopped, leaving everything battered and dripping. The funniest part was that the sun had been shining out of a blue sky when I walked over to the Casita. I had no umbrella, no jacket, nothing!
Still, nice and dry now by the fire.
Billie Jean has gone broody and is sitting

CHESTNUT, CHERRY & KIWI FRUIT SPONGE

on 6 eggs. She left the first lot then changed her mind again. I think Buffy may be broody too (they usually start the same time) so hopefully we will have chicks by the time you arrive in June.

At last, I have tomatoes. All the self-sets are growing really vigorously. Why do I go to the trouble of sowing them? I should just scatter our compost where I want the tomatoes, since it seems to be full of tomato seeds. The asparagus is good this year and the peapods are just fruiting, along with the broad beans.

We have a Swedish helper coming in May for four weeks so S will have someone to help while I'm in England. Sadly for him, it's a man not a gorgeous blonde female Swede. Still, I told him you can't have everything!

I have posted a few pictures of the cleaned living room 'arched' wall and the stone well on Facebook. Get Jan or Mandy to show you. The wall looks lovely and even my plastering isn't too bad. S has fitted your nice new chimney damper (tapa) in the kitchen wall. That was a fun job - trying to plaster down the rather narrow chimney. I have now started on the garden/window wall in the living room. I'll be getting professional if I'm not careful haha.

Weds: Less rain and more sun today. Glad my letter arrived. Still not had your Easter letter so I'm guessing we probably won't now. I hope all went well with the solicitor.

APRIL 2015

Suppose I will find out when this week's letter arrives.

I am double cooking (especially cakes) at the moment, and freezing stuff so S and the helper (Lars) will have plenty of 'ready meals' while I'm away.

When S was on the roof yesterday, he says Eusebio came to tell him it was going to rain. He was right of course. He (Eusebio) keeps popping his head into the kitchen, and I caught Granny peering through the window last week. They are all anxious to see how we are getting on.

Thursday: Just got your letter. Need a brandy myself after reading that. Stupid solicitor. He has obviously not been doing much toward the sale, has he? Glad you are coming in June. Sounds as if you will be done all their work by then.

DON'T WORRY - all will be well
Love you tons and tons
xxxxxx
Keep taking the brandy!

When Mum visited the solicitor, he had asked about building regulations paperwork for removing the wall between the kitchen and dining room. Dad had done this work in the late 1970s while the house was still owned by the council. The wall was a non-supporting, plasterboard one but the solicitor was adamant the relevant paperwork was required.

Mum's house, being an ex-local authority property, had a number of special conditions written into its deeds by Mum's original (and now sadly retired) solicitor. These included the council being responsible for the sewerage system and a clause holding the Coal Board responsible if any subsidence should occur to the property. This is a standard clause for any sale in a coal mining area, though the house does not sit on a coal seam. The new solicitor seemed unaware of these things and was slowing things down.

I started to think that we would be much better selling the thing ourselves and cutting out the middle men. I did exactly that when I sold my own Peak District house before we moved to Galicia to live. S and I made a 'for sale' board for the garden and I sent out details sheets, created on my computer during slow working hours in the Fens, to anyone who rang. I discovered that one could download the house deeds, and in fact all the relevant forms, online exceptionally cheaply. And I was stunned to discover that neither an estate agent nor a solicitor is legally required to sell a house. I did my own conveyancing and the sale cost me less than £50 in total, including hiring a van to transport my stuff to S' house.

My buyer's solicitor was not impressed with me cutting out the 'professionals' and sent me what I considered an extremely snotty letter. I replied in my best legalese, pointing out that I had a right to do my own conveyancing. He soon backed down and became quite helpful.

When we sold S' house, we were working away from home so were forced to use an estate agent. They would ring us to say someone wanted to visit and I would point out that they had the key, whilst we were 300 miles away. We still ended up doing most of the work ourselves, including talking with the buyers (who only lived across the road and had apparently been wanting to buy the house for years... ah, hindsight) and sorting out all the problems their solicitor raised. We emailed back and forth, myself and Laura, our buyer. She would tell me the latest thing her solicitor had asked about and I would email our solicitor straight away.

At one point our solicitor had said to me; "Lisa, you cannot keep answering questions I haven't even asked you yet!" I could, and I did.

Stuck in Galicia, I felt helpless to jolly along Mum's sale and was getting increasingly annoyed on her behalf at the compounding problems she was facing.

I think I get my impatience from Dad too. I once had to ask my ex-boss for a 12-word description of me for a university project. 'Lisa is an exceptionally loyal friend but she doesn't suffer fools gladly,' he wrote.

Sunday 26th April 2015, 8.15pm. Damp
Dear Mum,

Just spent a most interesting hour. The pair of us trying to change the headlight bulb in preparation for the car's ITV (MOT) next month. The side light wasn't working and what a faff. You need three hands and a mirror to see what you are doing but there's only space for one (small) hand... that'd be me then! Then we finally get the clip on and the new bulb is exactly the same as the old one (i.e., not working). Good job we are better builders than we are mechanics.

Actually, we had a nice afternoon. Had lunch in Monforte along with Kath and Jorge, and Mike and John. Slow service but very nice wine so no one bothered much about the service haha.

S asks if you remember Debs' and Al's glass floor upstairs? He says the light coming through the skylights in your roof and then

CHESTNUT, CHERRY & KIWI FRUIT SPONGE

through the holey floor in the utility-bathroom is marvellous for lighting up the downstairs barn below. So, in the bathroom - a glass floor. Yes?

Did I tell you about my visit to José and Rosi at the construction yard? S wanted some more rubber washers for the roof nails. I called in and said 'the boss wants these'. Rosi found them but didn't write a ticket. 'How much?' 'Nothing, it's a present!' So, you have a tiny bit of free roof. I suppose we have been good customers over the last 8 years.

Tuesday: Dull but S has managed to do some roofing without getting wet.

Looks like the neighbours are playing keeping up with the English again. Eusebio and gang are having new windows... brown uPVC like yours! Last week they had a kitchen firm in. Copycats haha.

I found Eusebio sitting on your stone seat by the door this morning. He said he was tired and looked it poor thing. He has a mountain of firewood he is chopping by hand. I think the 'ladies' ought to take more care of him. Don't know how they'd manage without him.

Billie Jean is still egg sitting and Clarence is wandering about 'singing' like a... well, a love sick tomcat! It must be spring!

The lad is taking me to Bar Scala so I'll post this on the way - though as our bank

APRIL 2015

holiday is Friday (the first of May) and yours is Monday I don't hold out much hope for a fast arrival.

Bought a new notepad this week then realised I only have about 6 more letters to send... ever! Who can we bribe to send our Telegraph crosswords out??

Love you tons and tons.

xxxxxxxx

Dad was a working man but, despite leaving school with no qualifications at 13, he was one of the most knowledgeable men I knew. He read voraciously, as do most of the family. He could quote Shakespeare and the Bible with equal abandon though he was not a religious man. He also often quoted ditties and poems whose origins are lost in the mists of time.

"Old hippo with a sigh sat down, he'd had a tiring day," he would say as he plonked himself into a chair. Or; "he little knows (with a touch of the nose at this point) I saw him take, the largest slice of cherry cake," if Mum had been baking. A man carrying a mattress invoked a comment from Dad of; "pick up thy bed and walk": A lady with an impossibly large harp; "I took my harp to a party but no one asked me to play."

He would tell me stories of Moira of long ago, and silly local rhymes.

"Go count the chickens," he'd say. This was the beginning of a rhyme I'd learnt when I was a babe.

"There's one together, two by their sen (self) and three among one of Grice's," I'd reply, on cue. It's a variation on the 'how many beans make five' rhyme, but much more fun.

Dad and Aunty Jean were both Moira born and bred so had a connection their spouses, both from 'off', could never fully understand. 'Off' meant, in

CHESTNUT, CHERRY & KIWI FRUIT SPONGE

Mum's case, three miles away, but she wasn't considered a local.

"A man knocked on the door. 'Ayup lad,' says the lady of the house, 'yourn not fray round 'ere.' 'No indeed, I'm from Italy,' the man replied. 'Oer, 'av you come all that way this mornin'?'"

I loved Dad's little sayings and still quote them to myself at times. It makes me feel close to someone who has been gone far too long. Some of his sayings have passed into general usage amongst S and I. If someone says they live a few kilometres away we say, "Have you come all that way this morning?" and at New Year we always quote Dad's ditty of the one-eyed Moira man and the man with one ear meeting in the street...

" 'appy noo 'ear to you," says the one.

"And the same to you, you one-eyed bugger," replies the other.

Dad was also the organised half of a very loving and close marriage. Whereas Mum is happily and sloppily disorganised, Dad would have lists. I get my list making nature, which S laughs at me for, from Dad.

Dad's notebooks were legendary. Dad and I would happily make gardening lists and planting lists, and lists of lists. I had my brand-new notebook already filled with lists for Mum's move and I was secretly dreading what Mum would have done to 'help' pack by the time I got there.

MAY 2015
A time capsule

I would be needing all my considerable list writing skills, and any diplomacy skills I could find, come June when I travelled to England to help Mum pack up 63 years of goods and chattels. I was looking forward to her arriving, if not the chaos which would inevitably come first.

Monday 4th May 2015. Heavy winds and rain pm
Dear Mum,
  Hope this arrives. We have a post office strike planned here. With luck, I may just beat it!
  We had a good weekend. Cris and Steve were coming to the Monterroso meet up on the 1st May. They were back over to sort out their house but didn't make it here until Saturday in the end so there were only 7 of us at the market. Excellent meal at Luisa's. I had fresh tuna. Two big steaks so I brought some home for another day.
  Cris and Steve had been cleaning up their house after their tenants left. They said they spent four days cleaning, it was such a tip. That's why they were late arriving here. The

CHESTNUT, CHERRY & KIWI FRUIT SPONGE

tenants had left food in the fridge and freezer then turned them off. They had scratched the wooden floor and damaged the worktops. It reminded me of my only venture into renting out when I let my house in Barnet. Do you remember the mess my tenant made? And then she ended up trying to defraud the social security too. I was pleased to see the back of her. So, no, I don't think your neighbour's suggestion of renting the house out is a good one. Don't worry - it will sell. I do think renting a skip is a good idea though. It would save lots of trips to the tip and we can put you in it if you misbehave haha.

When Cris and Steve arrived, Steve helped S lift the septic tank back into place now he's finished making the soakaway. So that's another job done and another tick on the 'completed' sheet!

Tuesday: Damp but sunny. Glad your removals man was good. You should have the quote by the time I ring on Saturday.

Now, please don't start packing too much before I get there. Brother is going to get hold of some packing boxes for us and I have my lists ready and organised. If you want to do something you could start packing your winter clothes into suitcases to store but remember to leave two cases free for your clothes to bring here. You will only need summer stuff for the time being and I can always find you working clothes. Plus you have quite a few things here already. I am bringing just hand luggage but have booked two suitcases coming back so we should manage...

I think brother was coming over at the weekend to fit your new electric shower. I asked him how much power it used, as we thought we could bring it over rather than him bother fitting it at Coronation Avenue now. He said, 'not much, only 9.5kw'. Unfortunately, our supply is only 3.5kw so that's one idea out of the window. Brother thought it hilarious!

Weds: Sunshine... in parts. Concha was being 'helpful' again. When it rained on Monday, S cleverly thought to put some buckets under the end of the guttering to catch rainwater to fill the septic tank. Concha saw him and thought he was trying to stop the water running into the barn so suggested he ought to fit the guttering right to the corner. Of course, when he does exactly that she will think it is because of her advice!

Love you tons and tons
xxxxxx

Because the only 'land' we owned at the *Casita* was the large open barn area, it was the only area in which we could put the new septic tank. Pepe had been sure there was an existing *fosa septica* somewhere. If there is, we still haven't found it.

Our vegan Workawayer, Gabriel, had dug the hole, and our friend Geert had helped lift the tank in some time ago. But S wanted to make the thing bomb-proof and odour free. He added a brick-built box below the septic tank filled with carbon, rescued from our various fires, to help filter the waste before the cleaned water leaked into the soil many metres below ground. It's not ideal having a septic tank in a barn which is used for parties and sitting around drinking coffee, but it is now well-disguised and there have been no complaints so far.

Another issue we had was the electrical power. In the UK one pays for the amount of power used. The more you use, the more you pay. Here one has to estimate how much power you want to be able to use at any given time before applying to the electricity company. The standing charge is dependent on your power allowance and rises sharply with a higher number of kilowatt hours. Our supply was the lowest possible at the time, 2.2 kilowatt hours. This meant that in theory if we ran our water pump and the microwave simultaneously, the main fuse would blow. Luckily in all the time we have lived here we have only tripped the fuse board switch twice and have never caused the fuse to blow at the main box.

For the *Casita* we decided 3.5 kilowatt hours would be enough to allow Mum the use of her electric kettle (a ridiculous three kilowatts) and her prized washing machine, which she makes very good use of on an exceedingly regular basis.

Often there is no choice in the power supply one gets in Galicia. When our friend Jen wanted to install a couple of electric showers for guests in her house, she was told it was impossible as there was not enough power to the village to allow her to upgrade her meter. The lights at their house used to flicker of an evening when the nearby milking machine came on.

I think this system is a hangover from when Spain had a quite limited power supply, electricity stations and cables. As Spanish companies such as Iberdrola now own much of the UK's electricity supply, I can't see that it is any longer necessary. But it's the system they use so 3.5 kilowatts it was, and Mum's brand-new electric shower stayed in England when she moved here.

Diary Saturday 9th May Sunshine! Warm
Drove over the tops for lunch. Got stuck in a cow jam there and back. On the way back the cows were alone and not for moving off the road. I tried to herd them into a field but they just kept running in front of the car. By the time we got past we had herded them 2km down the road. Kept wondering what the farmer would think when he finished his comfort break and realised his cows had gone!!
Planted Melons and peppers in the polytunnel and repotted the self-set tomato plants.
BJ has one chick. Two eggs pipping. Popped them back under her but when I checked later, she had abandoned them anyway.

It was to be a poor year for chicks, and this one gained the name of Tonic Sol-Fa or Toni Solita Faith Jean. Why I was feeling musically minded with that particular chick I have no idea but Faith, as she became known, survived her complex name and lived a long and happy life.

Sunday 10th May. Still very warm
Dear Mum,
The crickets were singing away as I did my nightly slug hunt (the pests have systematically eaten every runner bean as they came up) and it feels quite tropical. Sadly, my French beans are poor too... only 3 plants up and just when we have a bean-loving guest arriving to live with us! Luckily the pea pods and peas are doing better, and

CHESTNUT, CHERRY & KIWI FRUIT SPONGE

the self-set tomato plants are romping away. No idea what variety they are of course so it will be exciting when they fruit!

Tuesday eve: Over 30°C today. Our man with the plasterboard, who was due this morning, finally arrived at 5.30pm just as S needed to get ready for his Spanish class. He (Antonio) is a lovely chap but so chatty. He liked your house. Examined every part of it. Then he examined the English rockwool insulation Richard brought over for us. He was most impressed with the price and said if we brought a container of it over, he would buy it from us as it's much cheaper (and better quality) than he can buy here. He didn't stop talking even as they carried the 60 large sheets of plasterboard into the house. Poor S finally got off about 6.15pm.

Weds eve: Warm but breezy. Just had a nice shower. I opted for the outside hosepipe shower as it's more powerful and such a good view looking across the valley. A bit nippy in the wind but pleasant inside the horno area. S is trying the bathroom solar - I'm listening for the screams if it's too cold haha.

We certainly needed our showers tonight! S was on the Casita roof in the heat. Last section over the alpendre. It really is a huge barn and a lovely space. I had promised Carmen I'd jetwash her steps and patio (as she had let us borrow her water and jetwasher to do the living room walls after mine packed up). Of course, I ended up jetwashing me too... and Carmen! She was very pleased nevertheless, and surprised how white her patio tiles were.

Carmen's son-in-law is standing for the local elections. We had a deputation on Monday. One chap looked familiar. Turned out he is married to one of Ben's granddaughters, and both his identical twin brother and his sister-in-law came to me for English lessons. At least we know all our candidates!

Just realised this will be the first year you will be here for Taboada festival in August. I think it's the week S' Australian cousin is here too so we will have to go and paint the town red.

Fiesta season starts Friday with a giant paella in the square. Yum!

Love you tons and tons
xxxxxxx

The *papeiros* festival in our home town involves a giant paella, cooked in a three-foot diameter paella pan in the market square. We had enjoyed the feast on previous occasions, even though we still had no idea what *papeiros* were. Luis told us it was a nickname for people from Taboada but couldn't enlighten us on what it meant, other than it was 'rude'. Knowing that any festival involving food was sure to be popular, we came straight back from our Friday night swim rather than staying for a drink in the poolside bar.

Of course, nothing had happened by 10pm, despite the boards advertising a 9pm start. Instead, we wandered into bar Scala for a drink. Us and the

CHESTNUT, CHERRY & KIWI FRUIT SPONGE

rest of the town it seemed. The front bar was packed with people awaiting the commencement of proceedings, so we went into the new back room where Luis had created a comfortable outdoor/indoor space. They had put out tables and chairs, built a fish pond and had a huge banana palm. I noticed Luis setting up a long row of tables with plates and wine for their family supper. We had just paid for our drinks and decided to go along and see what was happening in the square when Luis asked us to join them. I declined saying we were going for paella.

"You can eat paella here with us. Come, sit," he said escorting us to a couple of chairs around the table.

Someone appeared with a huge pot of paella from the market square, which they dished out with alacrity. Despite my feeble efforts, Luis refused the money for our share of the food. We were force fed (in the nicest possible way) two huge platefuls of paella washed down with the family's own excellent wine. Afterwards, there were desserts and cream cakes someone had brought in. It was a typically generous offer and a lovely evening – but I did feel guilty, not paying.

On Sunday our new Swedish Workawayer arrived. We had not had any volunteers, other than our weekender, Ramón, since the previous autumn. We were keen to have the help again and had missed the easy company of the young people passing through.

We collected Lars from the bus stop in town on Sunday evening and decided to go straight for a pizza – to our local, and only, pizzeria, in Taboada. A pizzeria in Galicia run by a Danish woman who met her Galician husband in Greenland. Now that's what I call an international restaurant. And the pizzas are darned good too! We thought Lars may enjoy chatting to the owner. They understood each other very well as the Danish and Swedish languages are closely enough related, though of course both Lars, and Lottie from the pizzeria, speak excellent English, as do many people from Northern continental Europe.

Monday 18th May 2015. Warm
Dear Mum,

Well, that's the heels gone on the second pair of socks from Millets. Rubbish for the price, weren't they?

Meant to ask if you have an old fleece, or if brother's working fleece is still at yours? It would save me bringing one to work in (if I will actually need a fleece in June haha).

When you book the Doc can you try for Weds, Thurs or Fri (10th, 11th or 12th June) as I would like to go to Burton the following Monday (once we are all packed up) for some essentials. I have it all planned out as you can imagine.

Tuesday: cool and cloudy. Not sure I am going to stick this helper for a month. He is a good worker but tends to do his own thing and wander off in the middle of something.

Yesterday he left S stranded on the roof as he had borrowed the long ladders and didn't take them back. Then he left a pile of ivy 'tree trunk' on the track so Eusebio couldn't get his tractor in. That got me yelled at by Concha! Today he went to have his wash after work but left the barrow, spade and fork outside in the middle of the track.

On the plus side he has found the

CHESTNUT, CHERRY & KIWI FRUIT SPONGE

sledgehammer head which Gabriel lost all those months ago. It hadn't gone into next door's field at all but inside the alpendre through a tiny gap in the slatted wooden sides and was buried in a large heap of rubbish in the corner. I emailed Gabriel to tell him haha.

Weds: cool again. Will have to relight the stove if it carries on like this. Brrr. Mind you Lars still has his shorts on so I guess it's warm for a Scandinavian! S is sorting out jobs for him so I'll let them get on with it.

I have been planting out leeks - 78, if they don't get eaten. The plasterboard man, Antonio, left us some compressed-wood spacers with holes in so I've buried those in the allotment bed with mesh below. The holes are just the right size for a leek plant. We get to recycle something - and it may stop the monster eating them.

The aubergines and tomatoes are growing well now and the melons and squashes too, so long as the mice/moles/monster leaves them alone! Talking of which... slug hunt time!

Later: Good haul. They were all crawling south to north along a piece of old lino on the allotment. The chickens will be happy tomorrow morning!

Oh, and Bob, Polly, Bob. Just think, we will be together for the next new moon.

Love you tons and tons and tons

xxxxxxxxxxxxxx

MAY 2015

Mum has some of the most wonderful superstitions I've ever heard. I have never managed to find the origin of her 'Bob, Polly, Bob', though my godmother used to carry out the ritual too – I always said they would have been burnt at the stake as witches a few hundred years earlier.

On the first night of the new moon each month they would face the moon and bow or curtsey whilst saying the words, 'Bob, Polly, Bob'. If this ritual was not undertaken, or if the new moon was seen through glass, they had to break a piece of wood into three. As I say, I can't find any reference anywhere to this bizarre practice, so if anyone has heard of it, please do let me know!

Diary Thursday 21st May Sunny but cool breeze Made cakes and pud. Gutted sardines for lunch (why do they never sell them cleaned?). S put the final uralita on the alpendre roof. Wow!

The roof of the *Casita* is a strange and organic shape. The house has a standard apex roof which is more or less rectangular in shape, albeit a skewed rectangle, but at the garden end the roof adjoins that of the *alpendre,* or open barn, to form a sort of 'L'. This roof is far bigger than we imagined and has some lovely wavy ridges on it. The back wall of the *alpendre* is contiguous with the back of the *Casita* whereas at the front it forms a 90-degree angle with the house wall, enclosing the courtyard garden on two sides. Finishing the barn roof meant yet another tick in the 'completed' column.

Monday 25th May. Sunshine but cold NE wind
Dear Mum,
It's officially summer – I decommissioned the cocina today. Cleaned and oiled the top

CHESTNUT, CHERRY & KIWI FRUIT SPONGE

and covered it with the oil cloth and stainless-steel cover. It looks very clean in there now, though I miss it already. We had trout with salad and new potatoes for lunch so I didn't need an oven for that, but I'll certainly notice come Sunday. We also moved the living room round to its summer configuration and oiled the stove upstairs. That's it... summer has arrived (it is bound to rain now haha).

S has Lars busy scraping the beam in the Casita living room. On Saturday he and S went to the tip. The car was bulging again. Don't know where we keep finding this junk from. They had cleared the alpendre of yet more rubbish, and the barns below the house, so we have more storage space for your furniture.

I've knocked off the last of the old plaster from the side of the house. Even Granny admitted it looked good. It certainly beats the garden as it was when we bought the place, and they have a more pleasant view from their window too.

We voted on Sunday. It was quite busy at the town hall but they found our names easily... we were on a separate page which said 'foreigners'! You go into a booth and there are shelves full of slips of paper. Each slip is a list of all the candidates for a particular party standing. You choose a slip and pop it in an envelope then pop that in the box. The floor, as you can imagine, is littered with slips. It was like wading through a paper forest.

Anyway, after doing our duty we walked back and had a rather tasty lunch of rabbit with chestnuts and spinach, roast potatoes, and a lemon meringue tart for pudding.

Wednesday: Just got your text... Oh well, good job this is your first and last house sale isn't it. Bet you had a few choice words. Don't worry, you are still coming in June and like I say, IF a sale hasn't gone through by then we will leave brother in charge and the estate agency can have a key. On the bright side we have somewhere to store the furniture for free for a bit longer.

Try not to worry. I have made up the spare room ready for our long-term guest. I hope you will be happy here. I'm told the hotel is not bad haha.

Love you tons and tons and see you soon xxxxxxxxx

Lars turned out to be a super Workawayer once we got used to each other. He was a fair bit older than our usual helpers and therefore much more independent. In Scandinavia he was a guide for hiking holidays in several countries. After he finished for the day Lars would take himself off for walks, coming back armed with plants he had found to identify with his field guide. Sometimes we would look at his finds together, consulting some of our plant guides. At the weekends he would journey further afield, managing to use a bus system I had thought rather inadequate, to go for miles. Lars even

CHESTNUT, CHERRY & KIWI FRUIT SPONGE

discovered a bus which left Taboada in the early morning and went all the way to Ferrol on the coast.

One of the outdoor jobs we had Lars doing was to tidy the garden at the *Casita*. Although Tara and Rupert had cleared it of its 25 plus years of brambles and vines, the area was still a bare brown space.

Six years on, that garden is still tiny but full of life. Inside the gate, next to the house wall, there is a large winter-flowering honeysuckle (*Lonicera fragrantissima*). It's a cutting I took from my own plant, that first year we bought the *Casita*. It is now a metre and a half diameter bush and looks and smells beautiful in winter with its white, fragrant, honey-scented flowers and pale green, semi-evergreen leaves. The bees love it.

Beyond this, also backing onto the house wall where it gets the morning sunshine, is a wooden bench and beneath it grow snapdragons and poppies. The snapdragons I had given Mum as a packet of seeds one year to sow in one of her pots. She had returned the packet to me saying it was empty. I had been sure it had seeds in when I gave it to her but thought no more of it. The next spring, we solved the mystery when dozens of colourful flower spikes appeared, right below the bench on which Mum had put the flimsy paper packet of seeds. The wind had done the rest of the work for her.

On the opposite side of the garden are the *hórreo*, or grain store, the steps up to it, the ex-dog kennel below and the brick-built ex-chicken house. Gabriel had managed to remove the roof from the top of the chicken shed prior to losing the sledgehammer head, and I had lowered the sides still further but we had done no more to the 'garden' than that.

Lars bricked up the front of the ex-chicken house, where the old wooden door had been, to contain the raised garden I wanted to create. It would be at hip height, so ideal for an older gardener to weed and maintain, and Mum could fill it with the plants of her choice. I also wanted the dog kennel bricked up as we had no intention of having a dog in there. I planned to make a flower bed in front of it, in the space created in the angle of the steps and the protruding raised bed. Lars happily did this job for me, but he had an idea of his own too.

"I thought I could put a time-capsule inside the dog kennel before I brick it up."

I was intrigued. "What sort of thing?" I asked.

"I don't know, just something to say what I have been doing."

In the end Lars wrote something out in Spanish, English and Swedish about who he and we were, about the house, and what we were doing to restore it. He wrapped the whole thing carefully in plastic along with a local newspaper and sealed it inside the dog kennel. It is an interesting thought that maybe, many years from now, someone will uncover Lars' little scroll and wonder about us and our lives here in Galicia.

Above and behind the chicken pen, now it had been reduced in height, was a small bricked over part of the stone plinth on which the *hórreo* stands. Thinking back to the hidden cupboard in our bedroom at *A Casa do Campo*, I wondered what was behind the bricks.

It didn't take us long to find out.

Once the thin layer of bricks was removed, we found a small niche around 12 inches cubed. This hollow was not empty, though. It was full – of roof tiles, old leather boots, and glass bottles. A later Workawayer theorised this was a shrine: to a roofer who died after his boot slipped on the roof following a heavy lunchtime drinking session. As explanations go, it was as likely as any other.

On the last Thursday in May we took the car into Lugo for its annual ITV (MOT) test. Our Ford Escort had been ten years old when it made the journey

CHESTNUT, CHERRY & KIWI FRUIT SPONGE

here. It had served us well but its time was coming to an end. On this occasion it failed on the brakes - hardly a surprise given how bad they had become of late. The handbrake had been a disaster for years, stretched well beyond the point of no return.

The same day we dropped Lars at the bus station in Lugo, he was off exploring further afield for a few days.

JUNE 2015
I – Departures

Lars returned from his travels on the 2nd of June and the old Escort passed its ITV test on the same day. It had a stay of execution... for the time being.

Lars was staying to help S while I was in the UK helping Mum pack. Yet again, the promised sale had fallen through. Yet again because of the wood-framed construction.

This time the surveyor had highlighted a potential problem with the condition of the vapour barrier between the timber framing and the brick-built skin on the house. There had never been any problems with the house which had always been dry and damp-free. Mum's cash buyers were not convinced and pulled out. My brother told Mum not to worry, the house would get sorted and I told her she was coming back with me no matter what in just two weeks' time.

She had, though, vetoed the idea of us 'storing' her furniture in the house until it sold. To me, and to my brother, it seemed a simple and economical solution but Mum was adamant. She worried it would get stolen, even though she often left the house for far longer whilst holidaying here. We arranged one of the removal firms to collect it on the final Tuesday I was in England and keep it in storage until we could make space here in Galicia.

CHESTNUT, CHERRY & KIWI FRUIT SPONGE

Tuesday 2nd June 2015. Very hot
Dear Mum,

An historic day. I have just realised that, all being well, this will be my last ever letter to you. In future I can just tell you my news and since you will be part of it from now on, there will be little to tell. This does mean that I now have an almost full writing pad to scribble in. I shall have to make up an imaginary friend or get a penpal!

It was busy at the meeting yesterday. 11 of us for lunch, though not the best we have had. We tried a new place. Leo and I had a type of mackerel called Jurel - not a very big fish and quite bony but we were only served half each. Poor Leo was staring at his plate wondering where the rest was. A few had churrasco (barbecue grill) and it was burnt. Not just a bit charred either but completely black. Won't be trying that place again.

I hope you are all ready and the house is not too much of a tip from your 'packing'. Please, please don't do anymore! I have my lists and am organised, worry not! And it really doesn't matter that the house hasn't sold yet. The estate agents can take care of it and I'm sure being empty of furniture won't make a difference. People like to see where they can put their own stuff anyway.

I am busy making up meal packages for the lads while I am away so they can get on with working without worrying about what's for lunch. I am making a main course for each day and a pudding to go with it. Some need a little preparation like making custard to go with the jam tarts (I've left instructions for that), others just need reheating. I am labelling them all with dates too so they know what goes with what!

I am also potting up the rest of my tomatoes before I leave. I'm hoping they will be ready to plant out when we get back. I have plenty now, so you can have some for the Casita garden. I thought against the stone wall adjoining your neighbours' plot would be warm and sheltered.

The little space in front of the hórreo is looking good. I thought you could put a nice bush in the flower bed we have made at the bottom of the hórreo steps so you can see it from the living room window. We will need to find a supplier of garden soil for your raised bed. We are filling the bottom of the ex-chicken house with rubble to provide drainage but we don't have enough soil to fill it (the bed will be about 3 feet deep and 4 feet across so quite big).

My summer planting is coming on well. We had our first 'new' potatoes out of the polytunnel on Sunday and the first outdoor peapods too. I have planted the sweetcorn out, and the squash. The rainbow beans are growing (for drying) and I even

CHESTNUT, CHERRY & KIWI FRUIT SPONGE

have some aubergines planted out.

S has started fitting chipboard in the living room where the holey bits of the existing flooring are, so we can eventually lay the new floorboards over the top. I've knocked off the last bit of old plaster from your 'front' wall next to the barn and mortared most of it. It's a lovely straight wall with big granite stones and looks so smart. Need a new barn door now. I think we will put a herb bed next to that wall. It will be handy to reach when it's your turn to make dinner haha.

It's nice working outdoors on that side of the house as it's cool most of the day, and temperatures have soared the last week or so. It's quite thundery today.

Anyway, I suppose I had better post my historic last letter. I feel it ought to have something of more importance in it somehow. It is the end of an era after all. Maybe I can ask the post office for a special stamp haha.

See you in a week. Please don't pack any more...

Love you so much
xxxxxxxxxx

That was it, my last ever letter to Mum. After 32 years of writing home, I would be hanging up my pen and reassigning my writing pad. It felt strange, but I had no time to ponder as I needed to get organised to bring the old woman home to Galicia.

JUNE 2015

On Tuesday the 9th of June I caught the plane from Santiago to Stansted, leaving the boys to carry on with the *Casita* whilst I had the arguably more difficult job of organising Mum's move.

My trip did not start well.

I had arranged a hire car from the airport, ordering a 'B' size as I was concerned about the amount of stuff I would be needing to ferry about. I arrived, to be confronted with a Fiat 500. Now I know many people love the cute little Fiat Cinquecento but I'm afraid I'm not one of them. I like my cars to have a bit of muscle and, on this occasion, a bit of luggage space.

The chap on the rental desk was completely underwhelmed by my argument, even though he agreed I had booked the larger size vehicle.

"We will reimburse you the difference," he said.

"I don't want reimbursement," I replied through gritted teeth. "I want the car I ordered. Or..." I continued, "shall I try Avis across the way?"

Surprisingly my threat worked. Or maybe he had just had his fun. I was upgraded to a decent sized Toyota and finally made my way to my childhood home, and Mum's of six decades. As I drove, I turned over in my mind what needed to be done and ran through my lists. They were many.

Wednesday, I wanted to clear the smallest bedroom, the built-in cupboards on the upstairs landing and the bathroom shelves. These would be the easiest spaces to clear... in my mind, and I could then start to stack boxes in that bedroom. I wasn't entirely sure about the cupboards on the landing, as there were things in those going back to before I was born, and I was sure each item would be vital in some way.

Thursday, I was going to look at the garden and the back bedroom, which I slept in. Thankfully that room didn't have too much clutter in it as I periodically and surreptitiously cleared it when I

CHESTNUT, CHERRY & KIWI FRUIT SPONGE

visited. Most of the stuff had been mine and we had got rid of that on our last visit: taking my college books to Stafford University as a donation and taking my clothes home to Galicia, and as many of my books as we had been able to transport. There was a large metal box in that room, some RAF thing of my brother's, which I thought would be ideal to pack our bedding in on the final morning.

Friday was going to be a difficult day, as I had earmarked the shed to be emptied. S and I had made a start on this in February – throwing away old empty paint tins, broken plant pots, and tools with no useful function, but there was still so much in there. I was hoping my brother would be over to help with that little job.

Saturday, being the weekend, my brother was definitely helping as was my sister-in-law and my niece. That was going to be the kitchen, living room, and dining room day. I also had my brother pencilled in my notebook to disconnect and remove any electrical fixtures and fittings which were coming with us.

On Sunday, we would take cuttings of anything Mum wanted from the garden and do a last check round before transporting anything we didn't need to the local charity shops or, as a last resort, the tip.

Monday, Mum and I were going to Burton-on-Trent for my shopping to take back home and would have lunch out, since by then most of the pots and pans would be packed.

Tuesday, the removals people were coming first thing, then a quick clean and check around and we would be off to my brother's house to spend the next couple of days relaxing before our flight home on Thursday the 18th of June.

By the time I reached the turn off from the motorway I was convinced it was going to be a cakewalk. I relaxed and enjoyed the drive; happy I hadn't had to stick with the tiny Fiat.

JUNE 2015

Mum's house was a standard three-bedroomed semi-detached ex-local authority house. Emptying it shouldn't have posed much of a problem to an experienced house mover such as myself, even in a week. I just needed to be organised.

Unfortunately, there were two flaws to my careful plans. One was that although the house was not huge, it was very, very, full. Mum, as I believe I may have mentioned, is a hoarder. She doesn't believe in throwing things away. This meant there were items decades old whose original purpose was probably lost in the mists of time. The second problem was that Mum wanted to help.

I opened the door that Tuesday evening to a smiling mother and a pile of 'stuff' right in front of the door.

"What on earth is that?" I asked pointing to the pile.

"I'd thought I'd make a start," said Mum. "Look, I put some things in here."

She opened the door of a newly appeared wooden cabinet at the bottom of the stairs. It was full of crockery. I tried counting to ten.

"Why did you move the crockery from the kitchen cupboard to this cupboard in the hallway?" I asked, trying for calm.

Mum's face fell. "I thought it would help."

How to put this gently, I wondered. "How does moving stuff from one place where I know where it is, to another where it doesn't belong, help in any way, shape, or form, Mum?" Maybe it was late. I needed to sleep on this. "Okay, never mind, we'll sort it out in the morning. What's on the box tonight?" I distracted her and kept counting, silently in my head. It was going to be a long week.

By Wednesday morning, I was more sangfroid about the whole 'Mum packing' situation and decided to just ignore the elephant in the room –

CHESTNUT, CHERRY & KIWI FRUIT SPONGE

or rather the cupboard in the hallway – and get on with my plan of attack.

The little bedroom was as easy as I'd envisaged. There was a large wicker basket of material in the wardrobe which Mum wanted to bring with her and a bolt of peach satin which I had entirely forgotten about.

"Oh dear, I was going for traditional in those days, wasn't I?" I laughed, eyeing up the pattern which went with the bundle. "I'm glad I ended up with the wedding I did. And the man I did," I added thoughtfully. "But what should we do with this bridesmaid dress material? I can't think we'll have a use for it in Galicia, can you?"

"What about the charity shop in Ashby? I think they take most things. We can take some of the other things I won't need too, I suppose."

Poor Mum. I felt rather cruel, albeit briefly. Anyway, she cheered up when I suggested lunch in Ashby since we'd had a good morning and achieved our first success of the week.

The grandly named Ashby-de-la-Zouch was our nearest market town and where I went to school for seven years. It had grown over the years since I lived there and the number of pubs had diminished in proportion, but there were still plenty of places to eat.

Having parked in the car park behind the main street, we walked through one of the many alleyways, all filled with small, independent shops. One was a children's clothes shop. I paused.

"She looks like she makes the clothes herself, I wonder if she would like that cloth you have?" I mused. "Shall I ask?"

Mum readily agreed so I popped in. The conversation began awkwardly for two reasons; firstly, the young woman in there thought I was trying to sell her the material, and secondly, she seemed to think we were shoving Mum into an old

JUNE 2015

folks' home. Once we got that sorted out, she was delighted with my offerings and I returned later in the week with more.

"My friend runs a vintage dress shop in town, I'm sure she would love some of this velvet if you don't mind," she said.

"Of course not, we're happy it will be used," I replied.

The small charity shop on Market Street was also happy to take anything we had. It was one of the few charity shops which didn't seem to have a policy on electrical goods or secondhand books.

"We have an electrician, volunteers with us. He checks all the electrical stuff. We'll take anything you've got. There's a large storeroom behind," the man added, noting my doubtful look at the small and crowded store.

I often wonder if he realised quite what he had let himself in for that week.

Back at the house, after an enjoyable lunch, I started on the 'phone calls.

We had to cancel the telephone, electric, water, and council tax, and change Mum's address with the bank and other organisations. I started on my telephone list (I had a list – of course) explaining that I was calling on behalf of my mother and what we wanted to do. Each time I had to pass the 'phone to Mum for the 'security' questions and for her to confirm she was happy for me to speak on her behalf. By the fourth or fifth 'phone call I was fed up with this, so I'm afraid I have to admit to committing fraud. I rang as Mrs Wright (which I am) and gave the required answers to date of birth, address, and all the other silly security questions which anyone who knew Mum would easily pass. I even put a waver in my voice to signify age. It was much quicker to get through my list and Mum could get on with causing chaos in another part of the house.

On second thoughts, I should've kept her near me.

CHESTNUT, CHERRY & KIWI FRUIT SPONGE

'My' bedroom was easy to pack, except for the fact that the metal trunk I had thought to put the bedding in was full – of photographs, and programmes for long ago concerts.

"Why did you put those in there?" I pleaded.

"I thought it was a good place."

"Do you know how much paper weighs?" I asked, inconsequentially. Of course Mum didn't know. "That trunk is heavy to begin with, stuffed with photos no one will be able to lift it," I sighed.

I reorganised the family photographs into smaller, easily lifted boxes – I was thinking of us at the other end as much as the removals' men this end – and taped them down. Another task done.

As the weather was fine, we spent the afternoon in the garden digging up the odd plant or spring bulbs we could bring back with us in our luggage and taking some cuttings from Mum's favourite shrubs.

Of all the rooms in the house, the garden was the only one which it caused me pain to leave. There was so much of Dad in that plot and so many magnificent specimens which had been grown over so many years. There were two huge camellia bushes, which Dad had bought for Mum as a gift early in their marriage; the amelanchier tree, a favourite spot for the birds to sit with its carpet of daffodils below in spring; and Dad's bonsai conifer garden.

I remembered planting that garden with Dad. We'd drawn up a detailed plan of which conifer was planted where and their binomial Latin names. I still have that plan somewhere. Dad said the trees would grow very slowly. He was right, but 40 years later some of those miniature conifers were a good three metres tall and threatening to take over the path in front of the bed. I didn't envy the new owners having to dig those out. I would have loved to have taken some of my favourites with us though. Sadly, with

JUNE 2015

the furniture going into storage and us on a plane there was little we could do.

On Friday, we had Mum's GP appointment. Dr Tailor was a wonderful fellow. He had been Mum's doctor for a good number of years and knew her well. When he had first diagnosed her as needing a new hip, she had been her usual argumentative self, telling him it was just sciatica. After her hip replacement, I asked if she had apologised to Dr Tailor and got a 'look' for my trouble.

As we entered the surgery, the doctor stood and shook hands. He had produced a neat printout of Mum's medication and medical history. My kind of a guy. I nudged Mum.

"You have something to say to Doctor Tailor I think," I prompted.

"Oh, yes. My daughter tells me I have to apologise for arguing about my diagnosis," she said.

I looked at Doctor Tailor, who guffawed loudly.

"That was supposed to be an apology, Doctor," I said.

"Do not worry," he laughed. "It is fine, I am used to these independent ladies."

We shook hands again and left.

Saturday was going to be a major packing day, with the troops joining me. My stacked, neatly labelled and numbered boxes were growing: as were the entries in my little notebook - box numbers and corresponding contents climbing down the pages.

It turned out to be a fun day with everyone working hard and a restorative fish and chip lunch from our favourite chippy, The Admiral, just down the road.

By Monday we had got most things sorted. Mum's bedroom had caused some angst as the built-in wardrobes in there were stuffed full of treasures. There was Dad's birds' egg collection, now illegal even to own, toys and games from our childhoods and more books - including probably a full set of the

CHESTNUT, CHERRY & KIWI FRUIT SPONGE

Ladybird series of children's story books. My favourites, *The Princess and the Pea, Mick, the Disobedient Puppy,* and *The Billy Goats Gruff* (which Mum and Dad bought to keep me quiet one wet summer holiday in South Wales), I kept. I made a pile for my nephews' kids and another for the long-suffering charity shop.

"What about Chucky?" I asked.

The large celluloid doll was Mum's pride and joy. It was larger than a real baby and dressed in hand-knitted clothes. Its head sported a crop of painted on curls and its eyes closed when it was 'asleep'. One detachable hand was clad in a tiny mitten, the other bare. That mitten poorly disguised the fact that there *was* no hand on that side. I couldn't ever remember it having a hand, though Mum insisted it did once upon a time. The doll usually sat in the third bedroom but my niece, Belle, had been staying and she hated the doll. It was Belle who nicknamed it Chucky. Her condition for sleeping at Nana's was that the doll was moved for the duration.

"Oh, don't be horrid," said Mum, cuddling the doll. "I've had him for years."

"I didn't even know it was a him!" I laughed. "Do you think he will be able to breathe in a box for a bit? We'll put the other dollies in with him for company."

Whereas I was always a teddy bear type of child, Mum adored her dolls. She had them arranged around her bedroom and once told me Dad had threatened to leave her if she bought any more.

The removals' van arrived promptly on Tuesday. Mum was flitting around 'helping' and asking if the 'lads' wanted tea and biscuits after they had been there all of ten minutes, which of course they did. We would never get sorted.

Luckily my knight on a shining Honda Goldwing, in the shape of my brother, arrived at the exact moment I was thinking of leaving her to it and taking myself off for a walk. Between us, we dragged a protesting mother next door to her friend then left them to chat whilst we sorted out the removals.

Mum's large bamboo-wood wardrobe was causing a problem. The men couldn't get it out of the bedroom door.

"Well, it must've gone in that way," I said, not entirely helpfully.

"Maybe the door wasn't on then," said my brother, taking a screwdriver to the hinges.

Those hinges hadn't been unscrewed for decades and had at least five layers of paint on them. Even without the door, the wardrobe wouldn't turn in the tight hallway outside the bedroom.

"The storage radiator!" I shouted. Even I knew that was a later addition than the wardrobe. Out came brother's toolbox again and off came the storage radiator. At one point I seriously thought we were going to have to take the banister rail off to get the wardrobe down the stairs but somehow it was successfully manoeuvred. I was pleased Mum had been moved on.

Mum, when she did reappear, immediately began to vacuum.

"For goodness' sake, Mum," said my brother. "You don't need to clean everywhere. The house will be empty for ages." In frustration, he picked up the vacuum cleaner and tossed it in the skip. Mum looked aghast. I laughed.

Eventually the house was cleared except for the sofa – which Mum had sold privately – three mugs, tea bags and kettle, and our sandwiches for lunch. As I was pouring the tea a car drew up. It was one of my cousins, who I hadn't seen for years, with his wife.

"Oh no!" said Mum when I told her. "We haven't got anywhere to sit or any more bread."

"I doubt they are expecting lunch," I said. "And there are plenty of biscuits left. I'll borrow a couple of mugs from Aunty Jean."

CHESTNUT, CHERRY & KIWI FRUIT SPONGE

My brother abandoned us after lunch. He said he couldn't stick it any longer as Mum was now 'cleaning' the floor on her hands and knees, picking up specks of perceived dirt. We would make our own way to his house in time for supper.

I was having a final check round on Tuesday afternoon when I spotted something at the back of the wardrobe in my bedroom. The built-in wardrobes were deep so I had to stretch, but eventually my hand closed on... a hand!

I must have screamed because Mum came dashing into the room. "Oh, you've found the doll's hand!"

"Yes, and it frightened me to death," I replied. "What on earth was it doing in my built-in wardrobe?"

Mum didn't have an answer, though she was happy it had been found. I was more worried about Chucky's night-time activities which resulted in him losing a hand in my wardrobe. I was quite glad we were leaving that day and I hoped he didn't cause any chaos in the storage unit.

Part II
And Mother makes three in Galicia

JUNE 2015
II - Arrivals

Our plane touched down at Santiago de Compostela at exactly 15:05 on the 18th of June 2015 - 'another on time flight from Ryanair', according to the announcement which preceded the storm of clapping throughout the cabin. I had always wondered about that. Who started it, and more importantly, why? Anyway, this time I told Mum it was her welcome home. She liked that. We'd had a good flight, despite my having a minor panic at Stansted airport.

The hire cars were no longer collected and returned to the section adjoining the terminal building but to a 'car village' some ten minutes away by bus. I had already worked out that taking Mum and her two suitcases, plus my rucksack, on a crowded bus would not be fun. I determined that I would drop her off at the airport with the luggage, take the hire car back to base and catch her up in departures. Mum had wheelchair assistance booked at the airport as she struggles with the distances and the less than considerate crowds when faced with a slower, older person in their way.

I couldn't see the wheelchair person as we drew up in front of the drop off point but I did spot a telephone. A friendly voice answered.

JUNE 2015

"Hello, is that you in the yellow?" he asked.

"Erm, yes," I replied, looking around.

"I'm waving to you from inside the building," he said. "I'm on my way. You go, or it'll cost you a bomb."

I was still saying goodbye, or *au revoir*, to Mum when he caught up to us.

"Come on, I've got her. And that luggage. We can manage it all if your Mum can carry this one on her knee. Go on," he urged. "The prices go up after ten minutes. And they don't give you any leeway. Hurry up!"

Ten minutes! I gave Mum a kiss and sped off. He was right too. The charge for drop off was £2 for the first ten minutes then soared to £50. I was used to free drop off at Santiago airport and hadn't given it a thought. By the time I had queued endlessly behind a long row of cars at the barrier, I was just inside the time limit. I paid my £2 and silently thanked the friendly man.

Unburdened by bags or mother I was in and out of the car hire 'shed' and back to the airport in record time. Nevertheless, Mum was looking anxious by the time I joined her at the departure gate.

"I thought you weren't coming."

"Where else would I go?" I laughed, giving her a peck. "I don't have the advantage of dodging all the crowds like some people."

There was no wheelchair available at Santiago, according to the overworked disability helper there. But our local airport is so tiny, it really wasn't a great hardship to walk slowly down the corridor. Our slow progress had the advantage of meaning the luggage was already on the carousel by the time we arrived, so we were soon out of the doors and into the capable hands of my S. Right on time.

CHESTNUT, CHERRY & KIWI FRUIT SPONGE

We arrived in our tiny village at 5pm after stopping for our traditional cuppa on the way. It was good to be home. For all three of us.

§

Whilst I had been sorting out a sometimes annoying but always delightful mother, S and Lars had been working hard fitting a new plasterboard ceiling in the living room and pulling up the remains of the old wooden floor in the dressing room-to-be. They had also taken off one of the large and decrepit barn doors to the *alpendre*, leaving the right-hand one in place. This gave the open barn a more airy feel, whilst still retaining some privacy for those sitting inside. With the clearing away of yet more junk in there, it was starting to look like a cosy garden room. The boys had even cleaned the doors and windows of the *Casita* ready for the arrival of *La Jefa*.

They had also knocked out the concrete base to the ham cupboard in the corner of the living room. This revealed another wonderful quirk to our new house. The floor of the living room, as I've said, is lower than the top of the door frame for the barn doors below, with all that entails. What I hadn't realised was that the ham cupboard bench had been an afterthought rather than by design. Once the concrete slab was removed, the wooden flooring beneath was revealed as being chopped and hacked, as if by someone in a hurry or a temper. Not one edge was neat or square.

I had the most wonderful thought...

Señor decides to create a new room above the barn as a surprise for the wife. He buys some floorboards and takes his time laying them neatly over the beams. He gets to the end and, proud of his work, he wanders off for a smoke. Seconds later his wife finds him.

JUNE 2015

"*¡Hombre!*" she shouts. "I cannot open the barn door!"

Puzzled, Señor follows her to the barn. He pushes the door, then pushes it again. It doesn't budge. Suddenly he realises his mistake. Without a word, he runs upstairs to his neatly laid floor and begins to hack at it, removing pieces of board until there is a gap of 30 centimetres at the far end.

"Try it now!" he shouts.

The doors open but his nice new room has a jagged hole in the floor. Ever the genius, Señor builds a bench over the gap and creates a ham cupboard as if that was what he intended all along.

This is of course just my idle imagination but... do you have a better idea?

That floor issue also caused problems when I ordered the new barn doors some months later. I had decided that if we ordered tri-fold doors they would take up less of the precious living room space above when open. They would also be useful if we needed to get larger items into the barn. I very carefully drew the design and we showed the window man the problem we had. I even made a little folding paper pattern for him.

Did we get the doors we wanted? Given our experiences with Spanish window companies it's not a difficult quiz question. They are tri-fold doors, after a fashion. They don't lay flat against each other when open so catch on the upstairs floor, rending the folding bit inoperable. No matter how I explained, I couldn't get the company to see a problem. I was tempted to make them uninstall the things but really couldn't be bothered. What we are left with is a single opening door and a non-folding, folding bit. Highly useful.

Our problem of what to do with the gaping hole in the living room floor was eventually solved in an ingenious manner by another of our Workawayers some months later.

CHESTNUT, CHERRY & KIWI FRUIT SPONGE

Lars had left a couple of days before Mum and I arrived home. He had been a good companion for S and a hard worker. We had more Workawayers booked for July but for now the party season was already to hand - it was Arde Lucus that very weekend.

Each year, for four days, the city of Lugo is time shifted 2000 years backwards to its Roman beginnings for one of its biggest festivals of the year.

Lugo's documented history goes back to 14BC with the founding of Lucus Augusti (the grove of Augustus) by the emperor's representative Paulus Fabius. The 2nd century walls were built to protect the city from marauding attackers and became an UNESCO World Heritage Site in 2000. Soon afterwards, the festival of Arde Lucus (burn Lugo) was born. Arde Lucus is always held on the third weekend in June (unless some official randomly decides the first weekend in July would be better... as happened one year after a number of people had booked to visit us especially for the festival).

My favourite thing about Arde Lucus is the way everyone gets into the spirit of the occasion. There are barbarians stalking the streets with painted faces and Roman senators in robes and purple sashes drinking coffee. Lepers beg for alms, acrobats perform incredible feats of balance, and stalls line the streets selling everything from posies to swords, sweets to helmets. And then there are the Roman Legions.

Each Legion has its own uniform, which provide a wonderful touch of colour to the streets as they march past. The Pretorian guard, dressed all in black, are in charge of the Roman gates, the only entrances to the old town. They are frighteningly realistic with their gleaming helmets and armour plate.

We had our trusty potato sacks and Celtic trousers at the ready. One year, Richard made some

JUNE 2015

Celtic torcs from twisted copper wire; they were very authentic, if not exactly comfortable. I have an old, soft white kid-leather bag I found at *A Casa do Campo* for my apothecary goods, and a wooden knife in my leather belt. A red cloak (an old tablecloth, also found at the house) keeps me warm if it's cold. If it's a hot year I wear leather (look) sandals, if cooler, my suede boots with genuine bunny fur edging look the part.

One year I decided I was going to be Boudicca after reading the Manda Scott series of the same name. I had 'kill' feathers plaited into my hair and a bow and arrow set (made from some of our buddleia wood) complete with a leather wrist guard bought from one of the stalls in town. S wears a pair of genuine corduroy 'Celtic' trousers and a woollen hat (found at the house... surprisingly) and has a very smart leather wallet which once held Dad's tools, on his thick leather belt. He abandoned the idea of wearing furry slippers on his feet after he skidded down the steps from Jayne and Richard's house, landing on his behind.

That year, Mum wore a pretty white sundress, with a Roman-look sash and a very fetching bright orange sunhat. A friend, who accompanied us, arrived at our house wearing a towelling dressing gown. We were waiting for the big reveal but were to be disappointed – she continued to wear the dressing gown all day. Maybe she thought it was a general fancy dress event or maybe she was one of the 'asylum escapees' who wander the streets begging for alms during the festivities. I didn't dare ask!

Preparations for the fiesta begin early. The 'Euro' shops start to sell Roman costumes from April onwards but the re-enactment groups will have been practising their moves for much longer...

In the Plaza Mayor the Pretorian guard fight a tribe of Celts trying to take the city. The battle is ferocious. The guards form a tortoise (*tortuga*) with shields held over their heads, but the Celts are stronger and more determined and come away victorious. In another square, a battle goes on between gladiators, fighting for their freedom. Swords clash but thankfully no blood is spilled despite the violence of the encounters.

A Celtic wedding, meanwhile, is going on in the village set up just outside the walls, where Celtic stalls sell (real) swords, furs and arm bangles. In the Plaza de Constitución, a blacksmith is fashioning nails and chains, a stonemason is sculpting a large column of granite, and an elderly lady is sitting cleaning an animal fur.

In the evening there is a parade around the Ronda da Muralla, the road which encircles the walled old city of Lugo. The spectacle goes on for a while as each Legion and each Celtic tribe marches past. The Roman ladies look beautiful in their finery, their senator husbands resplendent in their robes of office, whilst the befurred Celtic tribes brandish their spears and bang their drums, painted faces looking suitably terrifying in the evening light.

The best place to watch this spectacle is from the top of the Roman walls themselves. There, cradling an artisan beer from the nearby Aloumiña brewery, I could imagine the scene 15 metres below might, just might, be real.

The final night of Arde Lucus is given over to a firework display. Being Galicia, safety protocols are few and far between. One year a firework spectacularly set alight a large and rather dry pine tree. That was quite a sight I have to say and almost gave Arde Lucus its genuine title as the flames threatened to engulf the city.

This was the first year Mum had been here for Arde Lucus and it was a fitting beginning to her new life here in Galicia. On an even more positive note, Mum's house had another buyer and everything

JUNE 2015

seemed to be going well this time. I had been emailing with my brother:

> *On 22 Jun 2015, at 09:59, Lisa Wright <lisarosewright@msn.com> wrote:*
> *> Hi Bro,*
> *> Well, she is here. So far has fallen in the sage bed (no damage to sage!) and cut her arm trying to prune dead rosemary. Considering chaining her to the bed! We had to go out to the fiesta to save more damage to mum or my plants LOL*
> *> Anyway other than that all is well. It is hot and mum seems to be enjoying herself and settling in. She is on washing up duty and cleaning the guest room for our helpers!*
> *>Any news re the survey?*
> *> Oh yes, that neighbour didn't want the sofa so can we try BHF again or other ideas?*
> *> love Sis (and mum)*
>
> *From: m wright*
> *> Sent: Monday, June 22, 2015 12:13 PM*
> *> To: Lisa Wright*
> *> Subject: Re: removals*
> *> Hi Sis*
> *> I'll contact the British Heart Foundation and let them know that a key is next door. Not heard anything re survey, I'll give the estate agents a ring later in the week. Weather rubbish at the moment, wet and cold. Love to all xxx*

That week, we had a new Workawayer for a few days. Lola was a loan from a friend of ours and was coming to help with the soft fruit harvest. My little redcurrant bush had done so well at the top of the allotment that I had propagated four more from cuttings. They were all growing and producing plenty of currants. The blackcurrants were also

CHESTNUT, CHERRY & KIWI FRUIT SPONGE

thriving and the tiny wood strawberries needed picking daily so they didn't rot.

Lola enjoyed picking the fruit. I think she was the slowest picker in the entire history of the world. She would peer at each and every currant as she picked it, turning it this way and that to admire its translucent beauty and declaring each one to be a tiny 'jewel'. This is all fine and good – but not, it has to be said, much use when I'm waiting on the morning's pickings for redcurrant jelly.

Lola was a delicate bird-like American girl who looked as if a stiff wind would blow her away. She loved to cook, though the reality was less than ideal if one wanted a clean bowl, knife or pot left in the house afterwards. I have never seen anyone over the age of five manage to make such a mess whilst mixing a cake.

She also had an interesting way of eating, which fascinated Mum. Being so tiny she declared she couldn't eat a full plate of food but, being a foodie, she refused to miss out so simply kept the second half of her meal in the fridge for later. She always ate this cold in the afternoon, whatever the meal had been. Whilst some meals are fine cold, others looked distinctly unappetising. Still, it was her choice and it saved me cooking twice over.

Our helper was only with us a few days but did have the opportunity to visit our local *sardiñada* with us on the 23rd of June, the eve of *San Juan*. I'm not sure what Lola thought to the pushing masses of Galicians fighting for the sardines, roasted over a charcoal fire, or grabbing pieces of hot bacon as soon as they appeared, but Mum loved the atmosphere and the food in equal parts.

That was Mum's first *Sardiñada* too. We found her a plastic chair and treated her like the royalty she is: bringing her wine, choice sardines, and bacon sandwiches far into the night. She even tried the *queimada*: the Galician hot toddy made with *augardente*, sugar, coffee beans and lemon rind, though she drew the line at jumping the embers of the bonfire at midnight.

> *On 25 Jun 2015, at 09:30, Lisa Wright <lisarosewright@msn.com> wrote:*
> *> Hi Bro*
> *> I must've taken the sun back with me, too hot outside here! Old woman was out boozing again on Tuesday eve (photo attached). Eve of St John the Baptist's day, so our council provides fishes and bread, and vino of course, then sets fire to a stack of brush and everyone jumps over it (we just went with the fishes and vino). >It keeps her out of trouble!*
> *> love Sis*
>
> *From: m wright*
> *> Sent: Thursday, June 25, 2015 12:13 PM*
> *> To: Lisa Wright*
> *> Subject: Re: removals*
> *> Hi Sis*
> *> Just thought I must start using a new email subject can't keep using 'Re: removals.' Just spoke with estate agency, the buyers received the survey yesterday and have passed it to the lenders. There were some issues raised but I would have been amazed if there hadn't been. Don't know what the issues are but we don't have much of a say anyway. I have arranged for the settee to be collected, again! It'll be 7 July. Love to all xxxx*

In between fiestas, we carried on renovating the *Casita* and hoped for good news on the house front. S made a neat set of steps down into the lower barn where we had stacked the firewood. I, meanwhile, had a go at replastering some of the kitchen walls.

CHESTNUT, CHERRY & KIWI FRUIT SPONGE

The west wall of the kitchen abuts the neighbouring house as the *Casita* is semi-detached. Because of the slope, it is next door's barn which adjoins the kitchen, and there seemed to be a problem with damp seeping into the walls. The plaster, when we first bought the house, had been blown and sodden on that wall. We had chipped off the old plaster and dried out the wall beneath. I had painted on some anti-mould liquid and a coat of PVA glue to seal the wall. Our neighbour had been happy for us to inspect his barn which was as dry as could be, so the water had to be condensation. We hoped it would no longer be an issue once the *cocina* was up and running.

Now Mum was here full time we could decide how to lay out the kitchen for her use. She'd had an eye-level built-in oven in England which my brother had disconnected and boxed up for its trip here. We thought it would fit neatly into the built-in cupboard next to the kitchen stairs. We removed the old glass doors, and the remains of the tins of food, and I started to clean the old white paint from the sweet chestnut-wood frame. Sadly, the opening was slightly smaller than the space needed for the oven so S had the job of rebuilding the cupboard to fit.

The second-hand cupboards we'd bought from the charity shop in Lugo, and which were still taking up space in the dining room upstairs, would make a good run of base and wall units along the wall next to the new oven housing. There was even room for one of the cupboards next to the new fridge-freezer installed in the space left by the old *lareira* or open *chorizo*-smoking fire.

Diary Saturday 27th June Very hot. Thunder in the evening. No rain
S busy cutting the beams to fit the chipboard sub-floor in the old smoking room (Dressing room-to-

JUNE 2015

be). It's lovely and uneven so he's having fun trying to level it.
L did two plaster mixes on the kitchen wall.
Lunch: Ham and cheese cobbler, first French beans. Blackcurrant and raspberry smoothie using new (not very efficient) juicer.
Moved the chickens to their summer quarters.

It was always an adventure moving the hens. This time they were coming up to their summer quarters near to the house and beneath the fruit trees, giving welcome shade and some protection from buzzard attacks. Although normally easier with some help, I had decided to wait until Lola had left as I just couldn't see her safely carrying a full-grown and wriggly chicken over the stone stile and up the narrow stone steps from the allotment to the wired in pen at the top.

Buff Puff, our half Buff Orpington, had gone broody so we left her in the allotment run. We were relying on Buffy's next brood to augment our stock this year. I was already thinking up some more names beginning with 'F'.

We had to do our chicken removals in shifts. The hens start to get nervous after a while, with much clucking and flapping of wings, and occasional hiding in inaccessible corners. S caught them one by one and brought them to me. I sprayed for red mite using an organic solution then released them into their new home. We did the two oldies, Buzz and Sarah, first, as was their right as the patriarch and matriarch of our flock. Damson was our only remaining 'D' year hen, the others having been cockerels, and therefore dinner, or killed by the dreaded buzzards. Next came Buffy's last brood, Edwina, Evelyn, and Emmeline, followed by Billie Jean's previous year's pair Ester and Eliot. Billie Jean herself and her single chick, Solita Faith, were

CHESTNUT, CHERRY & KIWI FRUIT SPONGE

already in the top pen so that was our job done for another five months.

Diary Tuesday 30th June 36°C on allotment
L sanded down the newly plastered kitchen wall. Looks okay if one doesn't inspect it too closely! S fixed the last of the sub-floor in the dressing room. The village cats are running out of bolt holes into the house now!
Lunch: Salmon and courgette quiche with beetroot and almond coleslaw. Orange curd ice-cream.
Buffy on five eggs (since 24th). Due 14th July.

The village cats loved the *Casita* and its many perfectly positioned holes through windows and floorboards, and from roofs and balconies. It was their playground and they were not happy at our interference. To this day, our tomcat, Clarence, turns up his scarred nose at our renovation efforts.

The cats may have been unhappy with our work but Mum was delighted and, better yet, she was enjoying her new life in Galicia.

JULY 2015
Party month

July is party month in Galicia. It is the beginning of the long summer break for the *Galegos*, the local outdoor swimming pool opens, kids are on holiday, and Mum and S both have birthdays mid-month. Mum would be 84 on the 14th of July. Buff Puff's eggs were due to hatch on the same day.

We also had two lots of Workawayers due in July. Hal and Jack were arriving on the 12th, but on the 2nd of July our other helpers appeared unannounced.

Roy and Francesca had emailed to say they would probably arrive sometime at the beginning of the month but were vague as to the exact date. They were driving, and it depended on their itinerary. We heard them arrive before we saw them, as the deep puttering sound of a Volkswagen camper van echoed around our tiny hamlet.

Francesca was first out. An attractive girl of Italian descent, she was all black curls and wide smile. Roy, when he appeared, was tall, and so thin as to be nearly invisible. His hair was tangled in grunge plaits all over his head, held in place with a myriad of silver beads. His beard was as unkempt looking as his hair and his teeth were mainly missing or rotten, but his smile was genuine and I immediately liked them both. I explained we had another couple coming on the 12th but that they could have the Workaway room until then if they wished.

CHESTNUT, CHERRY & KIWI FRUIT SPONGE

"Naw, we sleep in the van," said Roy. "It's cool."

"I would appreciate it if I can use the bathroom sometimes though," added Francesca. "And do some washing?"

"Of course, that's no problem," I said. "Now, where do you want to park up? It's not very flat round here." I pointed at our sloped garden. Then I had a thought. "You could park down the track aways if you didn't mind being further from the house?"

"Naw," said Roy. "That'll be cool."

I was beginning to think Roy's communication skills might leave a bit to be desired, but his van was an Aladdin's cave. As he opened the side door I saw a bed platform, and below that was the largest stash of tools I've seen outside of a garage.

"I do up VWs," said Roy by way of explanation, more animated than I'd seen him so far.

They both agreed the turnaround down the track was a perfect camping spot. They hung their washing line between two trees and set up their solar shower bag to heat. They even hung a toilet roll from a small branch. I began to wonder what the neighbours would think of this gypsy encampment appearing in our midst. Still, all our neighbours thought we were mad anyway so what would one more nail in the coffin matter?

We soon found that Roy lived to work. He would start work early in the morning, or occasionally sleep in and then work until late evening. We couldn't get him to stick to the five hours daily maximum we expect and struggled to persuade him to come on trips out. In the end we took Francesca for visits around the area and left Roy to get on with his own thing.

They both worked hard but were erratic when it came to mealtimes. I always tell Workawayers that we aim to be flexible. If they want to work a longer day, or two, as Lars did, and then go off for a few days to explore that is fine. Equally, I expect Workawayers to be flexible enough to complete a job if it runs over the five hours. The only thing I'm not flexible about is dinner.

Dinner time in our house is 2pm, not earlier, not later. If I have spent the morning producing a meal, the least I expect is for everyone to turn up on time to eat it. Twice Roy and Francesca were over half an hour late back from town. The second time I didn't even bother to save their portion of the meal but told them we had eaten. Francesca must have noticed that there were leftovers but didn't comment. They did work extra hard that afternoon though, and were never late again.

Timekeeping aside, these two got so much done.

Roy was a decent carpenter and builder. He pulled up the old rotten floor in the ironing room (the bathroom-to-be) and fitted plasterboard to the internal brick wall in there. He cement-rendered the wall and balustrade around the outside stone steps to the bedroom and made a rustic gate for the top. Francesca joined in, working as hard as her boyfriend. In between jobs, she chatted to Mum, while shelling pounds of walnuts for me.

Sunday 12th July Very hot
S cut hay whilst our helpers worked at the Casita.
Decided to have lunch at Luisa's but Roy wanted to carry on working so we took Francesca alone.
Met up with our new Workawayers, Hal and Jack, and did the grand tour.
Found 10 eggs! 8 hidden in a hole in the corner of the outside pen. Wondered why we were down. Buffy still sitting on her 5.

Hal and Jack were as different as granite and soap. Hal was tough, hard-working, and a go-getter. Jack was inclined to sneak off, and each time I saw him he seemed to be lounging about smoking leaving Hal

CHESTNUT, CHERRY & KIWI FRUIT SPONGE

to do the bulk of the work. Our Workaway profile clearly states 'non-smokers only' but that didn't seem to bother Jack.

The pair were also very strict on their working hours. At lunchtime each day they stopped work, and after lunch they would go exploring. I was happy they were exploring the area, but since they generally started work at 10am and had a half-hour tea and cake break, as we all did, at noon, they were doing less than four hours' work. Still, while they were working, at least one of them worked hard.

As it was Mum's birthday on the 14th, we decided to throw a surprise garden party for her at her new home. We invited all our friends, including Pepe and Mercedes from whom we bought the *Casita*. We hoped a party would also take Mum's mind off the fact that yet another sale had fallen through.

On 13 Jul 2015, at 09:39, Lisa Wright <lisarosewright@msn.com> wrote:
>Hi Bro,
>You said we needed a different header but after puzzling for ages I still can't think of one...
>Mum is bearing up surprisingly well after being told the house has fallen through and the bailiffs have her furniture!!! I had visions of someone carting the sole bit of furniture away before BHF got it but as S pointed out the removals company already have all her furniture anyway so they can just sell it. You'd better transfer the money though just in case LOL.
>We have a couple of fabulous helpers at the moment. A sort of hosts' dream. They have a VW camper parked down the lane. Roy seems to be one of those blokes who has done pretty much everything and works very hard.
>Mum has not been idle either. She has sanded down 2 drawer fronts and the door to the well.

JULY 2015

So we are keeping her busy... I've told her she has to work for her board LOL.
>The estate agency left a message saying they couldn't get hold of the buyers. Not sure how hard they tried. Let us know if you find anything out!
>Otherwise all well here. Still really rather hot. Mum seems to have settled in really well. She is up to 8 lengths at the swimming baths, walking to the next village (2Km round trip,) and guzzling for England at home and away!!
>We have a surprise party tomorrow for her. 24 people coming at last count!! Hope the cakes hold out haha
>lots love to all
>Sis
>xx

From: m wright
> Sent: Thursday, July 13, 2015 1:01 PM
> To: Lisa Wright
> Subject: Re: blank
> Hi Sis
>House update: the buyers weren't interested in our offer so back on the market. Same price but advert says 'cash buyers only.'
>Settee should be collected tomorrow (Tuesday), the British Heart Foundation van broke down last week!
>Keep forgetting to transfer the money for the removals, promise I'll do it before they sell all her stuff! Love to all xxxx

The buyers' lender had decided that £20,000 pounds worth of work was needed to bring the house up to standard and reduced the mortgage offer by that amount. In an attempt to salvage the sale, we offered to go halves on the costs, dropping the price by

CHESTNUT, CHERRY & KIWI FRUIT SPONGE

£10,000. The buyers declined, so Mum's house was once more back on the market.

Bastille Day dawned hot and sultry. After a 'special' birthday lunch of sausage and mash, we left Mum washing up (her 'job' which she did religiously each day) while we all busied ourselves over at the *Casita*.

S and Roy carried the old, large wooden dining table across to put food on, Francesca decorated it and laid the plates, while Jack had the idea to make the garden prettier using some of our pelargoniums. It was as he was carrying these over that Mum spotted him.

Later, after we had finished the party, she said to me, "I thought he was stealing your plants you know."

"Why on earth would you think that?"

"Well, I couldn't think where he was taking them."

"And you really didn't guess we were having a party?" I said, amazed.

"No, I thought I'd had my birthday lunch."

Mum is really quite easy to fool - thankfully.

The boys blew up and hung balloons while the girls prepared the food and prettied the *alpendre*. Francesca asked Mum to put on her new birthday dress, which she had bought on one of our trips out, so she could see it. This was a clever ploy as I hadn't thought how to get Mum into a party outfit without giving the game away. She did however keep her lime green Crocs (plastic sandals) on - a 'disaster' she still reminds me of to this day!

When everyone was assembled, Kath came over and asked Mum if she would give her a tour of the new works to date.

"I haven't seen it for ages," she said artlessly.

Mum readily wandered over with our friend, and stopped short at the sight of the overflowing *alpendre*.

JULY 2015

We had set up small coffee tables inside and out, and all the chairs we could find. Friends had brought more chairs and more food. There was food everywhere: cold sliced meats from the rural shop nearby, *empanadas*, cheeses from our local dairy, bread, tomatoes, and fresh fruits donated by friends. I had made half a dozen different cakes, suitable for all allergies, and all tastes.

Poor Mercedes was most upset as she had ordered a special birthday cake for Mum but when they had got to the bakery, she had been told it wasn't ready. An example of Spanish *mañana* timekeeping not being welcome. I assured her we had plenty of cakes, and that it was the thought that counted.

Everyone had brought a bottle or two with them and Jack set up a wet area near the barn door with a dustbin full of iced water for the beer cans, a table for the wine, and plastic glasses. He even remembered the bottle opener and was in his element as barman. It was the most work he had done since they arrived.

Mum sat like a queen on her throne as friends came to wish her well and chat to her. That was the first of many garden parties we have held at the *Casita*. We have had live music and barbecues and fun and laughter over the years – but only that first one was quite such a surprise.

Diary Wednesday 15th July 31°C terrace.
Tided up from our party. Jack and Hal picked plums (well, Hal did while Jack complained and smoked endlessly. If he leaves his ciggie ends in the chicken pen I'll go mad). S is fitting a new joist hanger in the bedroom-to-be as the floor joist only just reaches the wall and doesn't go into the hole in the stone. Looks very technical. Roy and Francesca moved boards around in the second bedroom, after demolishing the wall to the en suite,

CHESTNUT, CHERRY & KIWI FRUIT SPONGE

to provide a level and non-holey floor for Mum's furniture when it arrives. I painted the first coat of white on my newly plastered walls in the kitchen. What a difference. And what a crowded little Casita!
Visited Buff Puff in the evening. One chick hatched, one partly hatched but struggling, and three infertile. Gently helped the struggling chick out of the egg and popped it under Buffy. Went back 20 minutes later to find she had moved herself and the first chick away from the other one and was ignoring it. Decided to try and warm it up then reintroduce it to Buffy once it's stronger.

It wasn't the first time I'd tried to hand-rear chicks. One year a whole batch was abandoned by Buff Puff and I popped the eggs under the quilt in the spare bed with the electric blanket on full. It was just as well no guests were staying at the time. Sadly, the eggs had been abandoned too long and nothing hatched. Another year I'd rescued a similar, half-hatched chick. Penguin lived for five days but was obviously underdeveloped and couldn't eat or drink properly. He waddled about the sunroom, trying his little best but my efforts weren't good enough and he died one sunny morning.

S was sceptical about my new attempt, but this time I had an idea. We had recently bought a small propagator from Mike and John for my seedlings. I plugged this in and lined the base with old face cloths to prevent the chick getting burned. S' Celtic woolly hat was called into service as a bed. This was already lined with fleece and another cloth ensured it was cosy. I put a tiny, shallow dish of water in one corner and popped the chick in its new home.

The next morning, not only was the chick still alive but it had transformed from a damp squib to a fluffy energetic bundle. On seeing me it cheeped surprisingly loudly for such a tiny thing. I lifted it

JULY 2015

out to take back to Buff Puff. Although it had only been gone 12 hours, she would have nothing to do with the little yellow ball. If I pushed it too close, Buffy actually pecked the intruder. Knowing she wouldn't relent once her mind was made up, I carried my chick back to its little nest.

Sunday 19th July Hot and sticky
Spent most of the morning playing with baby chick and catching crickets for it. Spent the rest of the time scraping the beam Hal and Jack had started then abandoned.
All to Luisa's for lunch then back to catch more crickets.

I knew that chicks live off the egg sac for the first 24 hours, but after that Baby would need feeding. I had watched our broody hens enough to know what to do: they would pick out the choicest bit of grain, usually a piece not too big but not too dust-like, and repeatedly lift it up in their beak then drop it to the floor, all the time squeaking at the chicks to grab it. Using my thumb and finger, I did the same. My new baby caught on with amazing speed, leading me to think it was a very clever chick. I would lift it out of its nest box onto the sunroom floor and, sitting in a ray of sunlight, I would cluck and drop my gift of food for the mite. The chick would race around then eventually tire out and clamber onto my lap for a nap.

As chickens are omnivores, I thought I'd try to vary its diet a little. The first cricket I caught was tiny, half the length of my little finger nail, but Baby made a valiant effort to chase it as it bounced about the sunroom. Once I had partially disabled it, my little chick did the rest, devouring the creature with obvious relish.

My days were sorted. In between painting, cooking for our helpers, gardening and watering, I

CHESTNUT, CHERRY & KIWI FRUIT SPONGE

would collect crickets in a catching bottle I'd made. Soon, Feliz (happy), as my chick had been renamed, would recognise the green plastic bottle as I came into the room. It would begin to jump up and down with excitement and squeak unremittingly until I lifted it out of the 'nest' and we proceeded to play our 'catch the cricket' game. It wasn't long before Feliz was swallowing crickets bigger than it was. I was fascinated to watch it gulp, gainfully trying to get the insect down its throat.

Our Workawayers even joined in the catching process, having fun diving around the garden trying to catch the lively insects. Jack only ever caught one. The scream he let out when it moved inside his closed fist echoed around our little valley and had me in fits of laughter.

Roy and Francesca left on the 23rd of July. We were very sorry to see them go. They had done an awful lot of work and helped us get much closer to the *Casita* becoming liveable.

Hal and Jack were with us until the 30th. They had also been helpful: Mum now had a beautiful black-painted wrought iron gate to the garden and Jack had built a low stone wall for a flower bed next to the house wall. They had also scraped and cleaned the two painted drawers from within the *cocina* surround, having taken over the task from Mum. Once varnished, these ancient wooden drawers looked beautiful: one was fully two feet long and seemed to pull out forever. The other was wider but shorter, as that was the side with the large granite rock forming part of the surround behind.

On the 29th of July we decided to take Jack and Hal out for the day. It was already hot and the sun was blazing as we set off, the five of us, for Os Peares where the three rivers meet.

Os Peares is one of the strangest and most picturesque villages in Galicia. It sits in a valley where the mighty river Miño and the deep and

JULY 2015

forbidding Sil meet a third river, the gentle Búbal. Here, these three rivers join before flowing west together towards the sea and freedom.

The road to Os Peares follows a winding path down through tiny hamlets. There is a house at the edge of the road where we always stop for a photograph. The owner is a friendly chap who is used to our stopping to admire his view and his garden full of climbing roses and bougainvillea. The views from this *casa* are stunning. It perches on the top of a green verdant valley, looking down into a landscape of ridges, peaks, red-roofed houses nestling in valleys, and way, way down, the ribbon of the river. People have described the view from here as Austrian or Alp-like, so steep are the valleys and so incredibly green.

Os Peares itself is at the bottom of one of these valleys, in a favoured spot where oranges and lemons, figs and tropical fruits grow with abandon. One garden had squashes bigger than any I've ever seen. The whole town is a fascinating place in which to spend time, overlooked as it is by the hills on all sides and the high, concrete bridge that is the main Ourense to Ponferrada trunk road.

Walking alongside the river Búbal on a newly-built pedestrian footpath we noticed one part of the river had been dammed to create a delightful and welcomingly icy bathing pool. People were splashing around and lazing on the grass alongside. We had planned to visit the thermal pools in Ourense that afternoon, but a cool river swim was much more inviting than a soak in hot water on a stifling summer's day. S, Hal, and I quickly stripped off and dived in.

Oh, was it cold, but so refreshing. There were patches of warmer and cooler water as the currents eddied around, and now we were in the water we saw that the dam was a series of metal sluice gates which could be removed to allow the river to flow

CHESTNUT, CHERRY & KIWI FRUIT SPONGE

unimpeded or slotted into special brackets to allow the 'pool' to fill up. What a great resource for the locals.

Jack decided against a swim, though he did put his shorts on, lounging on the grass smoking. Mum found a spot to sit on a bench with grass growing thickly around its base. The grass cutters obviously hadn't quite finished their job as the rest of the area was neatly trimmed and covered with brightly coloured towels. It was a lovely afternoon, swimming and exploring this peculiar village.

We came back home via Monforte, as Hal and Jack wanted to visit our second city. As we sat at one of the many terrace bars, enjoying a drink and people watching, Jack announced that he had left his shorts in Os Peares when he changed back into his jeans. More importantly, his tobacco and lighter had been in the pocket.

I shrugged. "Well, we're not driving all the way back today, Jack. You can go and look on your way tomorrow, they'll probably still be there."

"Hm, doubt it," he mumbled.

Thursday 30th July Thundery
Hal and Jack left at midday after picking some (more) plums. L tiling the kitchen floor. S cutting the edge pieces and chiselling the beam on the mezzanine at A Casa do Campo.
Lunch: Lubina (bass) and vegetable rostis.
Wonder if Jack found his shorts??

Our hot and sultry month ended with some ferocious storms which whipped around our little valley overnight, turning the sky purple, white, and red as the lightning flashed. The view from our sunroom was spectacular and I was reluctant to go to bed, but little Feliz needed his beauty sleep so I covered his nest and left him to the flashes and bangs, which seemed to bother him not at all.

AUGUST 2015
Feliz

Feliz was growing fast. Although we had raised many chicks, it was far more interesting to see one changing on a daily basis. After the first week he (it was obvious now that my baby was a he) had begun to grow in his wing feathers, the first to emerge from the fluff. They were a beautiful mix of chestnut, black, and white, showing promise of handsomeness.

By the time Feliz was two weeks old, he had outgrown his little propagator nest. I made up a large box in the sunroom with straw on the bottom, a water bowl and food bowl, and the propagator base in the corner. Initially, I would plug the propagator in at night to keep him warm, but as he grew and the weather remained in the 30s centigrade, I left just the woolly hat, to which Feliz would retire to sleep every evening.

When I came into the room, Feliz would start to do a dance, hopping up and down and flapping madly to try and get out of his box. I'd put my hand in and he would immediately jump onto my arm and thence to my shoulder, affectionately pecking my ear or pulling my hair. From there we would play our 'catch a cricket' game. Feliz no longer needed me to pull a leg off his snack to enable him to catch it. Instead, he would jump high into the air and grab the unfortunate insect mid-leap, turning it in his mouth until he could swallow it head first.

CHESTNUT, CHERRY & KIWI FRUIT SPONGE

The chick was taking up rather a lot of my time but I still managed to work on the *Casita*, tiling the kitchen floor, and of course cooking our meals. On the 1st of August I had no cooking to do as we had a picnic at Monterroso, in the woods next to the river Sirgal and the outdoor swimming pool. The weather had returned to its sunny summer norm after the thunder storms of the previous week.

The local council has made a lovely spot down by the river. There are stone picnic tables and stone barbecue grills. There are walks alongside the river and a camp site just beyond. There is a café, changing rooms, and less than salubrious toilets. The swimming pool is clean and warm, the river clear and icy.

There were around 20 of us that day enjoying a shared picnic, chatting, and welcoming Mum to her new home.

Diary Sunday 2nd August Hot hot
Lovely boiled eggs and soldiers for 3. Have another Workawayer wanting to come mid-month for a few days, which is fine as S' cousin will have left by then and we will have had a week of relaxation! Haha. First ripe tomatoes and first melon.
Loin of pork with roast spuds, carrots, onion and courgette. Orange pudding and custard.
L varnishing the door to the living room which Mum has been scraping clean of blue paint. S was in our Big Barn sorting where the new cupboards will go on the mezzanine. More space for my books! All to Taboada pool in the evening. Mum sat at one of the tables outside the café while we swam, lazed on the grass, and ate ice creams.

I had been passing emails back and forth with my brother during this time. We were becoming less optimistic about Mum's house selling quickly now it was back on the market yet again. Although a quick

AUGUST 2015

sale wasn't an issue for Mum as she was here and happy, she was paying her full council tax of £120 a month on an empty property. My brother had been looking at alternatives and found there was an auction house nearby. This would be a cash buyer's market and an instant sale with far less chance of disappointment further down the line. There had been little interest from buyers since the third fiasco so we agreed to go down the auction route and withdraw the house from sale.

Diary Wednesday 5th August Cloud pm (because visitors are due)
Made plum cakes, plum vinegar, plum ketchup and plum chutney. And still there are more! Mum busy sanding the bedroom door.
Lunch: Sausages, onion gravy, mash, carrots and spinach.
Mum working even more enthusiastically now after her favourite lunch!
Tidied the bedroom ready for our guests.

S' cousin, Gerry, lived in Australia and was 12 years older than my husband. They hadn't seen each other for 14 years until the previous year, when we'd flown to Barcelona to meet him and his wife after their cruise ship docked there. It had been a fun couple of days and they'd decided that they wanted to come back sometime and see our house. This year their cruise was docking at Lisbon, not a million miles from us. Gerry had hired a car and was driving up to join us *casa nosotros* for a few days.

Gerry and Jeanette arrived on the 7th of August having made good time from Lisbon. We had a week's worth of entertainment planned for our guests and a welcome week of leisure for ourselves...

On the Saturday, we went to Os Peares again to show the Australians some of our spectacular

CHESTNUT, CHERRY & KIWI FRUIT SPONGE

scenery. Wandering down the river walk once more; I noticed the bench where Mum sat a week earlier had now been cleared of its weeds. On the arm of the bench something had been laid. On closer inspection it was found to be a pair of shorts complete with tobacco and lighter in the pocket. Jack's shorts! After a whole week they were exactly where he had left them. Only, I felt, in Galicia would people be so honest... or indifferent. We took the shorts home and left Jack a message saying we had recovered them. He never did return to collect them.

That weekend was the annual fiesta in Taboada. Our local fiesta runs for three days and nights and involves huge '*orchestras*', as the salsa bands are called. There are bouncy castles and side shows and many more people than have ever lived in our sleepy town. It is a spectacle not to be missed for the outsider.

It was the first time Mum had been here at fiesta time. We ordered her to bed in the afternoon for a siesta so she would manage to stay up until the early hours. We set off into town at around 10pm and stayed until 3am the next morning. Mum was a real party animal, it turned out. She stole my French fries and demanded ice cream at 2am. She also made a beeline for the fairground stalls lining the streets.

One chap had a stall called, appropriately, Arco Iris (rainbow – after Iris, the goddess of the rainbow, and my mother). It was a darts stall. Having never thrown a dart in her life, stopped Mum not at all. She collected her three darts and threw them for all she was worth. After the first dart, the stall owner prudently moved slightly further down his stall. I felt he might be safer further away still, but he was brave that chap. Mum must have done something right because her second set of darts won her a tiny sequinned purse which would have cost a fraction of the amount she paid for the darts. Still, Mum was over the moon and has that purse hooked over her dressing table mirror to this day.

Monday was the folk festival in town. It was a dance festival with troupes of local traditional *Galego* folk dancers and a troupe from overseas. Each year a different country is invited to take part and it has been interesting over the years to see folk dances from around the world. One day I would love to invite an English Morris troupe. The Galician dances are quite similar to some of the Morris dances except that both sexes take part here. The youngsters had their own dance troupe and it was a delight to see the tots twirling around on the stage set up in the market square.

Diary Tuesday 11th August Very hot again
Watered then all off to Monforte. Visited the Torre de Homenaje, had lunch at the wine centre (good) and visited the Casa del Torre.
Back 8pm to water again!

We had visited the castle keep tower in Monforte many times and always enjoyed the spectacular views from the top, but John had recently told us of a manor house or *pazo* nearby which also did tours.

The Pazo de Tor is a 15th century manor house, home of the Garza family until 1998 when its last owner Maria de la Paz Taboada de Andrés y Zúñiga donated it to the provincial government. In 2006, the house was opened as a museum.

Although originally built in the 1400s, most of the existing structure is from the 18th century due to a fire which destroyed much of the earlier building. The entrance to the *pazo* is along a narrow road, but as one enters the gates you get a real feeling for the grandness of this building.

The sun was scorching that afternoon as we parked in a designated space near the gates. The gardens were beautifully laid out and I could see

CHESTNUT, CHERRY & KIWI FRUIT SPONGE

outbuildings which I was anxious to explore. The Tor did free hourly tours of the property, but the outbuildings were at the end of the tour so I had to wait. In any case, there was so much to see inside (and it was much cooler within the thick stone walls).

The first thing I noticed as we entered were the cat-sized holes through the walls at skirting level. A friendly guide confirmed that they were indeed for cats to come and go at their leisure and hopefully earn their keep catching mice and rats. I loved the quirkiness and could imagine a group of animals playing their own version of cat and mouse throughout the house. The first room we entered was the arms room – full of suits of armour, swords, muskets and a tiny litter for carrying the nobility around. There were rooms every which way from this point and I was soon disorientated.

One of the bathrooms, off the master bedroom, had a stunning bath carved out of a single piece of marble which I coveted madly.

"That's a Stafford pottery toilet," said Mum, pointing at the white porcelain WC with its intricate pattern of hand-painted flowers around the inside of the bowl and on the high-level tank above.

Our guide obviously understood English, or enough to get Mum's drift, because she smiled. "It is from Trent," she said. "Made in England. Is that where you are from?" she asked Mum.

Mum was delighted. "Yes, Stoke-on-Trent. It's not far from us. I recognise the flowers. There were lots done like that years ago. But not now," she ended sadly.

In the dining room, Mum spotted yet more Wedgewood pottery and decided these Galician nobles had good taste.

Once we had toured the billiards room, the chapel, the bishop's room, and the morning room, I had been 'big housed' out and Mum was flagging.

AUGUST 2015

She went to sit on one of the chairs littering the games room but was told it was an antique. I had to stop myself from saying 'so is my mum'.

The library held some 3000 books, many huge and leather bound, and I could have happily stayed all afternoon. The last part of the house on the tour was a balcony with spectacular views overlooking Monforte to the rear and an interesting stone maze in the garden below. Then we were onto the outbuildings.

One was decked out as a henhouse, one a forge and one, my favourite, a carriage room complete with ancient horse drawn carriages, saddles and other paraphernalia. All in all, it was a fascinating tour which we have repeated many times since with guests, though they have yet to provide any chairs for visitors to rest on. Just a thought.

Diary Wednesday 12th August Very hot
Collected Mum's empadronamiento from the town hall. She is now officially living here! Wandered by the river in Monterroso and had lunch at the parillada grill in Baiuca.
Stuck a few more tiles on the kitchen floor and checked on Feliz who was very happy to see me and managed to jump straight out of his box in his excitement.
Off to the club nautico for drinks.

The Club Nautico, where S had his stag party five years earlier, was another good spot to spend an evening chatting and drinking. The ownership had changed since those times but the new owners, a couple of chaps who looked like doubles for the Hairy Bikers, had made some welcome changes for us - they now stocked artisan ales. The brown ale was delicious and S enjoyed the stout. Gerry, however, was less than impressed with his 25cl glass.

CHESTNUT, CHERRY & KIWI FRUIT SPONGE

"Call that a beer!" he said in his Aussie accent. "That's not a beer!"

"Well, you can have two, or three if you want," I said, trying to pacify him.

"I don't want two, I want a proper sized beer," he insisted.

Jeanette sighed. "Ignore him," she said. "He's just being a pain."

We did, and Gerry drank his miniature beer, complaining all the while. We spent the rest of the trip teasing him about it and he continued to whine at the tiny measures; despite the fact that six of them would still be cheaper than a 'proper beer' in Melbourne (as we found out four years later when we visited their delightful city... which is another story entirely).

Gerry and Jeanette left on the 14th of August and our next helper, Joseph, arrived on the 16th. We'd had a lovely relaxing time with our guests and Jeanette especially had been taken with my chick.

Feliz was growing apace. He was now almost fully feathered in beautiful browns and blacks with chestnut highlights and perfectly able to flap out of his box in the sunroom whenever he wished. S asked me what I was going to do with a second cockerel. I didn't have an answer for that but had decided that it was time to get Feliz used to the other chickens, and they to him. He was already joining us outside for tea break, enjoying flapping about the terrace and dipping his beak into my tea. I thought he would enjoy some time in the small chicken pen, watching his relatives from the safety of his bars.

The problem was that Feliz didn't know he was a chicken. He had been brought up with humans, and from his viewpoint he was a human. He showed no interest in the other chickens, who crowded around the wire mesh peering at this intruder in their home and complaining loudly, but would fly onto my shoulder as I turned to leave the pen and squeak forlornly when I left him there. It broke my heart, but he had to become one of the gang. He was too big to stay in the sunroom.

I thought if Feliz got used to the chicken pen, we could move his sister, Foxglove, the only other chick from Buff Puff's brood, up to share the space with him and she could teach him how to be a chicken. Buff Puff was fed up with her mother hen role now, and neither chick needed her warmth overnight. I would give Feliz a few hours a day in the pen alone, letting him continue to sleep in the sunroom, then move Foxglove in the next week.

My plan was working well – until I killed him.

Diary Monday 17th August Cloudy
L and Mum into town. Registered Mum with the GP and did our shopping.
Joseph filling holes in the back wall of the Casita with cement. S on the roof fixing the ridge tiles.
Lunch: nut and courgette balls with cheese and tomato sauce. Rice. Plum pie and ice cream
Finished grouting the floor tiles in the kitchen. After tea L put Feliz in the chicken pen but missed him running out again and stepped on him, crushing his lungs and killing him. Words can't express how I feel – so so sorry my beautiful Feliz. RIP, 6pm 17th August, one month and two days old.

I still don't know what happened that day. My diary entry is typically melodramatic but my grief was all too real and it still hurts to read this, six years later. I had popped Feliz into the top, enclosed chicken pen after tea, meaning to leave him there for a couple of hours until supper time. As I closed the door, the other chickens came running, thinking it was time for their food. Laughing at their antics, I was watching them instead of Feliz who evidently tried to follow me out again.

CHESTNUT, CHERRY & KIWI FRUIT SPONGE

I remember laughing at the chickens then there is a blank space in my memory until I looked down to see Feliz doing his little dance in front of me. He was flapping around and twirling. I smiled and picked him up. His head flopped and he stopped moving. I had broken his neck.

Completely at a loss I called my usual rescuer, but even S was unable to do anything for my poor chick. Joseph must have thought us an odd household that week. I was riven with guilt and virtually monosyllabic. Mum was upset and wanting to comfort me, but I didn't want comfort. I didn't deserve it.

I buried Feliz on the allotment where he had never been, cleared away his box and the newspaper strewn on the sunroom floor and tried to forget. At the latter I failed dismally and am still crying writing this all these years later. If only I'd checked before closing the door, if only I hadn't got distracted by the other chickens. 'If onlys' bounced around my head for weeks.

Diary Wednesday 19th August Hot hot
Have another Workawayer booked for next week. Pat is another Aussie so we shall look forward to his company. Made tomato sauce with Mum and cut tomatoes to sun-dry them. S went off with Joseph and Geert to collect some soil for Mum's raised bed. It has taken a bit of finding. Geert also had a load of unwanted roof tiles going begging so they brought those back.

Joseph left on the 20th of August having had only a few days holiday before he began his next teaching job. He was a lovely, polite, softly spoken Englishman who was willing to chip in with anything that needed doing. He would take himself off to our little river in the afternoon and swim in the shallow pool which had formed as the water level fell. I would have liked him to stay longer and wished, above all else, that he had been with us in better circumstances.

Pat was the opposite of quiet, polite Joseph in many ways. A tall skinny Aussie, Pat was a puppy dog, full of enthusiasm and bounce. He was more than happy to get stuck into any job so long as it didn't mean an early start. We have never minded which hours our helpers do, so long as they do their hours. Pat certainly did his allotted hours, his day just started somewhat later than most.

"Pat, if you aren't down in five minutes you'll miss morning tea break," I yelled up the stairs, the second morning. No response. "Pat!"

"I'll have a go," said Mum. "I'm used to teenage boys."

I was about to point out that Pat was in his 20s but she had gone. Standing right outside the attic room door, Mum shouted, "Tea time! Now!"

There was a groan from inside the room and a sleepy Pat emerged some minutes later. He soon woke up with a mug of tea and a slice of cake inside him and got stuck into the endless task of picking plums. Unlike Jack before him, Pat was more than happy to pick plums, scrape beams or do any other task we set him.

As I put on my review 'Pat is a perfect Workawayer, so long as you don't need someone to milk the cows at dawn'. Luckily we didn't, and Pat suited us well. Each evening after he finished work, he would get changed and head into town for a drink (or rather more, I believe). We would occasionally hear him come in at two or three in the morning but he was a quiet burglar, and rarely disturbed our slumbers.

Once he was particularly late back and I asked him the next day what had happened.

"I got lost," he said, sheepishly.

"Lost? From Taboada?"

CHESTNUT, CHERRY & KIWI FRUIT SPONGE

"Yeah, I turned wrong somewhere, ended up in another village."

I eventually found out that Pat had walked some two miles in completely the wrong direction before retracing his, I'm guessing rather wobbly, steps home.

Diary Wednesday 26th August Some clouds
L made tomato sauce, cookies, pud and lunch. Mum cutting nectarines to sun-dry. They are delicious in cakes. S up on the roof sticking on the ridge tiles before the autumn rains come. Pat happily sanding the beam in the living room, he hardly needs a stool never mind a ladder to reach! Lunch: Courgette and cashew quiche, green beans, tomato and olive salad. Cherry clafoutis and ice cream.
Pat continued sanding. L and S measured for the marble worktop around the cocina. Mum likes the pink 'rosa' granite. As the top is such a strange shape, we checked each other's measurements and made a paper pattern for the bit in the corner.

The kitchen was an odd room anyway, being a sort of lozenge shape. I'd had fun deciding where to put my straight edge for the floor tiles. We'd decided that the front of the *cocina* ought to be the straight edge as it more or less led in a line from the door and was the one feature which would draw the eye the most. Even the *cocina* surrounds were not square; instead, each was slightly out of true, meaning we had to be very careful with our measuring for the worktops.

We'd decided, after much consideration, to put the sink in the corner of the room. Where it was, below the window and within the 70-centimetre-thick stone outside wall, it would be impossible to fit a modern waste. But, if we fitted a new stainless-steel sink at an angle in the corner it would be

AUGUST 2015

possible to fit a U-bend below, in a fortuitous gap in the wall, and drill through to the outside for the waste pipe. This had been my idea and I was rather proud of it. The katy-corner sink would fit the quirky room perfectly.

Around the sink were to be two pieces of marble worktop. One would cover the existing stone sink and was almost square, the other long and thin – running as it did around the corner and behind the *cocina* as far as the chimney breast. A further three pieces would make the worktop around the built-in wood-burning range, and a final large square piece would make a shelf in Mum's new cool store in the well cupboard.

On our five-year wedding anniversary, we called into the marble workshop in Chantada with our paper plans. José, the owner, was more than happy to cut and polish the worktops for us, though he expressed surprise at the odd shapes we had produced.

"*No pasa nada, José*," I said nonchalantly. "Don't worry, they are fine. How long will they take to finish?"

"*Quince dias*," he replied. Of course they would.

SEPTEMBER 2015
Removing Rick

Fifteen days, or two weeks, is the standard Spanish reply to any question about time so we didn't worry too much about José's promise. We had become so much more pragmatic in the last eight years. *Mañana* was a wonderful word these days!

Pat was with us until the 6th of September. I had planned on having a break from Workawayers for a while afterwards. Much as we enjoyed their company, and their help, it was nice to have some time to ourselves and it had been a busy couple of months since Mum had arrived to stay.

Rick, however, was nothing if not persuasive. He was, he told me by email, a trained carpenter who could 'do anything' and would be the best Workawayer we had ever had. I should have known better.

It's a funny fact of life that often the more someone sings their own praises the less wonderful they really are, whereas those who are more modest or even, like our lovely Ramón, pessimistic, about their abilities, are often the treasures.

On the day Pat left we took him to Lugo, sorry to see our late-riser go. We hadn't intended to take him so far. Pat had arranged a BlaBla car in Lugo and was catching the bus there from Taboada. We dropped him in town and double-checked the time of the next bus at the café.

SEPTEMBER 2015

Although Pat had checked online, we knew better than to trust the bus company's own website. Sure enough, the timetable had changed and we had missed the bus he needed. As there are only four buses a day from our little town, we got a quick trip to Lugo in and Pat caught his lift.

The following day Rick arrived. A stocky blond American in a red baseball cap, Rick told us he had worked for years in the construction industry and could do anything at all in the building line.

"I've tons of skills and a work ethic second to none," he said, sounding like a marketing advertisement for himself. I left him in S' capable care while I continued painting the *cocina* surround and varnishing the shelves for the new oven housing.

At first Rick seemed fine. He scraped beams and helped S hang the newly varnished living room door. He cemented and picked apples, and generally got on with whatever was asked of him. Only at mealtimes was there an issue.

Mum loves to chat and I'd been pleased that all our Workawayers had been so friendly and happy to talk with her or listen to stories of 'the old days'. It helped Mum settle in and ensured a peaceful and happy existence.

Rick was different in a way I couldn't quite put my finger on. He happily ate whatever was put in front of him but seemed to have no social skills. He would either ignore questions, begin his own conversation midway through another, or just tune out completely. Only when he was talking about his ambitions to become a ship's captain did he show any animation.

"I'm going to get a job crewing on a yacht in the spring," he told us.

"Have you done much sailing?" asked Mum.

CHESTNUT, CHERRY & KIWI FRUIT SPONGE

Rick looked at her but ignored the question. "I'll get my captain's licence then."

"So, you're an experienced sailor?" I pushed.

"I've never been on a boat," he admitted, "but it'll be easy."

"I'm sure it will," I replied, bemused.

Diary Wednesday 9th September Drizzle am
L and Mum drove into Chantada to choose a stone plinth for her new living room stove to sit on. Mum liked the 'Orinoco' with swirls of red and black and grey, looking very dramatic and rich. José told me they had started on the worktops but worried what an odd shape they are. I agreed, they are. He does go on!
S and Rick were chasing the wall for the electrics and removing the ceiling in the bedroom-to-be ready for the new beams.
Lunch: Bacon and pork pie, creamed spinach. Chocolate and cherry 'Black Forest gateau' trifle.
Chatting at lunch time when Rick just got up and walked away from the table with no word of explanation. Very odd.

I had no problem with Rick's peculiar ways, but on this occasion he'd got up while Mum was asking him something and just disappeared. I didn't care if he was rude to us (and S said it happened frequently when they were working together) but no one is rude to my mother.

I found Rick and put it to him.

"Look, I can see you aren't enjoying it here and I'm sorry for that, but there is no excuse to be rude to Mum, she hasn't done anything to you."

Rick looked shocked, for possibly the first time. Maybe no one had commented on his odd behaviour before. "I, I do like it here," he said eventually. "I didn't mean to be rude."

SEPTEMBER 2015

I couldn't believe he didn't realise how his behaviour impacted others but I was starting to wonder if he was mildly autistic. "Okay, no worries, Rick. Let's all just try and get on, eh?"

"Of course, yeah," he answered.

From: m wright
> Sent: Tuesday, Sep 8, 2015 1:52 PM
> To: Lisa Wright
> Subject: Re: blank
> Hi Sis
>Auction date is 10 Sept, I'll probably go, better sit on my hands, don't want to come back with a property, unless it's somewhere warmer than here ☺.
>Xxx

On 9 Sep 2015, at 09:51, "Lisa Wright" <lisarosewright@msn.com> wrote:
>Hi Bro
>Haha. Some cheap houses in Galicia! Fingers crossed!
>When you speak to the removals on Weds can you make sure they have my fone number as they WILL NOT find us with GPS alone... If it's possible to get a mobile number for the driver too that would be even better!!!
>The house is progressing slowly tho mum still expects to be in by xmas! Really want to get it done for her but it has to be done properly too so catch 22.
>The marble tops are on order for the kitchen and the living room is looking pretty good... our last helper scraped and varnished the beam and painted thro. Will try to remember to FB some pics this week.
>Lots of love for now
>xx
>Sis

CHESTNUT, CHERRY & KIWI FRUIT SPONGE

Mum's house was sold at auction on the same day that her liberated furniture arrived here in Galicia. It had been in storage for almost two months and the costs were mounting. We felt that we could store it here just as easily. Roy and Francesca had strengthened the holey floor in the second bedroom-to-be and lined it with cardboard to insulate it. Most of the boxes and wooden furniture would go in there. The tougher things could go in the barns below, well shrouded.

The delivery company said they wouldn't help unload. Furthermore, as the van was a double trailer, they wouldn't risk bringing it on the narrow road down into the village despite the fact I'd specifically asked them to put all Mum's stuff on the inner, fixed trailer. That trailer was considerably smaller than our huge shipping container of furniture had been some eight years earlier.

That driver had been amazing. I still think of him manoeuvring back and forward to get out of the village, clutching his heart dramatically and sighing, "*mi corazon*", with affection. This company was adamant; they would not come further than the main road. We would have to transfer all Mum's stuff the one and a half kilometres to the village. It would be a long walk!

Luckily, we have some amazing friends here and by the afternoon before the furniture was to arrive, we had offers of three 'persons and vans' to help us. Richard and Geert brought along their large box vans, and another friend brought his smaller, but surprisingly spacious, Citroën Berlingo. With our long-suffering Ford Escort, we were set.

The removal truck was parked in the car park of our local supermarket by 10am. There were eight of us loading. We all swarmed around moving furniture whilst I tried to keep tabs on my inventory of boxes. I was dismayed to see that Mum's stuff had been divided between the two trailers, a part load in each, and squashed around with other people's goods. I had a bad feeling this wasn't going to end well.

By 1pm we had moved everything to its new home and I was only missing one box.

"It's box number 34," I told the driver, as I read from my list.

He sorted through a wad of scruffy, ripped pieces of paper to find our inventory from the warehouse. Only half of the 39 boxes were listed at all. Number 34 wasn't one of them.

"I can't check the van now; I've got more deliveries to do. I'm due in Alicante this afternoon," said the driver, rather sulkily. "If there's anything left over when we've unloaded it all I'll let you know, but you've got insurance don't you?"

What an incredibly professional attitude!

I spoke to the head office and complained at what I took to be gross negligence about inventorying the contents they had stored.

"It's not in the storage unit, it must have been lost in the shuttling process. Anyway, it's only pots and pans, nothing of importance," said the less than helpful contact.

"Well, A, that's not the point and B, do you seriously believe that it's possible to leave a box of around a metre square in a small van and not notice it? I'll be taking this further, trust me."

The driver declined to join us for lunch, even though Mum insisted on paying, and disappeared to his next job. The rest of our friends joined us for a well-deserved meal at Bar Mencía. Mum was finally here, chattels and all. There was no turning back now.

Diary Saturday 12th September Dull, then showers, then sun
Made cookies, meatballs, tomato relish, sun-dried plums and wine (from our grapes, with Mum's

CHESTNUT, CHERRY & KIWI FRUIT SPONGE

help). S and Rick fitting new ceiling beams in the bedroom-to-be. BJ on 3 eggs. Left her there.
Lunch: Pork and blue cheese meatballs in tomato and pepper sauce. Pasta. Fruit salad and ice cream.
L finally finished grouting the floor tiles in the kitchen whilst S redid the beams Rick had put in this morning.

The main bedroom, like all the rooms in the *Casita* bar the central dining room, is an off-square. It narrows considerably to one end. S had explained this fact to Rick and asked him to fit the new beams so they fanned out from the central beam where the plasterboard sheets would butt together.

"You won't be able to fit them with an even width apart," he explained. "As the ceiling widens, you will have to space them out or there will be nothing to fit the plasterboard to at one end."

Rick couldn't accept this oddity.

"It doesn't make sense," he insisted. "We always put them 16 inches apart."

We had already discovered that Rick's extensive building experience had been as part of a gang, barn-raising pre-cut, pre-fabricated houses in the US. Our *Casita* was anything but pre-fabricated. Our beams were ex-trees, still in the shape they had grown.

One of my favourite parts of the *Casita* is a cantilevered beam which is part of the roofing trusses and is in the shape of a bow. It doesn't touch any part of the beam below it on one side but supports a mass of beams above it. And has done so for over 150 years.

Rick was used to straight, planed wood of a consistent width, length and shape. Even our new 'straight' beams weren't really straight. No matter how S tried to explain what was needed, Rick couldn't grasp the concept.

SEPTEMBER 2015

Eventually, thinking he had the hang of it, S left our Workawayer to get on with fitting the new beams. Sadly, his work was no good. As feared, Rick had fitted the new beams in perfect straight lines, parallel to the first beam. This meant that by the time he reached the far end there was nothing to fit the last few beams to and nowhere to fix the new plasterboard ceiling.

At one point S came to find me.

"You have to look at this," he said.

I followed him and climbed the ladder to look where he indicated. There was one of the new sweet chestnut beams Rick had fitted and in its end was a mass of bent nails and twisted screws.

"What on earth?" I queried, looking down at S from my perch on the ladders.

"I told him that sweet chestnut is hard and needs pre-drilling before trying to nail it. He obviously thought he knew better," said my long-suffering husband.

"But the screws too. What was he thinking of?"

"I guess when he couldn't hammer the nails in, he decided to fix it with screws. I thought he was getting through a lot. When does he leave?" added S, plaintively.

Rick was booked to stay another week and a half. I didn't think my beloved would last that long.

The following day S showed Rick how to fit the noggins between each of the newly rearranged beams. Once more he came to me in a rare temper.

"He's cutting the noggins on his knee."

"What d'you mean? Don't you have the workmate over there?"

The workmate bench is a folding saw horse which we use to hold the wood safely and securely.

"Of course. He says he can do it as well on his knee, but he's not doing a proper job and the ends are splintering."

CHESTNUT, CHERRY & KIWI FRUIT SPONGE

It takes a lot, and I mean a lot, to get my even-tempered, blue-eyed man to see red, but Rick was succeeding.

Diary Monday 14th September Drizzly
S and Rick on the roof. I think S is trying to keep him from destroying any more expensive wood, or using our entire box of nails.
Made lunch and tomato sauce. Mum did some sewing repairs for me.
Lunch: Rabbit pie with apple and mustard sauce. Jam tarts and custard.

That afternoon S came into the garden where I was mortaring some holes, a big smile on his face.

"What are you looking so pleased about?" I asked.

"Rick's leaving tomorrow. He's got a job in Palma."

"Mallorca? Oh! Well, that's good I guess, it's where he wanted to go. Though he could have told me."

"I don't care," replied S. "I'm just happy he's going. He's costing us a fortune in ruined materials."

So pleased was my poor hubby that he didn't even mind getting up early to take Rick to the train station in Monforte. In fact, I think he wanted to ensure Rick really had left.

We celebrated with hot chocolates and *churros* at the wine centre in Monforte. The rain came down heavily and we stopped for lunch in Chantada at the Restaurant-Hotel Las Delicias. Always superb, the food tasted like nectar after removing Rick from our lives.

Diary Wednesday 16th September Poured all night and most of the day
Spent the morning fastening the runner beans back up and generally tidying the allotment after last night's storm. S playing with the electrics to the living room at the Casita.

SEPTEMBER 2015

Noticed Foxglove wasn't there when I let the chickens out, and the three eggs Billie Jean was sitting on have disappeared too.

I have to admit, that after losing my own chick, Feliz, I hadn't taken much notice of his sister. Each time I looked at her, now happily mixing with the big girls, I thought of how Feliz too would have had his final feathers. He would have been growing, sharing his life with the other hens and running around in the open air, climbing trees, pecking for grubs and having dust baths in the soil. It hurt too much, so I ignored her and let her get on with it. To be fair, Foxglove ignored me too. She was a different personality to her brother: independent and not needing of anyone.

That morning, when I had gone to feed the gang, I noticed she wasn't among the hens milling around my feet. I thought she was off grubbing for worms alone somewhere, but she didn't return. The following day, S found a pile of gold and white feathers below the walnut tree the other side of the house. We concluded that a cat had got in and somehow taken her. More bizarre still, Billie Jean's eggs just vanished. Gone. Disappeared. There was no yolk, no cracked shells, nothing. It was as if they had never been.

We later discovered that we had a weasel. Weasels are small mustelids, like stoats and pine martens. They are fast and can squeeze through the smallest of gaps. They are also clever enough to figure out a way to steal three eggs from under the beak of a broody hen. I was only grateful that Billie Jean had not been killed too.

The loss of poor Foxglove and the eggs meant we had a grand total of one chick surviving that year. Although I was sorry for Foxglove, I didn't mourn her as I should. Her loss somehow seemed fitting and *Solita* Faith really was the 'only' chick.

CHESTNUT, CHERRY & KIWI FRUIT SPONGE

Two days later our next Workawayers arrived.

Tony and Dan were a father and son team from the northwest of England. They could not have been more different from the disastrous Rick if they had tried.

Tony was a plasterer by trade but also a builder. He was my age, only slightly taller than S and, most importantly, he shared a very English and understandable sense of humour. Dan was in his 20s, somewhat new-agey in appearance with his woolly hat and incense sticks, but had his dad's easy ways. He was also a fabulous worker, and he and his dad made a great team. Dan did have one request though.

"You said if we didn't want to sleep together, you could find somewhere else?" he asked, that first evening.

Our Workawayer room has only a double bed and I'd already suggested to Tony that they may not want to share.

"It's no problem," he'd said by email, "Dan can have a rollmat on the floor."

Now Dan looked pleadingly at me.

"Sure. Come and have a look in the Big Barn. It's not finished but you can set up on the mezzanine if you like."

Dan loved the idea of his own sleeping space even if he did have to climb a ladder to get there. "It's Dad," he admitted to me. "He snores!"

Once that was sorted, and Tony had indignantly denied his night time snuffles, we all got on like the team we were. Tony and Dan both loved Mum, happy to chat to her, and to listen. Dan in particular kept Mum enraptured with tales of his travels around the world. I was just content to have a happy household to feed again.

Tony was a vegetarian, but I couldn't have asked for an easier person to feed. He would happily tuck into anything I cooked and even, at a meal we were invited to, picked the meat out of his dinner, rather than complain. Easy going doesn't come into it. In fact, the only time Tony wasn't laid-back was when S thrashed him at chess.

These clashes, at our coffee-table-come-chessboard in the sunroom, became a battle of wits. Sometimes Tony would triumph, occasionally Dan would get the upper hand, but more often than not S' logical brain would win the day. Tony even played Mum – who has no idea about chess and was moving her pieces quite randomly around the board despite S' instructions.

"No, that one can't jump," he said, as she leapfrogged her pawn across four pieces to reach the space she wanted. "It's not draughts, you know!"

Mum was convinced she had gained a victory that night and Tony was happy to concede the game. Another tick by his name in my books.

Diary Wednesday 23rd September Hot
Made three batches of cookies for Phil's party this afternoon. Mum was busy still sanding the door to the bedroom, trying to remove layers of blue paint. Tony and Dan were fitting the sewerage pipes from the bathroom and S was finishing his beams in the bedroom. Things seem to be shooting ahead. Funny what a bit of real help can do.
All off to Phil's party.

Our friend Phil has a party each autumn, nominally for his birthday though the date varies. He tries to pick a hot day and more times than not, he succeeds. Phil is an excellent cook and using an old and fairly decrepit *cocina* in a tiny, dark and ancient kitchen, he manages to produce two or three main courses for the masses. Chilli, Thai curry, bolognaise, and sausage and mash have all appeared out of that tiny space. To watch his six-foot frame bent over the 30-

CHESTNUT, CHERRY & KIWI FRUIT SPONGE

inch-high worktop preparing his dishes to the beats of the radio is to watch poetry in action.

The other must have at Phil's parties is a boules competition. Phil is very serious about his sports, and boules must be played properly. We are all given a lecture beforehand about how to play and teams are paired up using a proper league table with names drawn from a hat to ensure fairness.

I remember one year Phil had gone off to do something when we started the matches. We just played by throwing the boules in turn, the boule nearest the jack at the end declared the winner. When Phil discovered our heresy, he declared the entire proceedings null and void.

That Phil is an excellent boules player is probably obvious. That he should choose Mum as his partner is maybe less expected. But not only does Phil choose Mum, he insists on her being his partner. With Mum following his instructions, and continually being distracted by Phil calling her Doris, they have defended their title on a number of occasions.

"My name's Iris, not Doris," Mum would whine.

"I know, Doris. Now, see that little ball? Line your boule that way a bit and a gentle throw should do it. Aim for this edge here. Not too hard. Okay, Doris?"

Mum would throw in her bizarre and inimitable style and by some miracle it would end up exactly where Phil had told her.

"Well done, Doris," he would say, high-fiving her.

Diary Friday 25th September Sunshine
Day trip to Lugo. Dropped Tony and Dan in town to explore then drove up to the car showrooms at the north end of town.
Lunch at Recatelo and spent 20€ on cheeses from the cheese shop. I could live in there.
Back to water and feed the animals.

SEPTEMBER 2015

As much as my godfather's old Ford Escort had seen us through thick and thin, and as reliable as she had been, she was now 20 years old and the service bills were mounting. Even ten-year-old cars, with who knew how many drivers, were way more expensive than an English equivalent.

While Tony and Dan explored Lugo, me, S and Mum explored cars. We wanted something with three proper seats in the back, and a level loading area. One of the few faults of the Escort was having to lift heavy bags of cement over the boot sill. We saw a couple of options that day but with a potential cost of thousands it wasn't a decision to be taken lightly. In comparison, renovating a ruin was much more straightforward.

Diary Monday 28th September Hot pm, misty am
Bought 3 more bags of plaster for Tony to redo the kitchen walls. He has made such a good job of the utility-bathroom. Now S has fitted the toilet too that whole room is finally starting to look like a bathroom. Dan helping S with the plasterboard ceiling in the bedroom.
Lunch: Non-chilli sin carne. Chilli sauce separate for those who dare. Sponge pudding and custard. Coro Sold!

Mum's house had sold at auction to a cash buyer looking to renovate and now, three weeks later, the money had been transferred. Finally, Mum was free of UK ties.

OCTOBER 2015
La Casa Amarilla

What a team Tony and Dan turned out to be. By the time they left on the 3rd of October, we had a plastered bathroom with a toilet and plumbing in place. We had a bedroom with a new plasterboard ceiling, a newly cement rendered raised bed in the garden, and a replastered kitchen. They had even joined a gang of us to help lay a concrete floor for friends nearby.

We would have happily kept Tony and Dan longer but they had things to do, and we had a visitor coming: Mum's sister, Aunty Jan, was arriving on the same flight on which our star helpers departed. Before Tony left, we did ask if he would consider returning, as a paid worker, for a longer period.

Mum was itching to move in but we were reluctant to employ a firm we didn't know or trust. Tony, we trusted implicitly, and this seemed the perfect solution. Tony happily agreed. He would sort things at home and be back to help before the year's end. Result.

Diary Saturday 3rd October Dull
Took Tony and Dan to the airport, ate our butties while waiting for the flight to offload then collected Aunty Jan. All done with perfect precision. I do like a good plan.
Into Santiago for the day, calling at Leroy Merlin and the new DIY shop Britomart nearby to buy

OCTOBER 2015

some paint for the outside of the Casita. Mum liked the buttercup yellow, and why not? Then allowed Jan to enjoy Santiago which is more her scene than DIY shops!
Had coffees in the art deco café and wandered around the city. Bought Mum a new watch with a larger dial. I did say she doesn't need one in Galicia but to no avail.
Dinner at Dezaseis. Excellent. Home around midnight.

Sunday 4th October Wet!
Perfect eggs for four from the breakfast chef, S. Mum did a tour of the Casita with Aunty Jan, proudly showing her the doors she has cleaned and the mounds of furniture littered about awaiting a home. Chucky, I noticed, has been elevated to prime spot on Mum's lounge chair, peering out of the window. Very scary indeed.

It had been a warm and sunny autumn up until the previous day. Now the rain had set in, but the weather didn't matter as the sisters were enjoying chatting and shelling walnuts for me. S, meanwhile, ran around doing rainwater maintenance where it had leaked into the dressing room at the *Casita*.

On the third day the sun peeked out so we took a ride to the monastery of Santa María de Oseira.

This formidable stone building was first recorded in 1137 as the home of a Benedictine order on lands donated by King Alfonso VII of León. Documented history of the monastery is poor, but by the end of the 12th century it was run by a Cistercian order, the white monks. A fire in 1561 destroyed much of the original building, works of art and important documents but enough of the church, crypt, and the ancient stonework remains to make a most enjoyable tour.

CHESTNUT, CHERRY & KIWI FRUIT SPONGE

Unfortunately, on this occasion our tour guide spoke only Spanish and there was no sign of Mum's tiny Madrileño monk, who she wanted to introduce to Aunty Jan.

The monastery was rebuilt and improved upon in the 16th century with a new refectory and works to the cloister. It continued as the home of the Cistercian monks until the confiscation of church properties in 1836.

In much the same way as the English reformation of the 16th century, the Spanish confiscation act seized properties from the Catholic Church and sold them. The monastery at Oseira was abandoned, its treasures and its stones taken to be reused or displayed in Madrid and Ourense.

The monastery was in ruins, with many of the frescos damaged by damp when, in 1929, it was reopened. Those first monks must have wondered at the state of their new home, derelict and deserted.

One of the new brothers wrote of the desolation he felt looking at the ruins, overrun by brambles, parasitic plants and the plaster peeling from the damp walls. Despite the hardships, the new order flourished, making *augardente* and cheeses, and opening as a school for the poor.

By the time we visited in 2015 there were only eleven monks living there, just one of which was a novice. In 2021, as I write this, there are four monks left. Money is raised from the tours and the gift shop in which Mum happily browsed for aeons.

On the way home we stopped at the marble place and were happy to be told our granite for the *cocina* worktop was ready.

"But the shape is very strange," said José, when we called in. "*¡Mira!*"

"Yes, I can see, José. It's an odd shaped unit. Do not worry," I replied. "We will ask our friend to help us collect it tomorrow."

OCTOBER 2015

Geert happily obliged by bringing his van to collect the six large pieces of, admittedly very oddly shaped, pink granite. We stacked the worktops in the kitchen before enjoying lunch together. The sun had even shone all day.

On the Thursday, the sun was still shining so we decided we should go on our annual Galician road trip. We had pored over the map and chosen a section of the west coast S and I had visited in part before and a sight Mum would love, the Castro de Baroña.

Galicia is proud of its Celtic ancestry. We have bagpipes and Celtic music festivals, and Galicia is one of the seven Celtic nations. We also have plenty of surviving Celtic history. *Castros*, or Bronze Age villages, abound. We have a tiny ruin close to our house but my favourite is the Castro de Baroña on the west coast of Galicia.

We first visited this incredibly well-preserved *Castro* in 2005. The access at that time was down a narrow track wandering through pine and eucalypt woodland with an occasional wooden arrow saying simply *'castro'*. In the woods were multi-coloured VW campervans sporting wetsuits hanging out to dry: the beach is a popular one for surfing... and nudist bathing (a more bizarre combination is difficult to imagine). Around the next bend, across sheets of granite rock, lay the Castro de Baroña.

The ruins of this defensible village perch on a promontory reachable from the mainland only via a narrow isthmus. It is surrounded by treacherous seas on three sides whilst below is a beautiful and virtually deserted beach.

By 2015, the access had been improved and the surfers with their VWs ejected. There was a smart new interpretation centre and the café at the entrance had a name change, Castro, which also involved a doubling of the price of their coffee. I was saddened by the changes – the surfers and the narrow track gave the place an otherworldly feel, apart from the commercialism of the day. The interpretation centre, though, was excellent, with a reproduction roundhouse and an interesting video. The new paving meant it was easier for Mum to walk the half mile or so to the *Castro*. The sun shone and the roundhouses looked like they were just waiting for new inhabitants to appear.

In the afternoon we stopped for coffee at a small seaside town called A Pobra do Caramiñal. It was in a privileged spot facing the sea, with a new boardwalk along the front. Deciding this would be a nice place to stay overnight I set off to find a hotel. Eventually I asked a chap at what seemed to be the only open café.

"*¡No hay!*" he said. "The only hotel is up the hill behind." He pointed way up above the town.

"There isn't a hotel? Oh!" I was disappointed. We wanted to stay where we could promenade in the evening and find a nice bar... or three.

As we left A Pobra, I noticed a number of stunning, derelict old buildings along the waterfront with iron balcony railings and pretty gable ends. Not for the first time, I wished I could renovate all unloved buildings. I felt sure a nice little B&B would do well in this charming seaside town.

We arrived, a little while later, at the centre of Ribeira. A large and busy town, it seemed to have everything we would need and there was a hotel right on the front. I went to ask about rooms. Being out of season I managed to get two double rooms for 66€, no breakfast. No problem.

Our room was facing the sea and, unusually for me, I woke before sunrise to get the most glorious shot of the golden orb lifting out of the water and glinting on the sail boats below us.

The evening before we had wandered the streets of Ribeira looking for a restaurant. Although there were plenty of fast-food joints and pizzerias, there seemed to be a dearth of Galician restaurants. The ones we did find seemed to be reluctant to serve us. Finally, after walking out of at least one place which served all those around us but managed to ignore our table completely, we spied a busy looking café bar which did *raciones*.

The Café Patrón was perfect, the staff friendly and welcoming. We stuffed ourselves and drank the most delicious local wines, recommended by our genial host, before wobbling back to our hotel. At least the two ladies had sticks to keep them upright.

The following morning, we declined the offer of sticky buns in the hotel and walked along the sea front, sure there would be a café open. I spied one promising looking place up a dozen steps. I climbed the steps to look at the menu board and as I reached the top an elderly man stopped me.

"You want breakfast?" he asked me in English, grabbing my arm.

"Er, yes. I thought in here." I pointed, trying subtly to unhook him from my wrist.

"No, no," he said. "Go here to café Josue. Very good. Say I send you."

He let me go and I hurried back to the waiting family. "We have to go down here a bit," I said, bemused by the encounter.

The lady at the Café Josue was delighted to have customers for breakfast. We sat at a small wooden table just inside the open doors as she juiced oranges, made toast and tea, sliced tomatoes, and brought olive oil and pots of jam and butter to the table for us. Before we had finished the generous meal, she was offering us more. As we politely declined, my 'friend' from earlier walked in. Greeting the owner, he turned and smiled a toothless smile at us.

"Good, yes?" he said.

"Yes, very good." I couldn't help but think that with a marketing manager like that any business

CHESTNUT, CHERRY & KIWI FRUIT SPONGE

would do well. The cost of our breakfasts? 14€ for the four of us.

We arrived home in the late afternoon having visited another *Castro* on the way and collected some pebbles from the beach. At least Mum had. I felt her garden would be full of seaside pebbles soon.

"You do realise we brought back two boxes full of Galician pebbles from England when you moved here don't you?" I asked Mum one evening. "It gives 'coals to Newcastle' a whole new meaning!"

Diary Saturday 10th October Sunshine
Made lunch and tomato sauce. Tomatoes are keeping well this year, must be the late sunshine. Varnished the door to the bedroom while S measured the granite worktop to have it recut. Oops!
Lit both cocinas. Tira!

At least we weren't going to have a repeat of the '¡no tira!' saga when we first tried to light our own wood-burning range cooker some eight years earlier. That had smoked us out, and taken some six months and numerous disastrous workmen visits before S had ejected the mice and fixed the problem himself. Luckily, lighting the stove at the *Casita* was much more successful. Unluckily, our measuring for the granite worktops for the *cocina* surround had been less successful.

José, at the marble place, had insisted the worktop was an odd shape, and I had assured him that it was fine. None of the pieces were exactly rectangular. S and I had independently measured all of them and our calculations had tallied. However, when we put the second piece of granite into position on the stove surround it was some ten centimetres too long on the back edge where it adjoined the next piece, and stuck out at a decidedly odd angle. We measured the piece José had sent, but it was exactly the size we had requested. Somehow, both of us had independently got the measurements wrong. After poor José had told me on three separate occasions it looked strange, I knew this was going to be a fun call.

"José? The granite, it is the wrong size. We measured wrongly."

There was a hoot of laughter down the line. José had understood my Spanish perfectly for once. I got the impression he was waiting for this call.

"¡No pasa nada! Bring it back on Monday, I will cut it again."

The following week we returned sheepishly to José, who thought it a huge joke. He recut and repolished the worktop for us and refused any payment for the extra work.

"It is not so strange now, eh?" he asked, grinning hugely.

The weather continued kind that week. We took Aunty Jan to Ourense, to the thermal pools; much nicer in the cool of an autumn afternoon than the heat of a summer's day.

Mum spotted a carpet shop on Rua Progreso, in the old town.

"I want a new rug for the living room. Can we have a look?"

I demurred and we spent a good half hour perusing carpets in the huge shop. Mum of course wanted the one she had seen in the window. The assistant, as only assistants expecting customers to be spending silly amounts of money can be, was more than happy to completely destroy her window display to rescue Mum's treasure.

The carpet was huge.

"But Mum, how are we going to get it to the car?" I asked. Ourense old town is pedestrianized and our car was in the underground car park, a good ten minute walk away. "Anyway, it's too big to fit in the car with the four of us."

"I can fold the carpet for you," offered the assistant, obviously understanding and seeing her sale disappearing out of the door.

Even folded, the thick, three metre by two and a half metre rug was heavy and awkward. Leaving Mum and her sister in a café, S and I set off for the car.

"Hold on," said S. "This isn't going to work. I'll use my belt to tie around it. We can use that as a handle."

He did so, and luckily his trousers didn't fall down as we manhandled the carpet to the car. It was so heavy that the thick leather belt gave in as we approached the vehicle, broken by the strain.

My arms have never recovered, and are, I'm sure, three inches longer. But the carpet still looks nice in Mum's living room at the *Casita*.

Diary Thursday 15th October Warm in Lugo
Dropped Mum and Aunty Jan at the cathedral in Lugo for a wander then went off car hunting, visiting Seat, Citroën and Ford garages. After lunch we collected the new glass for the living room door. Mum saw a lovely stained-glass lamp with irises on it in the shop, which gave me an idea.

When we bought the *Casita*, there had been a small, high window in the wall between the bedroom and the dining room. We hadn't noticed it at first as there was a large wardrobe in front of it. We'd debated covering it up with plasterboard, but then Mum saw that iris lamp.

Why not make a feature of the oddly placed window by inserting a stained-glass picture in it? And what better picture than some flags, or irises, for the goddess of the rainbow herself? We asked the company to make us a design based on the iris lamp. It would be ready in '*quince dias*' – of course.

It was the start of the chestnut season again while Aunty Jan was with us. As usual, we were behind on the chestnut collecting front and once more letting down our village. Mum and Aunty Jan decided to remedy this situation by going out to collect some chestnuts for us.

I don't honestly think our little village has ever seen anyone picking chestnuts in October wearing gold lamé sandals. Aunty Jan is a fashionista of the highest order, but I think even she agreed that sandals leave much to be desired in long grass littered with spiky chestnut husks. Still, it proved to our neighbours once again that the English are *loco.*

Aunty Jan left on the 17th of October having had sunshine for all but three days of her two-week holiday. It seemed she was becoming our new sun queen – as the following day it began to rain.

Diary Sunday 18th October Drizzly
Perfect boiled eggs. Made lunch and cleared the allotment ready for the winter.
Lunch: twice cooked stir fry pork with peppers, courgette, onion and rice.
L and S fiddled with the new water pipes for the pozo. CJ arrived for tea and joined in. They are leaking everywhere. Took the pipes back out and left them in the alpendre overnight to uncurl.

The *pozo* at the *Casita* was an old fashioned, bucket-down-the-well type: a wide, stone-lined hole, eight metres deep. Hanging from a hook in the stone ceiling had been a blue plastic bucket, attached to a piece of string. We thought an electric pump might be altogether more modern, and simpler to use.

To pump water throughout the house, we first had to install some water pipes into the well. The piping came on a 20-metre roll. The first problem

CHESTNUT, CHERRY & KIWI FRUIT SPONGE

then, was straightening the rolled-up poly tubing so it went down the well without curling up on itself and forming an airlock. The second was the sheer length of tubing needed to reach the water – the pipework snaked across the kitchen floor and out of the door, making handling it as difficult as taming a python. The third problem was that a plastic pipe tends to float if lowered into water, rather than conveniently sinking. With CJ's help we eventually got it where we thought it should be and breathed a sigh of relief.

It seemed we were not the only ones having problems...

From: m wright
Sent: Monday, October 19, 2015 11:52 AM
To: Lisa Wright
Subject: Re: Bye bye Coro
> Hi Sis
>Looks like Jan had a lovely time. Coro is still haunting me. I think I mentioned that I picked up an electricity bill the Saturday before the completion date, it was an estimated bill from June until Sept - £72. I phoned the Electric Board, explained you had contacted them and the power had been turned off for that period and that I had just picked up the mail. The reply – it was no problem, they would cancel the bill. I confirmed there would be nothing to pay, which she agreed. Yesterday I received a final demand for £72 or court proceedings would be raised against me and debt collectors would be employed to collect the outstanding amount, plus an additional £40. As you can imagine I wasn't too happy, which I think came across quite well when I phoned the electricity board again. They tell me it has now been amended but there is a standing charge for the last quarter to pay - odds on it's still not right.

OCTOBER 2015

Oh and Saga house insurance won't let me end the policy, mum has to write to them - I fell out with them as well. Love to all Xx

On 20 Oct 2015, at 09:55, "Lisa Wright" <lisarosewright@msn.com> wrote:
>Hi Bro
>Noo, you didn't mention the electric bill. When I rang in June, I was told that the FINAL bill would be made up to the 16th June when we left, taken from mums direct debit and a copy sent to her new address here. That happened, so they know mum has left and that the electric is no longer her responsibility. I am happy to join in shouting at them if you like... or if you are having fun... haha.
>Jean says the chap has already chopped down mum's camellia round the back. Mum doesn't seem bothered thankfully. I was worried it may upset her to see dads garden destroyed
>Aunty Jan had a good time I think. Her and mum are sooo competitive with each other it's like having 2 kids in the house. Mum hurt her back walking too far trying to prove something to Jan and Jan kept trying to make mum buy expensive clothes. Mind you she did spend 50E on a scarf.
>lots love from all us here
>xx

From: m wright
> Sent: Tuesday, Oct 20, 2015 11:13 AM
> To: Lisa Wright
> Subject: Re: Bye bye Coro
>Hi Sis. I've cancelled DD for Saga. Told Saga supervisor I was cancelling and he said a letter would be sent to Coro, I said good luck with that. In the end he realised it was a pointless fight so DD cancelled. The electricity bill is for the

CHESTNUT, CHERRY & KIWI FRUIT SPONGE

*standing charge because someone has to pay
even when the property is empty. As you said
not the way it was explained to you, or me later.
Bill arrived today £16.49. Love to all xxx*

On the same day, the window company finally turned up to look at the kitchen door. We hadn't been happy with it from the beginning, with its odd tilt and turn handle, but it was getting worse. Poor Mum automatically pushed the handle downwards every time she went to close the door. This meant the mortise locks were engaged and the locking mechanism was being damaged. The company had argued it was our fault for not 'understanding' how the door worked. Then, at Mum's birthday party, one of our Spanish guests had done the same thing, bending the locking mechanism beyond the repair of a screwdriver. I insisted the company did something.

The company had the kitchen door all day. I told them it had to be back for the evening as we couldn't leave the *Casita* open to the world all night, not now we had Mum's worldly possessions in there. Plus, it was raining.

They duly reappeared at 7pm with the door: which was exactly and completely, utterly, the same as it had been before. I despaired.

*Diary Wednesday 21st October Back to sunshine
Prepared lunch while Mum hand washed one of
her jumpers then we took the opportunity to do
some planting in the Casita garden.*

It was a glorious autumn day. Next to the house wall I dug out a bed for the winter-flowering honeysuckle. In a half barrel, on one side of the entrance to the *alpendre,* we put a summer jasmine to climb up the wooden slats of the front of the barn. Mum wanted a camellia bush for the bed the other side, below the *hórreo* steps. That was to be a market day purchase.

Into the newly completed raised bed we put some crocus and daffodil bulbs, scattering others in the bed below the grape vine outside the garden gate. There was no point in putting anything precious here as the cows would eat it as they passed, so we planted rosemary, sage, mint and lemon balm – all guaranteed anti-cow plants. It was a nice spot for a herb garden, only a few steps from the kitchen door... if one could get in and out of said door safely that is.

Diary Thursday 22nd October Sunny and warm
S fitted the new slab of rose granite into the well cupboard to make a shelf. I started painting the outside walls of the Casita with our sunshine yellow paint.

Mum was terrified of the open well in the *Casita*: a fear not helped by our friend Mike telling of a neighbour who had committed suicide by diving headfirst down her well.

To be honest, the whole open well thing was also a waste of space in the kitchen. Space which could be better used. Once we had fitted all the water pipes to the electric pump, we would have water on tap and there would be no need to lower a bucket to collect it. Instead, we decided to cap the hole and create a pantry. One of our pieces of granite was for a solid shelf for the new cool store. The one metre cubed, stone-built cupboard behind the cleaned and varnished wooden door is now a perfect cool larder.

The outside walls of the *Casita* were mainly beautiful granite blocks like our house but, like ours, part of it was not stone. Around the kitchen door was an expanse of rendered over brick. We had first noticed this when the electricians fitted the new meter into the outside wall and when S had cut out

CHESTNUT, CHERRY & KIWI FRUIT SPONGE

the old door lock to allow us access to the *Casita* over a year ago. We assumed that at one time there was a double barn door there and the kitchen, as an inside room, was a later addition. It was certainly strange having the well and the old open fire in there.

I didn't know how far the brickwork extended and didn't want to knock off the render only to have to redo it later. I decided that, along with the newly rendered bannister of the outside steps to the bedroom, the kitchen wall was an ideal area to paint.

"What do you think?" I asked Mum, later that day. "It needs another coat but it's pretty, isn't it?"

"It looks really summery," said Mum.

"We can rename it *La Casa Amarilla*, the yellow house," I replied. "Like the White House but smaller."

Diary Sunday 25th October Sunny and warm. 22°C on terrace
All have winter colds! Just in time for our next lot of Workawayers.
L spent the morning in the kitchen making cakes and lunch then cleared the tomato beds. Good year for tomatoes. S cleaned the chicken's winter quarters ready for their move.
Lunch: Pork hock with borlotti beans, carrots, mash and Romanesco broccoli. Good winter fare. Orange cake and yoghurt. Feed a cold, Mum used to say. If so, that should stuff the bugs!

Our next lot of Workawayers were Australians. We have long since decided, in rather stereotypical fashion, that Aussies and Kiwis are our favourite Workawayers. We haven't had a bad antipodean yet and they all seem to be chatty and open with a great work ethic.

Tammy and Jake were no exception. They arrived on a showery day in a small Citroën which tilted alarmingly to the left.

NOVEMBER 2015
New cars and kiwis

"The suspension's gone I reckon," announced Jake cheerfully, jumping out. "It's the weight."

I peered inside as he opened the back doors. There was a large wooden wardrobe lying on its back in the rear of the car. The back seats had been removed.

"It's great storage," Jake said. "And we sleep on top."

Sure enough, there were sleeping bags on top of the wardrobe and below was a full-sized surfboard.

The back of the little Citroën was a masterpiece in organisation but the suspension on the car was never meant to deal with the kind of weight it had been subjected to, hence the sideways slump.

"Can I hang my suit to dry?" Jake asked, "It's still wet from the surf."

He hung it in the Long Barn as it was raining that day. Unfortunately, no one thought to tell Mum who came out white-faced some time later.

"What on earth's the matter?" I asked, alarmed.

Mum pointed at the barn. "There's a man, I thought he was hanging," she said breathlessly.

Hanging? With a jolt I realised it was Jake's wetsuit. It was dim in the barn with the kiwi vines outside and the suit was hanging limply from the washing line inside. Also, as I think I might have mentioned, Mum has a vivid imagination.

CHESTNUT, CHERRY & KIWI FRUIT SPONGE

One of the jobs we had for our new helpers was to remove part of the wall between the bedroom and the living room in the *Casita*. The corner between the two rooms was a strange angle, with many kinks and turns. It made that area unusable in the living room and prevented us fitting Mum's dressing table in the bedroom. As it was a lath and plaster wall, we took the decision to knock out the whole corner and remake it at a better angle.

Tammy and Jake started on the demolition their second morning. Jake called me not long afterwards.

"Hey! Look! It's full of rocks."

I wandered in from the kitchen where I was varnishing and sure enough the lath and plaster wall was actually lath and plaster filled with hand-sized rocks. I called S to see this new and interesting piece of Spanish workmanship.

"Why bother to make a lath and plaster wall then fill it with rocks? The weight must be enormous," I said. "No wonder the floor was sagging!"

The wall wasn't load bearing but was in itself a considerable weight. By the time Tammy and Jake had cleared the metre long section of wall they had a large pile of granite stone for Mum's rockery and enough to surround her other flower beds. Most were around four inches across but some were double that. It was yet another bizarre discovery about our new home.

Diary Monday 2nd November Drizzly
Moved chickens to their winter quarters on the allotment. So much easier having helpers. S caught, I sprayed, and Tammy and Jake carried. All very successful with no casualties (human or avian). S fitted the uprights for the new plasterboard wall in the bedroom.
Bathnight at Chantada pool. Stopped at a café on the way back as they had advertised a chestnut festival.

NOVEMBER 2015

The café was not one we had ever been into before, and as we walked in the door every head turned to us and all conversation ceased. I suppose we must have looked a strange group: one elderly white-haired lady sporting a track suit and stick; a young, good-looking tanned couple; a short 50-something year old with round glasses and long dripping wet hair; and an older man looking decidedly suspicious with a bushy chin growth and straggly grey-blond hair. All obviously not Spanish.

"Don't think they're used to strangers," Jake whispered.

"No, I hope we don't get lynched," I joked.

I managed to make my way to the bar, far more self-conscious than usual, to ask for five wines.

"*¿Son Ingleses?*" asked the barman.

"Yes, we are English," I replied, "and our friends are from Australia. We live near Taboada."

Another man at the bar looked up. "You bought Pepe Rey's place, didn't you?"

"Er, yes that's right. Mum is going to be living there. We live in *A Casa do Campo.*"

"I used to work for Pepe. I drive a *camion*. Look, it is a beautiful lorry."

With that he began to show me photographs of his admittedly rather swish truck on his smartphone.

"These English bought the place of Pepe," he announced to the crowd.

There were murmurs and *holas* and then a couple of back slaps. Everyone it seemed knew of 'those' English. Soon we were in the midst of a large happy crowd, being fed bacon sandwiches and juggling trays of hot roasted chestnuts as we supped our *vinos* and admired my new friend's photographs of his truck. And I pondered once more on how much acceptance is about who you know (or who knows you) here, rather than about who you are. It was another wonderful night in Galicia.

CHESTNUT, CHERRY & KIWI FRUIT SPONGE

Tammy and Jake's car was not going to last the next stage of their journey without some serious work. The left-hand side was sagging so much poor Tammy had to hang onto her door handle to prevent herself sliding onto Jake's lap while he was driving.

"The garage said they couldn't fix it because it'd fail the MOT, but to be honest we're ditching it after this trip. If it can get us to the airport in Paris, we'd be happy."

"I think I might know just the man," I said after a while.

Juan owns a garage nearby. I was told that he could fix anything. We arrived on a cool October morning and Juan let out a whistle as the Citroën bounced its way to a drunken stop.

"What you do to the car?" he cried in broken English.

As Jake opened the back door, Juan's eyebrows disappeared into his thick curly black hair. "This is *loco*!"

"Yes, but can you fix it?" I asked.

"You need it for ITV?" he asked. The ITV is the Spanish equivalent to the MOT.

"No. Just to drive to Paris."

Juan shook his head, seemingly marvelling at the craziness of the foreigners. "Okay, I can fix. Come back at seven."

"That went well," said Jake, ever the optimist.

It turned out he had every reason to be. At seven o'clock we returned to an upright Citroën and a huge pile of Tammy and Jake's belongings on the pavement outside. I was astonished at just how much had been stuffed in there. Juan showed us where the shock absorber had come straight through the lining on the left side and into the boot space.

"It is *increíble* the car did not collapse," he said, showing us where he had welded the shock. "It is not, how you say, legal. But," he added, shrugging, "it will get to Paris, I think."

Tammy and Jake left us the following morning for their long drive.

"Please let me know you've got there safely," I pleaded.

"She'll be right," answered Jake.

"We will," added Tammy.

Diary Wednesday 4th November Drizzle all day.
Fed animals then off to Lugo. Looked for tiles for Mum's kitchen walls but nothing she fancies. Commissioned Mum's 'Iris' window. The design the chap has drawn up looks beautiful.
After lunch we all took a test drive in the new Citroën C3 Picasso. Very nice drive though the chap (another Juan) looked terrified when I opened her up on the A6.

"Our car won't get above 110 kilometres an hour," I'd said to the gently perspiring Juan. I was thoroughly enjoying myself, seeing what the car would do. "Mmm, 136 and no wobble, that's not bad."

"But. It is not allowed," Juan had pleaded. "Please to slow."

I smiled and eased off the accelerator. I'd checked the car out and was happy with the performance for what is, in effect, a rather boxy car. How could he expect us to spend so much money without trying it properly? I could see Mum smiling in the rear-view mirror – she appreciated the need for speed, at least.

"Is it comfy?" I asked her.

"Yes, it's lovely," she answered, patting the seat cushion fondly.

We had, neither of us, ever bought a brand-new car. I'd had one as a sales rep, but that was a company car and not the same at all. Spanish driving, and Galician driving in particular, leaves something to be desired in the care and attention department so it was a worrying decision to make.

I've always thought that Galician driving is divided into discrete sections. There is the ultra-careful driver, as our neighbour Daniel was. He would drive so slowly I would sometimes think the car was at a standstill. At the other extreme is the crazy race-driver type. These are mainly the younger age group who enjoy speed but are not necessarily in complete control of the car. Then there are the weekend drivers who are used to ponderous but huge tractors and never quite make the transition to car driver.

Most accidents in Galicia seem to be due to driver error with, as the local paper always puts it, 'no other car involved'. I actually have a collection of newspaper cuttings about the more interesting or bizarre road accidents here. Far from being morbid most are hilarious, and thankfully the number of casualties seems to be small in comparison to the number of accidents.

One of my collection shows a car, nose down, its roof leaning casually against a tree trunk. The accompanying article states that the car 'left the road', bumped down a small incline and came to rest in that position. No one was injured but I felt a stuntman was in the making. Another of my all-time favourites concerns drink, a fiesta, and the best stunt I've ever seen.

The photograph shows a car sat four-square on a small terrace surrounded by perfectly placed pots of geraniums as if for a photo shoot. That terrace, though, is at basement level.

The car in question, being driven back from a fiesta early one January, had come to a T-junction. Opposite was a house with its bright front door at road level and its neat basement level terrace, some four metres below. How the driver managed to position his car so neatly after crashing through the street level barrier we may never know, as the police lost him.

When the local police arrived, the driver was incoherent and they decided to accompany him to the local hospital in case he was concussed. At the hospital the man asked to use the toilet facilities and never returned. By the time the police arrived at his home he'd had a number of medicinal drinks for the shock and could not be breathalysed.

My most surreal clipping is of an accident on the outskirts of Lugo. The picture shows a map of the immediate area and a photograph of a car, nose down in a bramble patch. So far, so bland.

The driver, having swerved off the national highway, the NVI, had decided to make his way to civilisation, and rescue, on foot. He set off walking, and walking, and walking. He clambered across a stream and through some woods. By nightfall he had still not found the road so he slept in a burnt-out car shell, continuing on his weary way the following day. Finally, he spied a house in the distance and tumbled towards the door. The owners of that house must have been startled by this poor man's dishevelled looks and immediately took him in. His sorry tale must have bemused them even more as he told of his two-day hike.

"But," said the rescuers, pointing out of their front window. "The NVI is there."

The police had found the intrepid adventurer's vehicle, but it wasn't until they discovered the burnt-out car in the woods, where he swore he had slept, that they believed his story. The unfortunate man had set off walking at 90 degrees to the road and had eventually completed a huge semi-circle to reach his rescuers' home just 100 metres along the same road.

It was no wonder I was terrified of getting the first scratch on that shiny new paintwork. The offer on the Citroën was too good to turn down though.

CHESTNUT, CHERRY & KIWI FRUIT SPONGE

At the time the Spanish government was trying to persuade people to upgrade to more eco-friendly cars and were offering a 1500€ sweetener for our 20-year-old Ford Escort. A secondhand Citroën with many miles on the clock, and who knew what abuse, would have cost us more. We swallowed hard and paid our deposit. This car would hopefully last us another 20 years and save us a small fortune on yearly ITV bills.

New cars in Spain don't need an ITV test until their fourth year and then only biennially until their tenth year. With the hopefully much lower annual service bills we reckoned it would pay for itself. At least that was what we told ourselves.

I intensely dislike boring-coloured cars but the choices seemed to be limited to white, black and shades of grey on all the new cars we had viewed. The Citroën C3 had a very fancy lilac colour that I craved.

S looked appalled, but Juan put his foot down.

"It is *imposible*," he said. "You can have the red. But this, *no!*"

I did wonder why I hadn't seen many of the lilac ones around. In the six years we have had Ruby (Naranja Rubi after her colour), I have still to see a lilac Citroën C3. I can't help but wonder if the colour was just in the brochure to appeal to the likes of me... or maybe I'm the only person to have ever wanted that colour? I'd like to think so.

Diary Thursday 5th November Rain all day
S spent the day raising the garage 'door' opening to fit the new car. Took Mum into the docs for her flu jab.
Lunch: Pork and black pudding stew in tomato sauce with green peppers and broccoli. Cheesy mashed potatoes and pumpkin. Apple pancakes and ice cream.

NOVEMBER 2015

The new car was bigger than our old Escort. The amount of space inside was similar, but the extra air bags and safety features meant it was a good 20 centimetres wider. We had feverishly measured our garden gates and knew it was going to be a tight fit, but the garage opening we had made all those years ago for the low-slung Escort was definitely too low for the much taller 'sit-up' type car. S slaved for two days cutting and refixing the slatted front of the barn so our new girl would fit in when we got her.

Diary Sunday 8th November Hot
21°C on the terrace. No fire in the evening and T-shirt weather. What a difference.
S making a deposito for the 'humanure' from the septic tank. We bought that pump last year in England so it's about time we had a go. He reckons once it's settled for a couple of years, we should be able to use it to mulch the trees. As the tank's never been emptied in 8 years, I don't think he's looking forward to it!

Actually, emptying the septic tank was a bit of an anti-climax. Instead of being full and stinking, there was little to empty and by the time the humanure pile had sat covered in straw for two years there was hardly enough to mulch a single tree. Still, it showed our tank was working and means we don't have to worry about it again for a good long time.

Tony was due back on the 13th of November with his girlfriend, Carrie. She was only able to stay a few days and they hoped to do some exploring while they were here. On our part we were more than happy to feed them both if they were prepared to pitch in.

The day they arrived, the autumn sun was shining as it had been all week. We decided it was as good a time as any to pick the kiwi fruit from the vines. It had been a great year for most of our crops and

CHESTNUT, CHERRY & KIWI FRUIT SPONGE

looked like being our biggest harvest of the kiwi fruits since we got the vines as foot high twigs some five years earlier.

We have found that kiwi vines do well in our climate; they flower late, generally missing the winter frosts, but they do need plenty of water. Had we realised quite how thirsty they were I'm not sure we'd have planted them, but they provide us with fresh fruit from November through to the following June stored in our cool barn.

That year we picked 1700 kiwi fruits.

The large wooden bread box in the bottom barn was full of cardboard trays with kiwi fruit in single layers. Having filled that box, which is over a metre deep and two metres in length, we looked for other storage solutions. There was another bread box on the balcony at the *Casita*. We filled that too. We gave fruit away to friends and I made pots of kiwi jam. Tony is a jam freak so more was always welcome when he was around. In the end we had 17 large trays of kiwi fruits stored in various places between the two houses.

Funnily enough we forgot all about those kiwi fruits on the balcony at the *Casita* until we were ready to start work on improving that section almost a year later. They were still firm enough to eat and very tasty.

Kiwi is a wonderful fruit, full of vitamin C, and a good meat tenderiser due to a protein-digesting enzyme, actinidin, which breaks down fibres. It also makes an excellent smoothie – those same enzymes acting to thicken milk almost instantly.

We also went fungi hunting while Tony was here. It was another good mushroom year with the fields full of horse mushrooms, field agarics, parasols, and wood blewits under our chestnuts. We picked, dried, froze and ate as many as we could. My storeroom was once more being refilled with produce as autumn came along.

NOVEMBER 2015

Carrie left on the Monday and Tony got stuck into plastering the new bedroom wall, which S had constructed in place of the old 'rock and plaster' affair Tammy and Jake had demolished. He also created a 'wellie cupboard' for Mum.

Just as one enters the kitchen there had been an incredibly low (four foot high) doorway on the left, leading down into the barn below. Of no use to anyone but cats and potholers, we decided to block up the doorway to create a handy alcove to store boots and shoes. Tony also had an idea that, if he fitted a hatch halfway up the new wooden 'door', we could pass firewood through from the store in the barn and stack it on a shelf in front of the hatch ready for use on the *cocina*. A clever time saving plan which still works to this day.

Diary Thursday 19th November Sunshine
Found Damson dead in the chicken hut. Probably a weasel again. S set the trap while I plucked and cleaned her. At least weasels just take the heads, yuk!
Tony spent the day ('til 8pm) plastering the bedroom. Looks very smart.
6 eggs despite the weasel attack. Checked the whole fenceline. No large gaps.
Paid the balance for the new car through the bank costing us an extra 1.5% for the privilege of using our own money. No wonder the Spaniards don't trust banks!

Our new car was going to be ready for collection on the 26th of November. I was surprised to find myself almost in tears as we emptied the back of the Escort for the last time and left her there on the showroom forecourt to await her fate. It was just a collection of metal, but it had been a good car.

CHESTNUT, CHERRY & KIWI FRUIT SPONGE

We had bought her, some ten years earlier, from my godfather when he decided he was no longer safe to drive. It had been a happy coincidence for us as both our cars had been written off the previous year. We had been on holiday thousands of miles away in Cuba at the time, and the cars had been sitting on the road outside our house in Rochdale. A car had careered around the corner hitting S' van and shunting it into my old Morris Minor. That had, in turn, hit the stone garden wall, demolishing it and wrecking my car. We had returned home to a scene of destruction and devastation.

Uncle George's Escort had only done 29,000 miles when we bought it from him. Now, it was 20 years old. It had gone round the clock, been re-registered as Spanish, and learnt to get along with the driver in the gutter. Its time was up. And we had to get used to a left-hand drive for the first time since we arrived in Spain.

Our first test was getting the car through the gates. There was a bare centimetre each side of the wing mirrors as I manoeuvred through the opening. Luckily the new barn entrance fit the car perfectly and Ruby was soon installed beneath the kiwi vines.

"Look," I said, pointing. "New cars and kiwis." No one else thought my alliteration amusing. Just me then!

That Friday was *matanza*. Tony, being a vegetarian, didn't want to assist in the pig killing. Neither did Mum. We left them to carry on at the *Casita* whilst we stood around a sunny field, trying to look useful and, as usual, failing dismally.

Diary Saturday 28th November Sunny
Off to collect piggy. 98kg this year. They're getting bigger! Back by 11.30am. Spent the rest of the day salting, chopping, and cooking pig bits while Tony fitted the shower taps in the Casita bathroom.

NOVEMBER 2015

Tony and Mum went for takeaway pizza at lunchtime so we could carry on cutting up piggy. Made black puddings, sausagemeat, and pork pies. Mum helped by washing up on a regular basis.

The following day we had our first frost of the year and a new and exciting fiesta at our village hall, organised by the parish committee. It was to be a *magosto* festival.

The word *magosto* comes from the Latin *magnus ustus,* or great fire, and is the oven used for roasting chestnuts. It has also come to be used as a term for any festival celebrating chestnuts and autumn. *Magosto* is born of the Celtic tradition of Samhain, the end of summer. It can also be associated with the Christian Harvest Festival, itself imprinted on the earlier pagan rites. Whatever the background, a *magosto* party involves autumn produce – pork, chestnuts, new wines, and of course fire.

When we arrived at our surprisingly spacious village hall there was a large barbecue set up on the square outside and over a hundred people milling around chatting and drinking local red wine. Our village hall sits next to the stone-built parish church, on a hill looking down on our tiny *aldea* or hamlet and the surrounding chestnut woods. It has huge glass windows facing the track and, on a sunny day, is filled with light. We chatted to a few neighbours before being ushered into the hall.

Trestle tables had been set up in lines along the entire floor and there were already people jostling for spaces. Our parish priest, Don Pepe, was already there and he called us over. In the centre of the tables were platters of sliced hams and *chorizo*, squares of tuna *empanada* and fried squid rings or calamari.

Luckily our 'vegetarian' helper ate fish so he tucked into the fishy offerings, chatting as he did so with his immediate neighbours. Mum, meanwhile

CHESTNUT, CHERRY & KIWI FRUIT SPONGE

was well looked after by Don Pepe, who gallantly kept her wine glass filled and periodically speared bits of cooked ham onto her plate with his knife.

Our main course was a *churrasco,* or mixed grill of barbecued meats. Tony of course didn't partake of this, much to the consternation of his new friends.

"You don't eat meat?" they said in horror.

Tony explained he was fine with the *empanada.* This statement caused the young man next to him to shout for another plate of *empanada* 'for my English friend', concerned Tony may starve before the end of the afternoon.

The *churrasco* was accompanied by mounds of fresh local bread and gallons of local wine. Desserts were sweet and cream filled. Then it was time for the star of the show, the chestnuts. These had been roasting on the barbecue, some a little too long judging by their charred exteriors, and were casually dropped onto the tables leaving diners to juggle and peel the hot globes themselves. To be honest, after a three course Galician meal, there was little room left for chestnuts.

Coffee was accompanied by local *augardente* and liqueurs. It was 7pm by the time we wobbled our way back home. Yet another lovely Galician festival had been partaken of. I was content.

DECEMBER 2015
Ding dong bell

I spent my birthday that year making hams and pork pies, head cheese and sausages. It was a most enjoyable day.

Even more special was the fact that at 7pm that evening the window company turned up with a brand-new kitchen door for the *Casita* – one which could be opened in a 'normal' manner by depressing the handle and which did not need a degree in engineering to figure out. I was happy. Mum was ecstatic.

Tony was a joy to have around. Not only was he great company and wonderful with Mum, but he was a demon worker. Having finished plastering the new bedroom wall, he moved on to Mum's dressing room-to-be. S had covered the old floor and the stone hearth with chipboard as a base layer, over which we would eventually lay new wooden flooring. I was sorry that we'd had to cover over the quirky firepit but there was no easy way to incorporate it, and the stone would have been icy underfoot.

The walls in this room were in a dire state; unrendered and unmortared, they were black with soot and a mess of small granite stones. S and Lars had mortared around the stones to prevent mice sneaking in but we felt the walls would be too cold and uneven to plaster directly, even if the tarry soot wouldn't come through... which it would. The room

CHESTNUT, CHERRY & KIWI FRUIT SPONGE

was a good size, though, so we decided to plasterboard out the walls with insulation behind.

This was Tony's job.

Diary Sunday 6th December Warm and sunny
All up early to go to Barbara and Martin's Christmas fair. Tony makes the most amazing metalwork pictures which I felt he should display but he declined, being ridiculously shy about his work. (No idea why as it's fabulous.) Enjoyed wandering round the stalls and partaking of Martin's Glühwein. Offered Kath a lift which led to some fun with the rear seat belts in the new car.

It was the first time we had travelled with five people in Ruby. The central seat belt was a proper three-point belt rather than an old-fashioned lap belt. It pulled out of the roof behind the centre seat but it didn't come with any fitting instructions.

We tried attaching one side into the belt clip, then the other. Eventually everyone had to scramble out of the car so we could work it out before we strangled someone inadvertently. It was good fun and another new discovery on our fancy modern car.

We had already found that Ruby put her own headlights on, decided if we needed windscreen wipers or not, or if I was about to skid. I couldn't help feeling we were becoming redundant.

Diary Tuesday 8th December Sunshine pm
L, S and T looked at the well again. We lifted the marble slab out first. The water pipe will still not sit properly in the bottom, it keeps curling up out of the water and sucking in air. Plus fitting the other end to the pump in the barn has proved impossible from above. There was no choice but to send S down the well.

DECEMBER 2015

S used to be a bit of a mountaineer, and luckily one of the things we brought with us to our new life in Galicia was his climbing gear. S had originally planned to use it whilst working on the roof at *A Casa do Campo* but it proved unwieldy and the roof is relatively shallow. Now we could finally justify bringing it.

S got himself fastened into the harness then lowered himself carefully down the well until he could straighten the pipe at the bottom.

"Not much water," he shouted back up. "Seem to be more than a few bats living down here though."

One of these flying mice proved his statement by whizzing past my head. I hoped Mum wasn't nearby, she is terrified of bats.

"Okay, I think the pipe is in the water properly, can you two go into the barn and feed the pipe from the *bomba* through?"

Bomba is the Spanish word for the water pressure container, a large red ball. We clambered into the barn and prepared for directions.

S' voice was muffled through the thick granite walls of the well. "Are you singing?" he asked.

"Um, yes. Sorry."

"Is it Ding Dong Bell?"

"Stewart's down the well! Yes!" I replied, pleased he had caught the tune.

I heard a groan in reply.

Despite my, admittedly dreadful, singing and Tony's giggling we managed to follow instructions. And after a whole day of S climbing up and down the well and fiddling with the inevitable leaks, we pressurised the system. Hey presto, we had water on tap. Admittedly it was filthy, muddy looking water, but it was water. We went on the town that night in celebration. It would take a while to clear but we felt confident that water would soon be flowing into all areas of the *Casita*. Of course, it wasn't quite that straightforward.

CHESTNUT, CHERRY & KIWI FRUIT SPONGE

We waited four weeks to test the water. The test came back 'not fit for human consumption'. We ran off more water, waiting another two months then testing it again. Again, it came back not potable. We wondered if there was a problem with seepage from old manure or an old septic tank somewhere. We considered cleaning the water with a chlorine blast but then, just as we were still pondering, the well ran dry.

It was late September by then and Mum was in residence. We needed to come up with an alternative, and fast.

I went into the town hall to discuss connecting to the local piped water system but was told the mayor wasn't in – twice. This was starting to feel like *déjà vu* from our attempts to find this elusive Scarlet Pimpernel when we wished to get wed here six years earlier. Eventually, I did the only thing I could – I enlisted the help of our friend, Luisa.

As soon as I explained the problem to her, Luisa rang the mayor. I could hear a loud and not entirely friendly sounding one-sided conversation.

"The engineer will meet you at your house in five minutes," she said, after ending the call.

I didn't ask how she had persuaded them. Probably better not to know.

Jorge was indeed waiting for us by the time we got home, sitting in his council truck. As we explained the problem, he looked serious.

"Okay, I will explain something," he began. "We have a long waiting list for the town water."

Jorge held up his hand to forestall my argument. "And, the council, we will charge 100 euros a metre to fit the water pipe from the stop tap here," at this he gestured to the top of the track down to the *Casita*, "to the house, maybe 10 metres, here." Again, he gestured, and again he held up his hand to tell me he hadn't finished.

"So, what we do is, we will dig the stop tap and fit a connector for your pipe. You, then dig to the house and put in a water pipe. You connect it to a water meter and when you finish you turn on the water and it is done. Then, in a few months you will have the paperwork agreed and we will start to bill you." Jorge smiled triumphantly at this neat and very Galician solution to a problem.

I was bemused. "So, we fit the pipework to the house?"

"*Si.*"

"And the meter?" asked S.

"*Si.*"

"But where do we find a water meter? Shouldn't it be fitted by the council?" S was obviously as bemused as me.

"No, no, you can buy one at the *ferreteria.*"

The ironmongers? Really? I was amazed.

S shrugged. "Okay."

"We will dig the stop tap tomorrow," ended Jorge, still smiling.

And they did.

Within a day the new T-shaped connector was fitted and our newly purchased water pipe attached. Jorge showed us how to bend over the end and tie it so the water didn't pour out until we were ready to use it. The workmen began to backfill the stop tap in the road whilst S began the painstaking process of hand digging a channel in the stone track into which we would lay the pipe. The foreman, Dion, came over.

"That will take you a long time," he said.

"Yes," replied S.

"I have a *picador* in my truck," he continued, miming a hammer drill. "You can borrow him while I have dinner."

"Great, thank you."

S drilled and dug, and drilled and dug, for two hours, pleased that he had the rudiments of the

CHESTNUT, CHERRY & KIWI FRUIT SPONGE

trench complete by the time the workmen's lunch break was over. But Dion didn't come back. When I asked one of the other men, he shrugged and said to ring when we had finished. He gave me a number.

S continued digging and drilling and after a while he had a perfectly neat trench which we lined with sand before laying the water pipe into it. I rang the number we had been given and left a message thanking Dion and telling him we had finished with the drill.

It was some three weeks later and Mum and I were in town shopping when there was a knock on my driver's side window.

"*Hola*, have you finished with the *picador*?" asked Dion.

"Yes, I left a message. I'm so sorry," I babbled, mortified he would think us rude.

Dion shrugged. "*No pasa nada,*" he said, smiling. It doesn't matter.

Within a few days we had connected the water, and the new meter which cost us peanuts at the ironmongers, and Mum once more had running water in the house – though she continued to get her drinking water from us.

Our neighbour had told us town water would kill you. I felt that was a little extreme given that there is a processing plant on the hill above the house, but it is heavily chlorinated and the taste is not pleasant, unlike our fresh, clean and pure well water. Oddly enough, the water for the piped system comes from our little river at the bottom of the valley. There is a pumping station in the next village which sends the river water up to the processing plant and thence back down to us.

Though the water was connected within days, the paltry bills took considerably longer to begin to come through, and I had to chase the council department on a number of occasions before they got the paperwork signed off and started to charge us.

It was yet another triumph of needs outweighing bureaucracy at work. I love Galicia.

§

Back in December 2015, this new disaster was still far ahead of us. Instead, we were looking forward to Christmas in Lugo, and shortly afterwards our pensioner holiday – this year to Fuengirola in Andalucía.

Sadly, we had been unable to register Mum with imserso in time for the pensioner holiday that year. It was her year to visit my eldest brother for Christmas so the two of us booked a New Year break with Leo and Margaret. Tony was staying on until January and agreed to house sit and continue working while we were off sunning ourselves. If we felt guilty, we hid it well, and of course there was Lugo to look forward to.

Our Christmas Chinese and pub crawl in Lugo had grown in numbers over the years. I was pleased that Sara, who ran the *pensión*, was getting more business as friends realised that staying over for the evening booze-up was good fun and the Pensión Gran Via was well-appointed, good value and incredibly friendly. This year there were ten of us booked in.

Diary Thursday 24th December Sun and cloud
L spent the morning in the kitchen. Tony is making a bench seat to cover the hole in the corner of the living room floor using some of the old bed headboards and footboards I cleaned up. His creation looks like an old church pew and fits the room perfectly. Debs and Al arrived 4pm. Had a walk around the area before dinner, casa nosotros.

CHESTNUT, CHERRY & KIWI FRUIT SPONGE

Stuffed Squash in Tomato sauce, roasted spuds. Debs' crumble and custard.

Tony's seat really was magnificent. We had to do something with the corner where the ham cupboard had previously resided and we had to leave the floor raised because of the doors to the barn below. Even with the new trifold design (which didn't trifold), the doors protruded 30 centimetres into the room.

"Why not make a seat there?" someone suggested. I thought it was me, but I was told it wasn't. Whoever made the suggestion, it was Tony who enthusiastically carried it out. He was determined to get his seat finished for Mum's return in the new year.

First, he used the wooden slats from the old ham cupboard to make a bench seat, then he made arms from an old slatted footboard. The headboard was made into a seat back, and I varnished the whole thing.

'Tony's corner' still looks magnificent to this day with one of his beautiful works of art hanging on the wall above the bench – a very different work of art. Above, the light shines through the glass brick, which S fitted in place of the mesh covered vent hole in the outside wall, onto some of Mum's decorative glass bottles sitting on the deep windowsill.

For Christmas morning, I had offered to do a brunch of smoked salmon and scrambled eggs to anyone who wanted to call in on the way to Lugo. Eight of us sat down to brunch, me constantly whipping up more scrambled eggs until everyone was finally sated. Then we set off in convoy to Lugo and our Christmas Chinese.

Two more couples joined us for lunch making the table long and noisy. We chose starters then a main course each to be shared out. Rice-loving Leo was concerned there wouldn't be enough.

DECEMBER 2015

"We can order more if we need it, worry not," I reassured him.

At the end we had more than enough and Debs and Al took a 'doggy bag' home to reheat the next day. After a soothing siesta we all met up for our evening jolly. There were 12 of us that night so we decided to pay the rounds in couples. Tony was paired up with the only other lone male in the group which meant we could spend the night making fun of them and asking when the wedding was.

Debs, as usual, provided the 'entertainment'. She had been sent a goody bag from England containing, amongst other things, a bag of flying saucers. For anyone who doesn't know, these old-fashioned sweets consist of two semi-circular halves of brightly coloured rice paper enclosing a sherbet filling. They are sweet and moreish and the sherbet fizzes nicely on the tongue. Not wanting to hog all the treats for ourselves, Debs began offering the bag to passers-by. The first few looked at us in horror and sidled past, worried looks pinned to their faces.

"They think you're selling drugs," I giggled, looking at the luminous sweets in her outstretched hand.

Eventually a group of young men, more adventurous than the rest, took one each and bit gingerly into the rice paper. One looked up in surprise.

"It's good!" he exclaimed, laughing.

It was unseasonably warm that Christmas evening and we stood outside the various bars drinking and enjoying Lugo's free double tapas with our wine.

Lugo has some fabulous bars, each of which has a different speciality tapas menu. One of my favourites offers mini burgers which seem just right with a local vino; another specialises in *pulpo* - Galician octopus served with potatoes; another flame grills *chorizo* sausages individually over a

CHESTNUT, CHERRY & KIWI FRUIT SPONGE

miniature barbecue. Wine flows, laughter gets louder and everyone is happy. I have never witnessed any trouble in Lugo, despite the heavy drinking, heaving crowds, and full bars.

Breakfast the following morning was hot chocolate and *churros* in a nearby café: a nice sweet carbohydrate hit, guaranteed to set you up for the day. The conversation over breakfast was Britain's upcoming EU membership referendum next year. To my surprise and horror, two of our friends thought leaving the EU would be a good move for Britain - citing stringent EU laws and lax immigration policies. I was amazed and upset that people could be so easily hoodwinked, but despite our best efforts, and Al's encyclopaedic knowledge of the facts, we could not persuade the two to vote remain. I often wonder if we could have converted just two people it may have made a difference to a future we couldn't then know about.

Diary Sunday 27th December Cloudy in Malaga
Scrummy boiled eggs and soldiers. S cleaned out the animals, L made butties for the journey. Left Tony in charge and drove to Santiago 12.30pm. Collected Leo and Margaret on the way and arrived at the airport in plenty of time.

As we passed through customs, S was detained.

"You have a knife?" asked the friendly customs officer.

S' face fell as he pulled his penknife from his jeans pocket. Everyone in Galicia seems to carry a penknife. I'd left mine with my keys at the car parking place. S had obviously forgotten about his. The customs man kindly measured the small Swiss army knife but was sad to declare that it was just too long to be permissible.

"Can I take it back to the car?" asked S.

DECEMBER 2015

"*Si,*" shrugged the official, as I stared at my hubby. The car had been dropped off ten minutes away and we'd had a lift to the departures' hall in the company's minibus.

S and Leo disappeared back into the hall as Margaret and I ambled through the duty-free shop toward our gate. The boys soon caught us up.

"What have you done with the knife?" I asked, unable to curb my curiosity.

"Hid it," smiled S. "Took a bit to find a place though. There's not many hiding places in an airport."

No, I couldn't imagine there were, to say nothing of the CCTV cameras which had probably captured them acting suspiciously.

The rest of the journey went without a hitch. The hotel was thankfully not the one Leo said was on 'Cardiac Hill' but was just across a busy road from the seafront and promenade. It also boasted an indoor swimming pool and nicely landscaped gardens, so I was happy.

The sun shone almost the whole week. The four of us took to walking along the seafront together in the mornings, walking further and further each day and returning to the hotel in time for lunch. In the evenings we played Leo and Margaret at Rummikub, a cross between cards and dominoes, a game we had never played before but which we caught on to far too quickly for our friends.

My only disappointment was the food, which was bland in the extreme. Leo and I purloined a bottle of hot pepper sauce for our personal use from a side table and used it to add flavour to the meals. On the table next to us were a couple who brought their own milk and orange juice to breakfast each day. We decided they were German, for no reason whatsoever, until one day the woman called out as the man passed our table.

"Hey, your stick!"

CHESTNUT, CHERRY & KIWI FRUIT SPONGE

I looked up as the chap turned around and saw his T-shirt for the first time. 'Stafford Morris Minor Club', it read.

"I used to be in that club," I said pointing. "Best car I ever had, my moggie."

Within seconds I was chatting away, oblivious to the fact that none of the others were joining in. As the couple left to enjoy their day, I turned to my friends.

"They seemed nice."

Leo was the first to speak. "I didn't understand a word he said."

"Nor me," piped up Margaret.

"I didn't follow much either," added S. "Where was that accent from?"

"What language was it," chipped in Margaret before I had time to answer.

"He was from Stoke-on-Trent," I laughed. "I didn't even think about it. I suppose it was quite a strong accent. Nice couple though," I finished, lamely.

As my companions had apparently really not understood the conversation, I filled them in. The couple came to Spain every winter, usually for three months. They would book a couple of weeks and if they enjoyed the area would ask to extend their stay. The hotels were rarely full and they usually got a good deal. They always booked bed and breakfast only, then hired a sunbed for the day which came with a free lunch and a pint. Sorted!

Tuesday was apparently market day. It was also the only day of the trip when it rained. Leo had laughed at us bringing our umbrellas to the south of Spain. He had laughed at us bringing our kettle too. Both proved invaluable. Being generous souls and having also packed waterproofs, we lent Leo and Margaret our umbrellas as we splashed our way to the open-air market.

It was huge. There were stalls selling everything from children's clothing to magnificent vegetables.

Had we been self-catering, we could have stocked up for a fraction of the prices at home. Having bought some pecans to try and grow in Galicia, we returned for lunch whilst Leo and Margaret decided to forego the delights of hotel blandness for the equally dubious pleasure of Burger King. Sadly, Leo managed to misplace the cover for his loaned umbrella. As a forfeit he did let us win five Rummikub games on the trot that evening.

Diary Wednesday 30th December Sunny and warm Up for an early breakfast. Collected by coach for our booked trip to the Caminita del Rey.

All the pensioner holidays include three meals a day, but trips are extra. Some are worthwhile and this was one of them.

The Caminita del Rey used to be dubbed the most dangerous walk in the world. The seven-kilometre walkway hugs the sides of a deep canyon, following the old wooden pathways erected at the turn of the last century for inspection workers at the hydroelectric power plant. For many years these wooden paths were unmaintained and broken, but a draw for any adventurous soul. Then, in 2000, a group of youngsters ziplining across the gorge fell to their deaths. Although unrelated to the pathways, this latest tragedy caused the local government to think seriously about the canyon and inevitably close off access to it.

Money was spent on upgrading the pathways and making the walkway into a pleasant ramble for most abilities. It had reopened that year, in spring 2015. Now there were compulsory hard hats, metal pathways above the old rotten wooden ones and guides to ensure no one enjoyed themselves too much. It is still an incredible walk, though, and the views are spectacular.

CHESTNUT, CHERRY & KIWI FRUIT SPONGE

No one was allowed on the walk without ID. This, they explained, was so they knew who was missing should a rock fall occur. The Spaniards always carry their ID cards, and I had my passport with me. Unfortunately, S had neither.

"If he can't go, I'm not either," I said. "They should have told us at the hotel."

I saw one tourist being turned away, tears in their eyes.

"What about other ID?" I asked one of the guides.
"Maybe. What do you have?" he replied.

That was a good question. S had only his camera as everything on the trip was included, even lunch. I rummaged around my bumbag, or fanny pack as Margaret insisted on calling it to our amusement (North American readers, look up fanny in a British dictionary).

I had our bank debit card. "Will this do?" I asked, holding it aloft. Luckily it was in S' name, though I had it in my wallet. I stood, fingers crossed, waiting.

The guide came back, smiling. "It is okay."

Leo was counting our mistakes so far. "Dangerous weapons, no passport..."

"But we did bring umbrellas, even if one of them has no cover now," I replied.

Our banter continued along the canyon. We all looked vaguely ridiculous in hairnets below white hard hats in the blistering sunshine, but it was a fabulous walk. Even our lunch, in the basement of a restaurant at the very top of a steep pedestrian-only hill following a seven-kilometre walk, didn't faze us. There was wine and there was laughter. What more could we need?

That evening we took Leo and Margaret to an 'authentic' British pub, The Rover's Return. Seriously. It had to be done. Margaret said she would get the drinks in. I coached her...

"Ask for: two an' 'alf pints o' bitter an' 'alf a lager," I said, bursting into laughter as Margaret tried and failed to get her lips around the odd phrasing. The barman joined in our teasing by asking Margaret what language she was speaking.

The beer was poor and the crowd noisy, but it was another fun evening in the company of good friends.

Thursday 31st December 2015 Sunshine 25°C
Walked the whole way to Solail castle along the promenade. Some 10km.
I had to stop off on the way to buy a pair of snazzy lime green shorts as it was way hotter than I'd dressed for. Ice-creams on the front before heading back for a late lunch and a laze by the pool.

New Year's Eve was gala night at the hotel. We'd had to pay an extra 25€ a head on our holiday price for the dubious pleasure of having to share long tables with a bunch of strangers, and eat a meal with no choices at a set time rather than sit at our 'own' foursome table, eating when we wanted and what we wanted. Still, the wine and *cava* flowed and I enjoyed the crab salad starter, though judging by the number of portions going back I was in a minority.

At 11pm we were all handed our goody bags of streamers, paper hats, *uvas de suerte* (lucky grapes, which have to be eaten before the last stroke of midnight sounds), and plastic moustaches, thrown out of the dining room, and told we could go to the bar to continue the party. They had fed and watered us enough.

We took a quick peek into the tiny bar area and opted for a walk along the front instead. We donned silly hats and blew our party whistles loudly until they stopped working, letting out nothing but a sad groan.

We were rather giggly, calling "*Feliz Año Nuevo,*" or "Happy New Year," randomly to everyone we saw.

CHESTNUT, CHERRY & KIWI FRUIT SPONGE

Leo spotted a man leaning out of an upstairs balcony to see what was going on and shouted loudly, "don't jump!"

This set us off into more giggles. When we thought to look at our mobile 'phones, it was almost midnight and there was no time to get back to the hotel. We stuffed in our *uvas*, trying not to choke as the countdown started around us, looking like overgrown hamsters, grapes in cheeks, chewing madly.

"Three, two, one... happy New Year 2016!"

JANUARY 2016
Painting the town

Our last few days in the sun flew by. We were unable to book any more trips due to the bank holidays, but we enjoyed our walks, reaching the castle on the headland each day. In the afternoons, S and I would have a swim and a sauna in the indoor pool then retire to our sunbeds to read and top up that tan. In the evenings, we would join Leo and Margaret for dinner and to play Rummikub. The final match, on our last night, was so satisfying I wrote the score in my diary:

'Thrashed L&M at Rummikub. 3 games L, 3 games S, 0 games Leo, 0 games Marg.'

Not that I was gloating, but we sure had caught onto that game fast.

We left Malaga on Sunday morning, the 3rd of January 2016. At Santiago airport, S and Leo went off to find the hidden penknife, coming back triumphant, and thankfully not in chains as suspected terrorists.

Our car was waiting for us at the off-site parking area. Not only waiting but also shiny and clean. It was Ruby's first wash since we'd bought her and reminded me why I'd christened her thus in the first place.

§

While we had been sunning ourselves in Fuengirola, Tony had accomplished an incredible amount. He had plastered the dressing room and the dining room walls, and plastered in the kitchen around his

CHESTNUT, CHERRY & KIWI FRUIT SPONGE

new 'wellie cupboard'. The whole house looked bright, and sparkled whitely.

Unlike us in the south, Tony had had a week of rain over New Year. That week soon became three long weeks battered by storms, rain, thunder, and hail. Luckily, we had plenty to do indoors at the *Casita*...

Back in December, on my birthday in fact, the boys had decided to remove the entire dining room ceiling. S had already cut new holes in the ceiling for the skylight windows he had fitted in the roof, but due to the numerous roof beams and the angle of the ceiling to the roof above he was having difficulty making the light tunnels work. Tony had suggested a vaulted ceiling instead. They'd climbed up into the roof space to look at the beams, and the roof above, and apparently agreed this would be a good idea.

It was an excellent idea. Sadly, it also meant a huge amount of dust and mess all over again.

"But, we're still on the demolition phase," said S, reasonably, when I complained that I had been cleaning up. Silly me. I had thought that after a year and a half we were now onto the rebuilding phase!

Once the ceiling was gone, the low, dim room was transformed. As a new year began, we scraped beams where they had been exposed, probably for the first time in a hundred years. S fitted plasterboard to the newly created window tunnels, now at a much better angle without the ceiling, and laths to the new vaulted ceiling which he and Tony insulated and plasterboarded. The window tunnels and the ceiling would be painted white to reflect as much light as possible into the room which, being in the middle of the house, had no conventional windows.

I continue to be amazed years later at just how bright and sunny that room now is. The skylights let in the sun all day long. Mum's house plants love it.

JANUARY 2016

Mum had said that she would move in to the *Casita* once the main rooms; the kitchen, living room, bedroom, and bathroom, plus that central dining room, were ready. We had already decided that the second bedroom and the dressing room would be completed after Mum had moved in, giving us a chance to finish the essential areas more quickly.

Mum was due back from England on the 7th of January, giving us time for a major clean through of the *Casita*. We tidied plaster splashes off the kitchen ceiling and fitted the granite worktop around the new corner sink. It looked as if it had always been in that position and was quirky enough to fit right in. We carried Mum's wardrobe, and the spare base-units we'd bought at the secondhand shop in Lugo for the kitchen, into the dressing room, together with a large rug brought over from England. This we threw on to the chipboard floor. The room could be used like this until we had time to lay the new floorboards. The second bedroom was acting as a storeroom for Mum's many boxes and would be sealed off until we were ready to start work on it.

Mum arrived home to a newly plastered dressing room, a plastered dining room with a partially plastered vaulted ceiling, electrics in the bedroom and dining room, and worktops around the kitchen.

Tony left us on the 13th after some two months here. We were even sorrier to see him go this time and he promised to return soon.

Diary Thursday 13th January Rain, cold
Tony left 10am. Mum in charge of lunch, cleaning Workaway bedroom, and putting the washing through whilst L and S continued working at the Casita.
L scraped and cleaned the beams in the bedroom and utility room ready to varnish. S put batons on

CHESTNUT, CHERRY & KIWI FRUIT SPONGE

the kitchen wall for the wall units we bought from Rastro in Lugo.
Lunch: Pork chops, mash, green beans (frozen) onion gravy. Egg custard. All excellently done by my sous chef and a pleasant change from cooking! Plastered inside the new wellie cupboard in the kitchen and helped S lift the kitchen wall cupboards into place.
4 eggs.

The day after Tony left, the rain stopped and the sunshine returned. The rest of January 2016 was mainly warm and sunny with overnight frosts.

Our next Workawayers were due on the 19th of January. Now being at the finishing stage (possibly), we planned to ask them to paint the bedroom walls and ceiling.

DeAnna and Maria arrived by bus in the afternoon. As they stepped off the coach, I couldn't help but think they were polar opposites. DeAnna was tall and skinny, with a mass of golden curls. Maria was shorter with coffee coloured skin and straight black shiny hair in a bob. DeAnna had on heeled cowboy boots, skinny jeans, and a leather jacket. Maria looked like she had been dressed from a rummage sale with ill-fitting jogging pants, a jumper which came over her hands and old trainers which obviously didn't fit.

I soon had an explanation for the clothing.

"Only one of our suitcases arrived from the US," said DeAnna, breathlessly. "Maria's was still in Texas. When we called American, they said they could send it to Madrid where we flew to, or back home. Well, we were already in Brazil then…" Here, DeAnna paused and looked at Maria.

"Portugal," said Maria.

"Yeah, that's it, Portugal, I always get those mixed up," continued DeAnna smiling.

JANUARY 2016

She seemed totally oblivious to the effect her statement had on me. I was standing with my mouth open, staring at her. Did she really say she got Brazil, largest of the South American countries, and Portugal, smaller of the Iberian ones, mixed up? It appeared she did. She was still in full flow so I tuned back in.

"We told them we couldn't go back to Madrid anyway from Brazil."

"Portugal," interceded Maria, helpfully.

"So, we're sharing clothes."

Maria smiled. "DeAnna's don't fit me too well."

We soon found out that DeAnna was the chatterbox of the couple and if anyone fit the description of a dizzy blonde, it was our DeAnna. Maria was the quiet, competent one.

I showed them their task the following morning.

"So, we're going to paint the walls and ceiling in white first. This'll act as an undercoat on the walls to stop the plasterboard soaking up so much paint and means you can get a neater edge where the walls and ceiling meet. I suggest one of you does the cutting in around the edges with the small brush and the other uses the roller to fill in. Okay?"

"What about this bit?" asked DeAnna, pointing to my newly varnished door frame.

"No, that's varnished, it's staying like that."

"Oh, okay. Does it matter if we get paint on the floor?"

"Erm, no, not really as this is only the chipboard underfloor. But obviously try to keep it on the walls," I laughed, keeping my tone light. Inside I was already panicking.

Maria started cutting in, neatly painting around the edges of the exposed beams. DeAnna decided to do the same.

I popped my head in two minutes later to find DeAnna standing with paint pouring off her brush, down her arm, and dripping onto the chipboard

CHESTNUT, CHERRY & KIWI FRUIT SPONGE

floor from her elbow. My newly varnished door frame had a nice long smear of paint down it.

"This is fun," smiled DeAnna.

I gasped. "Erm, yeah. Erm, maybe when you dip the brush it's best not to load it quite so much? And that varnished door frame didn't need painting. Erm, maybe you could wipe that off? Try following the edges? Maybe?" My speech was coming out as a series of questions as I tried to process the mess in front of me. "You have painted before, haven't you?"

"No! But it's great. We'll be able to build our own house when we've finished here, won't we Maria?"

Maria sensibly continued cutting in around the beam.

"Mmm, well, okay. Maybe you could do the rollering and let Maria continue with the cutting in for now?"

When I next returned, DeAnna had hold of the roller brush, which I'd carefully shown her how to load from the paint tray. It too was dripping. The floor had been painted in a wide strip a good foot out from the wall. DeAnna's lovely blonde hair was liberally splotched with gobs of white paint. I despaired of it ever coming clean, or of her touching any surface in the house before we managed to clean her up.

When we stopped for lunch, I ran in front of DeAnna opening doors and laying newspaper so her liberally painted cowboy boots didn't leave white footprints throughout both houses. I'm convinced she just thought I was rolling out the metaphorical red carpet as her acolyte.

S, in the meantime, was driving back and forward to the woodyard collecting the new sweet chestnut floorboards for the *Casita*. It was a test for our brand-new car, carrying such a weight, but I think he had the easier task that week.

We soon found out that DeAnna really was 'blonde'. I was still fascinated by her Brazil/Portugal error but it wasn't a one off. We were saying that our friends were hiring a car this time when they came over from the States.

"We could have done that," said DeAnna.

"Done what?"

"Hired a car and driven here."

"From Portugal?" I asked.

"No, from Texas. It would have been fun."

I looked to see if she was joking. She was not. I looked at Maria, who rolled her eyes and smiled. I looked at S, who had his jaw firmly clamped. I looked at Mum, whose face mirrored mine.

"Erm, there is the problem of the Atlantic Ocean to consider," I joked.

"Sorry?" said DeAnna.

"The Atlantic? Big ocean. Deep. Not good for driving through," I hinted.

"Oh! Yeah! I forget about that. Mm, I suppose we couldn't drive all the way then."

"Not all the way, no," I sighed.

Geographically challenged though she was, DeAnna was nothing if not a willing worker. Sadly, she was as skilled at painting as she was at geography.

By day three I'd had to find a hairnet for her, and a pair of old shoes left behind by a previous Workawayer. I didn't think DeAnna's cowboy boots would be rescuable, given their paint-splattered state – and in fact I was right as she abandoned them here when they left. We always supply Workawayers with overalls. Maria's were blue. DeAnna's were now white, with the odd blue patch peeking through where she hadn't quite managed to paint herself.

I had to buy a new 25 litre tub of white paint, the first one now being totally empty. That tub would normally have done three rooms the size DeAnna and Maria were painting. I had also decided there was no way I was letting them loose with the expensive, coloured top coat. That was a five-litre

CHESTNUT, CHERRY & KIWI FRUIT SPONGE

tub - plenty to do the 12 foot (un)square bedroom walls in normal hands, but not in DeAnna's.

Our chipboard floor was, by now, entirely white other than the odd piece which had miraculously been spared DeAnna's splashes. Her brush and roller were caked in paint from the tip of the bristles to the end of the handles, and there was as much paint dripped down the outside of the paint tub as was left inside it. Maria, on the other hand, was clean and tidy. Her brush was as pristine as when she started and her lines were neat and straight.

I was thinking of how to separate the two of them, finding DeAnna a different job while Maria painted the top coat, when they came to me. DeAnna was in a tizzy.

"It's my dad," she said. "He's ill. I need to go home."

"Oh, I am sorry. Is it serious?" I asked.

"No."

"Oh! That's good at least. Does he live on his own?"

"No, his wife is there, and her son. And my sister," she added.

"Oh." I was starting to sound like a broken record, but I was confused. "Why do you need to go then?" I asked. It seemed odd to rush half way round the world for a non-emergency when it sounded like there were plenty of family around.

"His wife says she won't help, and her son rang me and said I should be there," DeAnna continued. "But it's expensive."

"It usually is for a last-minute flight," I began.

DeAnna interrupted. "It's because he lives in Hawaii you see. It's an island," she added, unnecessarily.

"Yes, like Britain, only further from land," I said, half to myself, still thinking.

"Is Britain an island?" asked DeAnna.

I looked up. "Sorry?"

JANUARY 2016

"Is Britain an island? Only I thought they had to be hot."

"What, islands?" I asked.

"Yeah, like Hawaii. An island is somewhere hot, isn't it?"

"Erm, no. An island is land surrounded by water. That's the definition of an island. It doesn't matter where it is."

DeAnna smiled. "Oh! I've learned so much here. And we'll definitely be buying a fixer upper when we get home. We can do it all ourselves now."

I didn't bother to reply, but just smiled.

DeAnna and Maria left two days later, the family having paid for their flights back to the US. They had only been with us six days but they would be etched into our minds forever.

I often wonder if they ever bought a house. And if so, what the paint job looks like.

Diary Tuesday 26th January Sunny and warm
Got Mum scraping the blue paint off the doors for the dining room built-in cupboard. L started to tile the shower in the bathroom-utility.
Lunch: Smoked salmon and leek quiche. Carrot, raisin and walnut slaw. Mum's queen of puddings.
L continued tiling. S fit the waste pipes from the new kitchen sink.

We had been given some coloured wall tiles by Debs and Al. They had a number left over from their own project, and ever Wombles, we gratefully accepted. There was a mixture of royal blue, slate grey, moss green, and cream, six-inch tiles, and a strip of tiny sky-blue tiles pasted on a mesh background. I spent my evenings drawing out designs. I reckoned that if I bought some white tiles the same size, I could mix them with the donated ones to create a design.

The green and cream tiles I put to one side for the second, en suite, bathroom. I'd decided on a blue

CHESTNUT, CHERRY & KIWI FRUIT SPONGE

and white sea theme for the main bathroom-utility room: Mum had plenty of shells and Galician sea pebbles to add to the ambience. I used the tiny mosaic tiles above a white splashback behind the sink, and I eventually came up with a sort of wave design for the shower which I hoped would look like a splash against the white tiles. Design sorted, I got to work.

Diary Friday 29th January Sunny and warm
L off to visit Dr Sin for her back. He is a great acupuncturist and has a lovely sense of humour. He loved my explanation of his name in English and seems to be helping with my back too.
S pruned some of the kiwi vines. They have grown into the roof of the Long Barn, twisted around each other and completely obliterated my cold frame, all in a few months. The extra watering seems to have paid off.
Stuck on the last few whole tiles in the bathroom-utility and weeded in the allotment. Dr Sin says I shouldn't weed or use a broom. Haha. What does he expect me to do?
Out in the evening for the first night of the Tapas Trail in town.

Dr Sin is a Korean acupuncturist and Chinese medicine expert. He has wonderful hands for massaging the back, and the agony of my trapped nerve soon improved under his gentle administration and long needles.

Later, after I had finished my course of massage and acupuncture, and had run out of money for more, I booked into a yoga class nearby.

I've practised yoga since I was 12 and have always enjoyed the stretches and the flexibility which comes with it. Sadly, my back problem had put paid to my doing much of late so I thought I'd join a class to encourage me to restart. Now, I am aware that

JANUARY 2016

there are different types of yoga but didn't at the time realise the profound differences. I have always enjoyed yoga for the exercise. This class began with two yoga positions but as quickly as we had begun the teacher stopped us.

"*Ya está*. Now, everyone in a circle," he announced.

The rest of the class trooped obediently to the hard wooden chairs and draped themselves with the blankets laying there. Soon we all looked like refugees from a natural disaster waiting for hot soup.

"We will now meditate," said the teacher, walking behind us as he spoke.

It was disconcerting having someone talking to me out of my vision, his voice coming and going as he paced. I guessed he was encouraging us to relax but it wasn't working. I had come to exercise my back, not make it worse sitting on an upright chair covered with a scratchy blanket. I was just pondering how to make a rapid exit when there was a 'ting' in my ear.

"What the?" I screeched, spinning my head round.

Behind me, smiling serenely, was our teacher, holding a triangle which he was hitting at intervals with a small hammer.

"Focus on the sound and relax," he intoned, still pacing the circle.

I had no chance of relaxing with that racket going on. I dislike harsh noises intensely. Music, yes. Bird song, yes. Triangles tinging no, never, not on your Nellie!

Luckily the torment continued only for another day or so... oh, sorry, I mean 15 minutes, before teacher announced the end of class.

He came up to me as I was folding the blanket. "How was that?" he asked.

"Er, well, erm, great. I'm not sure I'll be able to make it again. Erm something's come up, erm..."

CHESTNUT, CHERRY & KIWI FRUIT SPONGE

I'm hopeless at lying and it probably showed, but I'm also too English to say I'd hated it. I blame the fact that it's still difficult to organise my thoughts in Spanish, but really, it's simple cowardice.

"If you want to join for the whole course, telephone the centre," he continued, oblivious to my panicked thoughts.

"Right, yes, thanks," I mumbled before pulling the door open and legging it as fast as my screaming back would allow. Another one to put down to experience.

Diary Sunday 31st January Mild
Up late to eggs with frozen bread! Oops. Made lunch while Mum sanded some of the cupboard door she has been working on. S keeps telling her she needs to remove every speck of blue paint. Mum says he's cruel!
S pruning the fruit trees.
Lunch: Pork Loin roast with mash, fried cabbage and roast squash. Orange curd tart.
L&S long circuit, across the valley and round via Taboada. Not sure if walking helps my back or makes it worse. Enjoyable though.
Final evening of the tapas trail in town... now, vino definitely helps my back!

The end of the month had brought another fiesta in Taboada. Nine bars, cafés and restaurants (yes, we have plenty of those for a small town) took part in the Tapas Trail - a competition to see who could produce the best tapa. The rules were that each tapa offered had to include pork in some form, and bread. They cost a euro each. Ever the foodie, I was excited to try each and every tapa there was.

We collected our voting cards at the first bar. All the participating bars were listed on the card and there was a space next to each one. Each bar had its own stamp. Once we had ordered the special tapa our cards were stamped, and once all the bars were ticked off, we could vote for our favourite.

We'd decided to divide the bars up into three nights of feasting (and drinking, obviously) as we could do justice to neither more than three wines, nor more than three tapas, in a night. The bars had gone all out in an attempt to win the competition. The tapas were huge and the variety incredible.

Luisa had produced a stew of roast pork, potatoes and vegetables. The Anduriña restaurant had made giant, ham-filled flaky pasties with a mushroom sauce. Bar Gema used the best of Galicia: ham, *grelos*, and sweet chestnuts set in a mould. Bar Scala had created mini barbecues – skewered *chorizos* were brought to the table flaming, with a side of mashed potato and a red wine jus. It was showmanship of the best kind.

The winner that year was Bar Mario. Their offering was a deep-fried potato basket filled with bacon, mushrooms, *chorizo*, green peppers, and a fried egg. It was a full English breakfast, even to the smear of tomato ketchup alongside.

I smiled at Mum as she wiped her mouth clean of grease and sipped her wine.

"Now, I enjoy painting the town much more than painting the *Casita*," I laughed.

"And it's nicer than scraping blue paint too," replied Mum.

Taboada's Tapas Trail was a lovely end to what had been an interesting and productive month. *La Casita* was finally coming together.

FEBRUARY 2016
To infinity and beyond

No wonder Mum was fed up with scraping blue paint. Whilst we had been tiling and plumbing, she had been kept busy in the open barn, cleaning doors.

All the doors in the *Casita*, including the cupboards, were of sweet chestnut, and all were painted. Galicians seemed to have had a love for a particular shade of powder blue with which they liberally painted all woodwork. Mum's job was to remove the layers of paint down to the original dark brown wood, ready for sanding and varnishing. She has done a sterling job but confesses that she 'never wants to see another blue door – ever'.

On this particular occasion it was the cupboard doors from the dining room she was working on.

When we bought the *Casita* there was a crockery cupboard in the corner of the dining room, above and backing onto the crockery cupboard in the kitchen. The kitchen cupboard was now ready to house Mum's eye-level oven, with space above and below for pans and kitchenware. This had been varnished and looked beautiful next to the four steps up to the rest of the house. The dining room cupboard had two glass doors painted in that delightful 'Galician blue'. S had taken the doors off so we could remake the interior of the cupboard. Whilst I was fiddling with the shelving inside, Mum was wrapped up in layers of jumpers in the *alpendre,* scraping away. No one could say she wasn't willing to join in with the work.

On the first Wednesday in February, we decided a day off was in order. The sun was still shining and Ourense beckoned. A day trip to Ourense is always a pleasure and a soak in the thermal pools was just what the doctor ordered for my back... I hoped.

Diary Wednesday 3rd February Sunshine
Lit both cocinas and stacked them well. To Ourense via the Euro store in Chantada for some kitchen bits for Mum. Found a nice bright red plate rack for her to match the new kitchen wall tiles.
Called at the Restaurant Rio Búbal for tea on the way, but stayed slightly too long as the road train was just pulling away as we rushed across the pedestrian bridge over the river Miño towards the stop. Wandered back and waited for a bus into the city.
Interesting ride through areas I'd never seen before, but we made it safely.
Lunch at Restaurant Maria Andrea as compensation, sitting on the sunny balcony looking down on the plaza. And managed to catch the train back again for our long soak. Home via one of the local bars for a restorative vino. Good day.

I'm not sure whether the thermals helped my back but I'd enjoyed myself, and missing the little road train had definitely been a bonus. Lovely though the train ride is, it's not exactly prime comfort.

The tiny Italian-made 'Dotto' road train runs regularly from the thermal park outside the city, bouncing its way alongside the river Miño, across the Roman bridge and into the city centre where it stops in the main square before doing the return trip. It is a more interesting and picturesque journey than the bus, which winds through built-up residential areas

CHESTNUT, CHERRY & KIWI FRUIT SPONGE

on its way to the centre, but the cushioned, sprung seats on the bus are a definite plus point.

The Maria Andrea restaurant was our new favourite place to eat in Ourense. It is a charming mix of old and new. Downstairs is gleaming wood, with a long bar counter and scattered, circular tables. Upstairs there is a gallery around the stairs with a newer, light-filled area beyond and, on sunny days, a small balcony with half a dozen tables overlooking the square below. The food is excellent and rotates daily so there is always something to look forward to. Summer is gazpacho, thick with garlic flavours, whilst winter is a time for *cocido*, the Galician pork and chickpea stew.

The February weather continued hot during the day with heavy frosts overnight. I pruned the grapevines, almost certainly at the wrong time again, and continued tiling. S pruned the sweet chestnut trees, did necessary winter maintenance outdoors in the sunshine, and scraped the ceiling beams in the dining room until they were smooth as silk.

That weekend was Taboada's famous 'bone stew' festival, *a feira do caldo de ósos*, and another first for Mum. We and our friends met in town before going on to the *parillada*-grill nearby for an enjoyable meal, and plenty of chatter in good company.

Diary Tuesday 9th February Wild and wet all day and all night
L finished tiling the splashback in the kitchen. Mum made a cake for brew time and S scraped more beams.
Lunch: Homemade pork pie and salad (leaves from the garden, walnuts, blue cheese and sun-dried plums)
L and S painted in the kitchen and S fitted Mum's candelabra ceiling light in the dining room with Mum giving helpful instructions the whole time.

FEBRUARY 2016

Having Mum here with us has been a wonderful experience. We laugh together often and enjoy each others' company.

When we first mentioned to friends in England that Mum was moving here, S got all the mother-in-law jokes and we got some 'be careful you don't regret it' speeches from people we didn't expect. By total contrast, all our Spanish neighbours and friends thought it was not only a great idea but the logical thing to do. Of course she would move over, why wouldn't she?

The way older people are treated here goes some way to explaining the differences. Certainly, Mum has never been discriminated against due to her age in Galicia. In fact, she wouldn't be considered old here. If she said something along the lines of 'I'm 84 you know?' the likely answer in Galicia would be 'and I'm 92, what's your point?' In England she found her opinion unwanted even when she had the answer.

Before Mum sold her house in England, there was an ongoing problem with the sewerage system. The drains had sadly backed up the very day a surveyor came to look at the property, though it probably didn't affect that particular (non) sale. Her deeds of sale from the council included a clause that they were responsible for remedying the problem should it occur. Over the years the contract for maintenance moved from the council to various private companies, none of which seemed to have the necessary plans or information to solve the problem.

On one occasion, they had dug up half the garden and had a camera down the sewer pipes to locate the blockage. Mum had explained three times that the issue was in the nearby wood but they ignored her. In fact, Mum says they gave her that 'what do you know, you're an old woman' look rather too many times. After a week of intensive investigations, they discovered the cause for themselves – a number of hefty tree roots had broken into the sewer pipes in the little copse and blocked them. There was, of course, no apology forthcoming, and Mum failed dismally to say 'I told you so.'

Here, older people have as much right to their opinions as young ones. Probably more so. If an elderly person talks, they are listened to. In fact, everyone here thinks Mum is amazing... and of course they are right.

In those early days Mum worked hard helping renovate her home, making the odd meal and more than a few cakes. As she enters her 91st year, she does less on the cooking and DIY front but still walks every day and can easily be persuaded to darn something or patch my jeans once again – although the complaints about the thickness of the patches upon patches and her poor darning needle, are the price I have to pay for having my own personal seamstress.

Having always been a voracious reader (something of a family trait, as I remember nights at home spent in front of the fire with us all reading), Mum has also discovered the delights of Kindle and reads avidly, especially the memoirs I download for her from my favourite Facebook group, 'We Love Memoirs'.

Mum has always been unique and I do tease her mercilessly, both in real life and in the pages of my books. But our life would be so much duller without some of her eccentricities.

§

We were sitting having our morning tea break when Mum started rattling change in her pocket.

"I owe you another shilling but it's all I've got," she began, placing five euros on the marble table top.

FEBRUARY 2016

I was confused, which is quite a normal state of affairs. S was laughing.

"So... why?" I began.

"I've got a confession. But I couldn't help it."

Mum's sentences tend to begin in the middle and radiate outwards. I knew we'd get there eventually. I waited.

"Well, I woke up. I had my PJs on. I didn't know what it was and it was dark."

I waited some more.

"It was making a terrible racket clattering about the kitchen. I threw it outside."

Now I looked at S for assistance. He was helpless with laughter and no use at all.

"And he said they were six shillings," finished Mum, breathlessly. "But I don't have another one."

"I'm totally flummoxed, Mother," I said into the silence.

"A mouse," supplied S at last.

"It was wriggling so I threw it all out," added Mum.

"The mouse trap?" I asked, twigging at last.

We have a problem with mice sneaking into the houses on occasions. I dislike killing them but when they get into the kitchen they need to go. We had put a trap under Mum's *cocina* and it had obviously been sprung in the night.

"You threw the trap out with the mouse in it?" I clarified.

"Yes."

"You didn't think to let it go?"

"I couldn't touch it." Mum shuddered dramatically.

"But you picked the trap up."

"I had my big gloves on. And I threw it out the door. Well, no. I put it on the step first but I thought someone might tread on it there."

"On the mouse?"

CHESTNUT, CHERRY & KIWI FRUIT SPONGE

"Yes. Then I went out with the torch to see if it had gone."

"And?"

"There were ten cats outside."

I could imagine. The poor mouse would have been a snack in a box. A takeaway mouse.

"So, the money is for it."

"What, the mouse?"

"Yes."

"For a funeral, or a survivor's fund?" I teased.

"Yes. No. The trap. I owe you another shilling for it."

"The mouse traps are not single use you know."

"No. Sorry."

"And if you catch another?"

"What do you mean?"

"Will you throw that one away too?"

Mum thought. "I'll put it in a drawer."

"A drawer?"

"Yes."

"With the knives and forks?"

"Or the tea towel drawer," supplied S. "It could make a nest."

"Oh dear!" said Mum.

We never did find that trap, but thankfully the mice have not visited lately so Mum hasn't had to resort to using her tea towel drawer as a temporary jail.

The stormy weather continued through the middle of February but as we were busy indoors tiling, scraping doors and laying floorboards, it didn't really matter.

Diary Sunday 14th February Cold wet windy hail and sleet!
Boiled eggs and soldiers as we all sat cosily in the kitchen watching the rain. Lovely.

FEBRUARY 2016

Made lunch (toad in the hole) and varnished the steps up to the dining room in the Casita. No one is allowed to walk in there until tomorrow.

Since our Americans had left early on their emergency dash home, we hadn't had any Workawayers staying. Instead, we had concentrated on doing the work ourselves. Now we were at the definite renovation stage, rather than demolition, I was more wary of who we had to stay. We didn't want a repeat of the painting disaster that was DeAnna.

Our next Workawayer was, by chance, also American. However, Lynda could not have been more different from DeAnna. Tall and slender with a head of grey hair, she was capable, intelligent and personable. Lynda had renovated houses of her own and had been a hippy chick in the 60s. She was such a complete contrast to poor DeAnna, I had to laugh. Lynda filled her brush to the exact degree required to paint a neat line. Her roller never dripped and the dining room floor remained strangely unsplattered even while she painted the ceiling. She was, in short, a star.

Diary Thursday 18th February Sunshine
S fitted the electric sockets in the dining room. L sanded the utility-bathroom floorboards ready to varnish while Lynda painted the dining room.
Lunch: Pork fillet with sun-dried plums and cream sauce. Mash, roast squash and creamed spinach. Apple and plum crumble.
S found me in the afternoon to say Buzz and Eliot had got into a cockfight causing the 'bike shed' to collapse. Buzz didn't look well.

When I got there, Buzz was inside the hut, hiding in a corner. He looked very sorry for himself with blood dripping in his eye and his feathers all ruffled. I

CHESTNUT, CHERRY & KIWI FRUIT SPONGE

hoped it was more because he'd lost his first fight than any injuries sustained from the falling shelter.

I carefully carried Buzz to the summer chicken hut in case Eliot wanted to continue the fight. Later, being sentimental, I decided to also relocate Sarah to keep him company.

Buzz Lightyear and Sarah Bernhardt were our two eldest residents now. We had been given them (in exchange for two breeding rabbits) by Anne and Simon back in 2008. Sarah had hatched a brood a year for her first four years with us, and Buzz had fathered around 20 chicks. Sarah no longer laid many eggs and had stopped going broody a couple of years earlier. Buzz did not seem to be as active of late either, but I felt they had both earned their retirements.

For the last two years we'd had two new broody hens; Billie Jean, a black and white Sussex cross, and Buff Puff, a golden fluffy half-Buff Orpington. These two were brood sisters, hatched by Sarah. They would go broody, usually within a few days of each other, and cause all sorts of trouble.

One year they sat together on a brood of eggs. I have a wonderful photograph of Buffy, fluffed up and gorgeous, squashing the smaller BJ out of the box they had chosen to share. On that occasion they hatched a single chick between them.

Charlie William Puff was a handsome white cockerel with an identity complex from being bossed about by two mothers with totally different ideas of mothering, but he always came when I called his name. I sold Charlie to a friend who insisted he wanted a cockerel but who then failed to feed him. When Charlie eventually escaped, looking for something to eat, our 'friend' left him outdoors until his dog, also not fed regularly, made a meal of poor Charlie.

We sometimes got fertilized eggs from friends and neighbours to vary the gene pool a bit. Later the

FEBRUARY 2016

same year that Charlie hatched, Carmen's sister donated some eggs. Those hens must have been huge. The contrast in size between the chicks from the donated eggs and our own, was ridiculous. The largest, an incredibly handsome and gentle black and white barred cockerel who answered to Harry C Houdini, because he inevitably followed me out of the door, was over four kilos and stood as high as my knee. Eric (Clapton) was in contrast tiny and almost pure white but he was definitely the boss of the pair, bullying poor Harry mercilessly.

Eggs fertilised by Buzz hadn't hatched for a couple of years now. That was the reason we'd kept Eliot. He had been one of Billie Jean's brood the previous year – his full name being Billy Eliot Jean. There had never been any major scuffles before, with Buzz keeping Eliot in line with a look or a quick peck. We had 12 chickens at that stage so I thought there were plenty of hens for the two males to share. I was obviously wrong.

Sadly, when I opened the pen the next morning Buzz was gone. My handsome cockerel was just a pile of feathers, lying in the corner. His injuries must have been more severe than I thought and he had not made it through the night. Sarah was sitting unconcerned in the furthest corner from the body and not for the first time I wondered what chickens thought about death, or if they even understood it. They never seemed to go near a dead hen.

I carried Sarah back to the other hens and her new cockerel boss, Eliot, then left S to pluck my beautiful patriarch to so many chicks.

"To infinity and beyond, Buzz," I whispered to myself. "Travel well."

Diary Saturday 20th February Sunny and warm
Mum walked to the supermarket for me while I made lunch and cookies and did a bit more floor sanding. Lynda rollered the dining room ceiling,

CHESTNUT, CHERRY & KIWI FRUIT SPONGE

doing a fabulous job. S pondered how to fit the track for the intended sliding door to the kitchen and dressing room.
Lunch: Lasagne. Coleslaw, pepper and cheese salad.
Spoke to the carpenter nearby about a possible new/old door for the dressing room.

The only two rooms in the *Casita* without old sweet chestnut doors had been the kitchen, which had a mouldy blockboard fire door – the outer ply sodden and peeling away, and the dressing room, which had no door at all. Because these two doorways were next to each other, we'd decided to fit a track and double sliding doors.

We had tried to source doors to buy, but finding old sweet chestnut doors was all but impossible. Our wonderful local priest had even given us permission to take some doors from a nearby derelict house owned by the bishopric. Thankfully for our consciences they were the wrong size. I had felt incredibly guilty that day, rooting around in someone's house measuring up doors to steal.

A local carpenter had said he could get doors for us; though when it came down to it, the only one he found the right size was a pine door. That door stayed on the dressing room for a while but in the end, Mum preferred the room open. After all, it was not a room for sleeping in so why did it need a door?

That left the kitchen.

The dilemma of the kitchen door was finally solved in 2019 by our good friend Leo, who, having bought a large derelict house, was systematically replacing all the old doors with brand new ones. His discards became our gains. We found not only a perfect fit for the sliding door to the kitchen but replacement doors for our newly completed Big Barn. Our friend Geert took most of the rest of Leo's unwanted doors. Between us we had once more

FEBRUARY 2016

actively recycled useful things every day folk leave behind.

Diary Tuesday 23rd February Mild, cloudy
S continued to think about the runner for the sliding doors while Lynda painted around him. Prepared the guest bedroom for Belle.
To the airport via Leroy Merlin, as S decided the sliding door track he has will not be of any use for what we want to do. Bought a different track.

My beautiful niece was due for her annual visit, something we always looked forward to. Belle tried to vary her visits to enjoy Galicia at different times of the year. This year she was in time for an early spring, and to help me unbox some of Mum's many possessions.

Diary Wednesday 24th February Sunshine
L and Belle started unpacking boxes into the kitchen. Hope there will be space for it all! Lynda painting the second coat in the dining room and Mum sanding the door to the second bedroom. At least that one is white not blue! S sawed off part of the top step to the kitchen to fit the door runner.

The top step was, like much of the flooring in the *Casita* and in our own *Casa do Campo*, not entirely level. The dining room had a marked slope toward the bathroom, meaning the sliding door idea wouldn't work without some serious carpentry.

In the meantime, Belle and I were having fun organising the kitchen. Belle opened a box labelled with a '40' in marker pen. I couldn't find a box 40 on my list.

"That's odd, there isn't a... Hold on," I said, as Belle pulled out the first item. "That hairdryer should be in the missing box."

CHESTNUT, CHERRY & KIWI FRUIT SPONGE

At that moment a piece of toughened glass dropped out of the bottom of the box.

"So should that. Something's up here."

I inverted the box - which said '34' on the bottom.

It was the box which had caused all the arguments with the removals company months before. I still maintain that during the frenzy of packing, someone - obviously not me, had turned one of my labelled boxes over and renumbered it. There was no box 40 inventoried because that box never existed.

I have to admit that I never informed the company we found that box. I had written numerous times since September, eventually contacting the chairman himself. All that got me was a cheque for £25 'in full and final settlement and without prejudice'. I didn't think their careless attitude deserved an explanation and as I had returned their measly cheque uncashed, in disgust, I didn't owe them one. The incident did keep us amused through the arduous task of emptying dozens of kitchenware boxes though.

As usual Belle only had a few days holiday, but we visited the thermal pools at Ourense again and Belle helped Mum scrape the hateful paint off the second bedroom door. Unlike most of the doors in the *Casita*, this one was a wide, and low, ancient, brace and ledge panel door. The paint was thick but the solid door beneath was sweet chestnut.

Belle had got bored.

"Can't we just repaint it?" she asked one morning.

"No," replied S. He handed the pair some sharp new pieces of broken glass and urged them to carry on.

We know how to treat our visitors!

Diary Saturday 27th February Snow!
Day out in Santiago. Very snowy and slippery in places and slow going. Lunch at Manolo's in the

plaza. We'd not been for ages but the portions are still huge. Belle had a whole rack of pork ribs, S two quarter chickens. A doggy (or catty) bag or three was needed. Wandered about in the sleet then had hot chocolates in the Casino café. Back to the car in the now teeming rain and dropped Belle off at the airport in plenty of time. Home to warm up!
7eggs

It was a leap year that year, and on the 29th of February the sun shone once more while Lynda pruned the rest of our kiwi vines. It seemed she'd had some of her own years before and was an expert pruner. I wasn't surprised.

MARCH 2016
A promise of spring

The old proverb states that if March 'comes in like a lion, it goes out like a lamb' – and vice versa. March 2016 started off beautifully calm and lamb-like.

Diary Tuesday 1ˢᵗ March Sunny
All to Monterroso market. Lynda had a look around and Mum enjoyed poking things, as usual. Eight of us for lunch. Tried a new place. The meal was fine but ridiculously rushed. Geert was still eating his starter as his main course was pushed under his nose. After we had paid our 12€ a head Jorge stayed behind to chat to someone. This meant he overheard the next couple being charged only 10€ each for their menú del dia. Did they overcharge because we are 'foreigners'? The Cañoto. Note taken!

Other than the fiasco over lunch, we had a nice day out in Monterroso and a long walk in the afternoon over the tops, through the deliciously scented golden gorse bushes. It was a good way to walk off lunch. I had been all for going back in and complaining about the price but the others said it wasn't worth it. I've been described as a terrier more than once, and I don't like to let go. I wanted to explain to the restaurant just how much business they potentially lost from trying to get

MARCH 2016

one up on the foreigners that day. Maybe they will read this instead!

The gorse was not the only thing in bloom. The fruit trees all had fat buds on: fat buds just ripe for picking by our visiting bullfinches. These stunningly beautiful pink-chested birds only ever appear in early spring, usually within a day or two of the plum buds showing. They pull off the buds with their fat beaks, chew them, then spit them out. They can be quite a menace on fruit farms in England, though I like to think they are eating the buds which have bugs in them and are therefore doing us a favour. Certainly, we seem to have plenty of plums ripen despite the ground around the trees being littered with half-chewed buds in spring.

Meanwhile, it was time to start sowing my vegetables for the new season. I'd sown the tomato seeds back in January and they were now big enough to grow on in the sunny sunroom, which was turning into a very satisfactory conservatory for young plants. My tomatoes were grown from saved seed from the previous year.

Saving the seeds worked well. I would choose the best fruit from the best plants in terms of productivity, growth and resistance to disease, drying the seeds on kitchen paper before storing them overwinter. I had a nice system going and got some interesting and tasty crosses. I also found my saved seeds inevitably grew quicker and stronger than any packet ones, having already been adapted to the Galician weather.

In went the parsnip seeds which I'd had in the freezer since autumn, and the carrots. Parsnips need stratifying, a sharp frost, to encourage the seeds to germinate and the freezer works as a satisfactory substitute in mild years. And in went the brassicas; cabbage, cauliflower, broccoli and romanesco.

CHESTNUT, CHERRY & KIWI FRUIT SPONGE

Lynda left us on the 2nd of March, having neatly and professionally painted the whole dining room bright white. Our next task in the dining room was to lay the flooring.

The floor in the utility-bathroom was varnished and looking good. The short chestnut floorboards, which we got at a discount because the company had six square metres no one wanted, were perfect in such a long thin room, drawing the eye outwards. The dining room floor had to be laid next; the central dining room, bedroom one, the dressing room and the living room were all on one level so the floorboards had to run through neatly. The only way to ensure this was to start in the middle – the dining room.

Diary Wednesday 9th March Sunshine
S continued flooring the dining room. L made lunch, puddings and cakes.
Lunch: Loin of pork with mash, roast carrots, broccoli and brussels (which even Mum ate!) Carrot and orange sponge with custard.
L&S walked to the 3rd mill. Lots of early spring flowers out.

That Sunday walk was delightful. It was hot in the sun and the birds were singing in the chestnut trees as we passed by. In the fields the crickets were already tuning up and I spotted a fox lurking at the woodland edge watching us warily. The gorse was still flowering and the early fruit blossoms were already showing.

The third water mill from home on our little river is hidden in a steep valley, overshadowed by tall birch trees, shady and cool. I loved listening to the water thundering down the mill race before disappearing into the woodland. It was peaceful down there in the woods, and not for the first time I thought just how lucky we are to live here in Galicia.

MARCH 2016

Diary Thursday 10th March Sun, frost overnight
Mum made a cake while L made lunch. Both planted out new strawberry runners in the stone trough at the side of the house. S continued laying the flooring in the dining room.
Lunch: Ham in orange sauce with peppers, carrots and rice.
L sanded the floorboards at one end of the dining room whilst S carried on laying at the other. What a team we are!

T S Eliot may have thought April the cruellest month, but here in Galicia March can be much more deceptive. The March weather can be sunny and warm, leading us to think spring has arrived. Our first year in Galicia, I had planted everything enthusiastically in February and March thinking the winter was over – only to discover I was wrong.

It was frosty that middle week of March 2016, with sunny days and cold, clear nights. I had 29 peppers and 65 tomato plants growing in our sunroom by then. I was desperate to plant them out but had learnt my lesson: it would be at least another month before it was safe to do so.

Diary Wednesday 16th March Sunny, frost overnight
L sanded the last of the floorboards in the dining room and swept up. Started to varnish them but ran out of varnish (could have sworn we had another tin). Just as well as Luis and Luis senior visited to view the Casita. Mum enjoyed doing the 'tour', and I was happy my floor hadn't just been varnished!

Mum was very proud of her *Casita* and loved to show visitors around. By the 18th of March we had finished varnishing the dining room floor and were ready to move the furniture in.

CHESTNUT, CHERRY & KIWI FRUIT SPONGE

Mum's dining room suite from England is dark oak – chunky and ancient looking. It is a brand called Old Charm and fitted the *Casita* as if it were made for it. The triangular corner unit was perfect next to the door to the living room with space for her Welsh dresser, filled with her Crown Derby plate collection, next to it. The oak dining room table, with its bulbous carved legs and the four leather-seated chairs, sat beneath the new iris stained-glass window. And the built-in cupboard, its newly sanded and finished doors devoid of blue paint, complemented the furniture and provided valuable storage for Mum's crockery.

The new skylights with their white painted tunnels reflected the spring sunlight into the room, making it bright and airy. The exposed roof beams below the vaulted ceiling shone now they were cleaned and varnished. And Mum's wooden candelabra, made for her by a dear friend some 50 years earlier, hung from the centre beam, perfectly at home. It was strange to think that all this furniture had travelled some 1300 miles, or more than 2000 kilometres, to look more at home than it ever had in England.

Diary Sunday 20th March Dull, mild and damp
L and S moved boxes and furniture into the dining room and finished dressing it ready for the jefa's inspection. Cleared out the dressing room so we can stack the remaining plasterboard in there.
Lunch: Pork and lemon tagine with mash. Apple charlotte with pumpkin custard.
Planted three rows of onions in the allotment. Left Mum happily polishing her furniture!
Salamander on the track in the evening.

I continued to plant my crops for the year. There is something particularly satisfying about growing and eating our own vegetables. It's not just that they

MARCH 2016

taste better – which they do, even Mum will eat her greens when they are home grown and fresh that morning. But I think it's also a primal urge to see new life appear every spring and the cycle start again.

My leeks and runner beans, peas and black peas went in.

Black peas are a variety of legume having pretty purple flowers and dark, almost black, peas once dried. In the northwest of England black peas are a staple served with vinegar on Guy Fawkes Night. They seemed to thrive in Galicia, and I loved the colour of the flowers. Black pea flowers are also a favourite with the honey bees.

The honey bees start to fly early here. The first warm spell and they are away. Our early spring can fool them too. Luckily, we have pollen-producing plants all year round so the bees always have something to feed on; from the winter-flowering honeysuckle in late December, through the spring bulbs and fruit blossoms to the ubiquitous marigolds and the late-flowering asters. Maybe it is this richness and variety which encouraged one honey bee swarm to settle in our loft at *A Casa do Campo*.

The first we knew of it was finding the odd dead and dying bee in the guest bedroom. It got to the stage where I was sweeping them up three times a day and throwing them out of the window. We searched everywhere but failed to find a gap where they could get into the bedroom. Then one day I was in the garden below. Looking up I saw a huge swarm around the eaves of the roof. When S investigated, we found they had made a very nice nest in the loft space under the eaves. By the time we found it, there were four oval honeycombs hanging from the beam and rather too many bees for us to be happy with.

Luis at the bar, whose dad keeps bees, told us that spraying would be a bad idea: left unattended,

CHESTNUT, CHERRY & KIWI FRUIT SPONGE

the honeycomb would deteriorate and the honey would start to drip out. As much as I love honey, the idea of it dripping through our ceiling didn't appeal. Luis offered us the use of his bee suit so we could investigate further.

The nest was virtually inaccessible, hidden as it was amongst the beams at the lowest part of the roof. Added to that it was a hot day, and S was sweating freely inside the bee suit with an old pilot suit of my brother's underneath and thick gloves. He managed to remove most of the honeycombs, having smoked the bees beforehand, but we couldn't get the lot. We popped the combs in the hollow of a tree hoping, but not expecting, the worker bees would find them. Whether our efforts worked or not I'm unsure but we had no more bees buzzing around in the bedroom which was good news for any barefoot guests.

The biggest swarm we've had was two years ago. I had been in our sunroom when the sky turned black and a vicious humming descended. As I photographed the scene, the bees, in a stacking formation from just above ground level to roof level, whizzed past the window and into our apricot tree. And there they stayed, slowly adding to their number until the poor tree bent to the ground under the weight. By now the swarm was a beach ball sized blob, and I was able to get up close to photograph it as the bees were obviously preoccupied.

I put a call out on social media for anyone who wanted to collect our bees, and soon a couple of friends arrived. Watching them carefully but quickly scoop the whole wriggling mass into a large wooden box was fascinating. After they had left with the bees for their new home, I found a tennis ball sized swarm still hanging around. Those poor bees stayed in the garden for two days before eventually dying. Without instruction they didn't eat so they didn't survive. What a hard life.

MARCH 2016

Diary Thursday 24th March Hot in the Sun
Made lunch and watered the flower tubs while Mum was put to work sanding one of the coffee tables we found in the Casita. S is laying the flooring in the bedroom.
Ramón arrived at 12.30pm for the Easter weekend. He helped L put Mum's new garden bench together and level the ground for it against the house wall in the sun. Perfect!

Our friend and Workawayer, Ramón, had asked to return for the long Easter weekend. We were delighted and had an enjoyable weekend of work and chat, with Ramón's friend Maria joining us on the Friday.

It was sunny on Easter Thursday, but Friday dawned drizzly and damp. This didn't stop Ramón and Maria getting stuck in cleaning and mortaring the back wall of the *Casita,* standing in the damp with their hoods up busily cementing away. We were so pleased Ramón had come into our lives.

We heard our first cuckoo that week, a little later than usual but a welcome promise of spring and summer despite his reputation for cuckolding the nests of others.

That year, the great tits decided to nest in the high stone wall which separates our garden from the much lower track beyond. I heard the cheeping one morning when I was going across to the allotment and spotted tiny mouths, open and showing yellow inside. It was a safe place to avoid the cuckoo but not to avoid being eaten by the many neighbourhood cats. Amazingly, the brood survived and safely fledged. We have many varieties of birds here and plenty of places for them to nest with all the open stone barns around

The first year Mum moved here, we had a redstart's nest in the open barn at the *Casita.* It was built in a thick hank of rope we had hung on the

CHESTNUT, CHERRY & KIWI FRUIT SPONGE

back of the barn door, somewhat too low for safety. The following year, they nested on the window ledge outside Mum's living room. The cats had fun that year, sitting on the garden wall opposite with their mouths open waiting for a snack to fly within reach.

The next year, these imprudent birds decided on a beam in the second bedroom as their nesting site. Unfortunately, that was the year we were renovating the guest room. Each morning we had to dismantle the nest which was inevitably rebuilt overnight. We couldn't explain to the birds that their access was about to be curtailed by new windows and doors. The redstarts, though, were the least of our difficulties in that space.

In Galicia we have a serious problem with the Asian Hornet, or *velutina*. These yellow-legged pests are smaller than the native European hornet and so can access honey bee hives. They also hang around outside the hives carrying off bees as they emerge or return from foraging. It's heartbreaking to see the bees being devastated in this way and every year we have a campaign of death to any *velutina* we see. Normally these hornets build their large wasp-like nests of papier-mâché high in tree tops where they are almost impossible to access, however that year they took a liking for our open barn.

We didn't notice anything until a visitor pointed out the, by then football sized, nest high in the roof. S and Mum are both allergic to wasp stings so I volunteered for the removal job on this occasion. Kitted out in three layers, hat, and gloves, and armed with the most powerful wasp spray we could buy, I clambered onto the balcony and reached across towards the nest. At least half a dozen hornets were patrolling their territory so I didn't have long. With a sharp intake of breath, I leaned as far as I could across the balustrade and sprayed a long burst from the can. Then I turned and ran into the house, banging the door behind me and taking a huge gulp of fresh air.

The spray had done its job most efficiently. The nest collapsed inwards before falling to the floor of the barn three metres below in a puff of soggy paper. The hornets were dead, though some of the fat white grubs were still wriggling, safe from the effects of the spray inside their cocoons. I was pleased with my morning's death toll but sad that I couldn't feed the grubs to the chickens due to the poison. A pity as it would have been a real treat for them!

The guest bedroom at the *Casita* is in a sort of annexe to the house, built out into the open barn or *alpendre*. Access is down two steps from the central dining room and through a beautifully stripped and varnished, sweet chestnut brace and ledge door. That doorway is less than five feet high. We had initially decided this was going to be the main bedroom, with its en suite bathroom, but Mum preferred the other room – the 'iris' room, which we were now finishing.

Diary Sunday 27th March Cloudy
Mum went to our local church for Sunday service with Carmen whilst S and I continued working in the Casita. Yet more flooring!
Lunch: Marmalade chicken. Roast potatoes. Orange curd tarts with fruits and ice cream.
Went for a walk leaving Mum frantically repolishing the dining room furniture. That will keep her busy for a while seeing as we are still making such a dust!

Towards the end of the month, we went on our annual road trip. This year we visited Salamanca in the centre of Spain, somewhere Mum had always wanted to go. It was much cooler than earlier in the

CHESTNUT, CHERRY & KIWI FRUIT SPONGE

month but even so we were astonished to return home to snow.

Diary Thursday 31st March Snow am!
Luckily the sun melted it quickly. Hope the fruit buds aren't affected by the cold and glad my tomatoes are still in the sunroom. S having fun trying to rehang the door to the main bedroom as, surprise, the floor isn't level!
Took our kitty, Yoda, to the vets to be spayed 12pm and collected her at 5pm, none the worse for wear. Left her in the kitchen to recover. She seemed to enjoy it, playing happily whilst we walked around her.

Although the snow didn't last, it certainly confirmed that my decision to hold the tomatoes back was the correct one. Even the fruit trees seemed to be fooled by the erratic March weather. That late snow flurry also proved the old proverb was correct. March may have started like a lamb, but it left in a most lion-like way.

APRIL 2016
A tale of two kitties

Please forgive the punny title – I've long been a Dickens fan and couldn't resist. There are actually three kitties in this chapter, though one was long ago and in a different country...

I love animals of all kinds but I happily admit to being a cat freak. As a child I didn't have a pet but my godparents next door had a beautiful long-haired tortie and white she-cat called Snuffy, who I adored. Once I left home and had a place of my own, one of my first actions was to get a cat. At the time, I worked every Sunday cooking dinner in a small nursing home near where I lived in Muswell Hill. The home had a tiny black and white St. James' cat which decided to have her kittens under one of the residents' beds. I fell in love with a jet-black kitten who I called Mister Mistoffelees (I was reading T S Eliot's *Old Possums Book of Practical Cats* at the time).

Clever, quiet, and black to the tip of his bushy tail, Misty was. But small, he was not. I had him castrated as soon as possible at six months and thereafter he grew, and grew, and grew like the eunuch he was. His tiny mother could have fitted under one huge paw and I often wondered in later years, after he had been dubbed 'the panther' by Mum's neighbours, just what his father was.

Misty loved visiting Mum, with the acres of green fields just behind her house which became his

CHESTNUT, CHERRY & KIWI FRUIT SPONGE

playground. In later years we would drive up in our old van, Misty standing happily in the back until we got within two miles of Mum's home whereupon he would start running round in excitement. I don't know what landmark he recognised, or if it was some Ashby scent, but it happened every time.

We'd started letting him loose in the back of the van because he hated the cat carrier so much. The first time I drove up to Mum's from London with Misty as a tiny kitten, he was in a cardboard carrier. That lasted as far as Luton before he'd scratched his way out. He happily sat on the back parcel shelf the rest of the way up the motorway with no problems.

Not long after I got Misty I found out I was seriously allergic to cats. I used to cycle home to Muswell Hill from work at Friern Barnet Psychiatric Hospital and suddenly could not climb the final hill without wheezing and gasping for breath. The doctor said I had asthma and blamed the cat.

"You will have to get rid of it," he said, with a complete lack of understanding.

"I can't do that! It's not the cat's fault."

"It's up to you," shrugged the doctor, writing out a prescription for a Ventolin inhaler.

It was, and Misty stayed with wheezy me through umpteen moves. Then, with a new job involving working away from home more often than I was there, and again now living alone, Mum adopted him.

Misty died, aged 21, the year we moved to Galicia. I had no intention of having a cat here. There was my asthma to consider, plus pets are tying and it was enough to have the chickens and the rabbits to look after. And that's the way we stayed for six years.

Diary Monday 4th April Wet
April showers then! Mum and L into town for shopping and a tin of sardines for the cats. Poor little Yoda needs a treat!

APRIL 2016

S finally got the door hung in the bedroom, though it now opens into the room with the light switch behind it. S says it's fine but it seems a tad awkward to me. Still, what do I know?
Went for a walk in the rain. Very pleasant.

Our village is what I term a 'cat village'.

In Galicia, many villages have hordes of dogs, chained up outside, day and night, summer and winter, barking and howling for all they are worth. A friend of ours was so stressed she bought one of those sonic alarms designed to stop the dogs howling. It didn't work and she eventually got used to the noise.

Our village, on the other hand, only has one dog; a quiet, friendly mongrel who lives at the other end of the single street. What we do have are dozens of cats. Our immediate neighbour Carmen feeds a good half dozen semi-feral cats, and Eusebio can often be spotted with a cat wrapped round his neck as he wanders about.

Clarence came to us, as cats have a tendency to do, one fine June day in 2012.

The first picture I have of him shows a handsome young tomcat, crouched on our stone wall, watching us warily but without fear. He got his name the first time we saw him close up. As I tapped on the kitchen window to him, he looked up, straight into my eyes – or more likely into all of my eyes, as his were crossed. Anyone who remembers *Daktari*, the 70s television series set in a South African safari park, will remember Clarence the cross-eyed lion, though ours is more of a tiger – a silver grey tabby with the bluest of blue eyes and the ears of a boxer.

How could a semi-feral cat survive if he couldn't see straight? How could he know where to pounce? These were questions I pondered, but it was clear he managed somehow as he became a solid bruiser of a tomcat with a tiger striped face, tail, and legs, and

CHESTNUT, CHERRY & KIWI FRUIT SPONGE

thick dense stone-coloured fur. He was almost perfectly camouflaged against our granite walls. One of our neighbours had a number of Siamese cats in their barns at the time, and the blue eyes suggested Clarence had some Siamese DNA in him somewhere.

At first, I would put food out, usually some leftover meat or fish skin, in the open barn-come-garage. Clarence would approach, hissing all the time, until I backed away. Then he would set to devouring his meal. Once finished he would disappear to do cat-things until the next meal.

By 2016 Clarence had been a 'resident' pussycat for three years, though he would still occasionally turn and hiss as I put his food down then look incredibly sheepish when I glared at him, as if he had momentarily forgotten he was not wild anymore.

Diary Wednesday 6th April Hot pm
Paid for our 'sponsored' walk at the bank. Surprisingly easy to use the machine to pay in. Another first for me and technology! S clearing the living room for his next lot of flooring. Chucky doll was ejected from its seat. Tony would be happy. He used to say it was watching him as he worked!
Lunch: Leek and sun-dried tomato risotto torte. Green salad.
First house martins back, and the hoopoe. Brown bunny has kits.
L and S finished off tidying in the Casita then did a circuit, 5km.

The last time we visited Ourense, we'd seen a poster in a café about a charity walk taking place at the end of April. It looked like being an interesting route and was five euros a head to enter, so we did so. It had been a while since we'd walked further than our usual circuit so we needed to get back into 'training'. We'd been walking at least three or four kilometres a day, often finding new routes or enjoying old ones at a different time of the year. Hopefully by the end of the month we'd be fit!

Diary Friday 8th April Early sunshine then clouded over
L sanded most of bedroom floorboards – making sure the door was firmly closed or Mum will need to repolish her dining room furniture, again. S has started on the living room floor, which will be interesting as it's such a weird shape.
Lunch: risotto with sardines, red pepper, sweetcorn (frozen) and 'Galician' pesto of walnuts, parsley and Galician cheese. Rather good. Saved the sardine heads for the cats. Happy moggies!

In September of 2015, while I was still mourning the death of my hand-reared cockerel, Feliz, Clarence had appeared one morning carrying what looked like a scrap of fur. The scrap was dropped onto the ground in front of our gate from whence it began to make a huge wailing sound. It didn't seem possible such a small pair of lungs could make so much noise. Clarence sat quietly waiting for me to understand.

"Okay, so I have to feed her, do I?" I asked him.

He sat silently while the fluff ball stood up, revealing a skinny Clarence look alike with pale blue eyes and a tiger striped face. The Siamese genes were strong in her, with her seal-point colouring and paler body markings. She also had long, silky fur, something I'd not seen in any of our village cats which generally have short, thick coats. A strange creature this one.

I found a spare cat bowl and put them side by side. The kitten dug in, Clarence sitting to one side watching her before starting on his own meal. Yoda, as I soon christened her, finished her meal and edged up to Clarence who moved aside and let her eat his dinner too. With her tiny heart-shaped face

CHESTNUT, CHERRY & KIWI FRUIT SPONGE

and huge pointy ears, she looked just like the Jedi master and Clarence had definitely felt the force.

I was fascinated by the cats' interaction. Our roughty-toughty boy was a bit of a legend in the village. Carmen told me, years before, that he ate kittens. I was on the verge of saying 'but only one at a time' when I remembered the Spanish don't do irony. To be fair, she had told me only that week that he didn't do so any more, so he was obviously considered a reformed character. What she'd have thought seeing him drag Yoda to our gate I dread to think.

Diary Monday 11th April Showers again
First coat of varnish on the bedroom floor. S fitted fixtures, handles, and towel rails in the utility-bathroom.
Lunch: Apricot and mixed nut pilaf, first asparagus spears. Crumble and ice cream.
Long circuit. 8km. Picked some wild flowers (wild daffodils, violets and rock roses) and planted them in Mum's rockery.
Caught a mouse in the loft. Offered it to Clarence but he wasn't interested.

Clarence had never been one for dead, furred, raw food. I still wonder how he'd survived as a feral cat. Yoda, however, was happy to play with the dead mouse for hours, or at least until I took it away before it decomposed on the terrace.

Yoda had quickly made herself at home at *A Casa do Campo* and she clearly adored her father. There was no doubt in my mind that Clarence was her father. When he was home, they would curl up in the cat box together on the terrace or she would drape herself across his massive shoulders on the wooden bread box, licking and grooming him. He returned the favour with a gentleness I'd never seen before. When Clarence was out on one of his visits Yoda would snooze, curled up on one of the chairs on the terrace, or clamber into the vines from where she could launch a surprise attack on the unwary. Although Clarence was by far the bigger, Yoda had sharper claws. They were like needles and honed for maximum damage. She was also the leader of their little two cat gang.

Clarence had always been a bit of a loner. A feral cat for so long, he'd never learnt to play, never miaowed or purred, and never, ever, ventured inside the house. Yoda had no such qualms. She would follow me into the kitchen, talking constantly and rubbing round my legs for attention. She knew she was beautiful and used her feminine wiles any way she could.

One day I had been on the allotment collecting vegetables for lunch. As I came up the path, I noticed the back door was ajar. I pushed open the door and heard a frantic scratching and banging from the attic room. Clarence shot down the stairs and past my legs, giving me a terrified glance as he disappeared outside. A few moments later, Yoda pranced genteelly down the steps, smiling gleefully and miaowing loudly. That she had been the instigator of their little adventure was in no doubt. That she was not the least concerned showed her true character.

Diary Friday 15th April Wet
L repainted Mum's wicker chair and positioned it in the alpendre along with a couple of folding deckchairs, around our new 'coffee table'. Mum wants some proper garden furniture she says but it will do for now. She also says the village cats sleep on the chairs at night, which I have no doubt about. Probably ecstatic for such comfortable surroundings!
L and S moved the furniture into the bedroom and made the bed up. It all fits perfectly. S fitted the

CHESTNUT, CHERRY & KIWI FRUIT SPONGE

lightshade and generally tidied round. Long circuit ending in town for a cola before walking home.

All cat lovers say their cat is the cleverest, funniest, or most beautiful – but Yoda was all three. Unlike her father, she soon learnt to play. Her favourite game involved a walnut which she could hoick into the air and catch double-handed in her front paws. So dextrous was she that I was convinced she was some kind of polydactyl cat, though she had the correct number of toes as far as I could see. She would fling the walnut around the terrace for a while before scoring a 'goal' through one of the drainage holes in the terrace wall. I, her faithful servant, would go round and collect the walnut from the herb bed the other side only to watch her do it again, and again, and again. Who was playing with whom?

Yoda was also fearless.

We have a number of foxes in the area and that year one of the young dog foxes took to visiting our garden looking for easy pickings (and probably cat food). The first thing I noticed missing was the metal cat bowl. Then one of my gardening gloves vanished from my bucket on the terrace. A few days later one of my sandals, left on the terrace steps to dry, was chewed to pieces by morning. I was bemused as to the cause but we were soon to find out.

We were relaxing upstairs in the sunroom one evening when I heard a hissing and squealing from the terrace. Running outside, I discovered the dog fox standing in the middle of our lawn with a very angry kitten facing it, hissing and arching her little back as high as it would go. Her fur was standing on end as she danced around the totally bemused fox. I was concerned that the fox would snap at her but he seemed disinterested in her posturing, trotting away as Yoda hissed and yowled behind him.

I found the bowl and glove some time later, hidden in the ha-ha, or ditch, below our house. The fox tracks through that overgrown area testified to its use as a pathway – though what use a fox might have for those particular items I never discovered.

Diary Wednesday 20th April Sunshine, hot
S cemented the glass brick into the living room 'window' behind where the ham cupboard used to be. With the plastered windowsill and Tony's seat below, it now looks rather smart and beautiful. L sowed french beans, runner beans (St. George) and pea pods on the allotment.
All to Pantón for lunch with Mike and John and friends at restaurant O Castelo.
Back to their house for a chat before shopping in Monforte.
L and S did a quick power walk up the hill to the Merca Rural and back.

By March of that year, it was obvious that Yoda was fully grown. At least she suddenly came on heat, to the delight of the village tomcat population.

Having been unsure of her age because she was so tiny, I'd left it too late to have her spayed. The vet suggested I kept her away from the tomcats until her oestrus cycle had finished, then bring her in. It was not safe to spay her whilst in heat, she said.

Knowing Yoda wouldn't stay indoors, and conscious of my asthma, we set her up in the unused chicken pen. They were still in their winter quarters on the allotment so the top pen was vacant, clean, and filled with straw. Yoda made her disgust obvious from the beginning by miaowing loudly whenever I went near. The rest of the time she was silent and seemed to enjoy rolling round in the dirt floor outside.

One morning, I went to feed her but there was no cat. That chicken pen has narrow chicken mesh all round, dug into the ground and with a skirt below the door to prevent weasels getting in. Nevertheless,

CHESTNUT, CHERRY & KIWI FRUIT SPONGE

Yoda had got out. She hadn't gone far, and I soon found her curled up happily asleep on my garden fleece. When I found her, she looked up and smiled contentedly before slashing my shirt to pieces as I tried to carry her back to her 'prison'.

Luckily Yoda didn't fall pregnant, despite her escapade, and eventually we were able to take her to the vet – a 15-minute journey which lasted a lifetime as she yowled and cried the whole way. When she was released after her operation, the vet sold us a cone collar to prevent her from licking or pulling at her stitches. The poor thing hated that collar which she kept catching sight of out of the corner of her eye.

"Sorry baby, it's for your own good," I soothed.

The first night, Yoda was still groggy so we bedded her down in the kitchen in a box. The next morning, I wandered into the kitchen to find a happy kitty snoozing in her box, collarless. A little searching discovered the offending item behind the *cocina*. It seemed our clever kitty had jammed her head between the bench and the wall, then tugged until the collar came off. She gave me her wicked cat smile. I couldn't bring myself to put the hated contraption back on and she never once pulled at the stitches, which healed perfectly.

Diary Sunday 24th April Sunshine
Up early to get to A Peroxa for our sponsored hike. It seemed rather busy as we circled the tiny town looking for parking. Walked into the main square to find over 600 people milling about, sporting pinned-on bibs. Luckily the organisers were efficient and we were registered and bibbed by 10am.

It was a most enjoyable walk, though I wasn't used to quite so many people on our normal daily wanders. We set off in a bunch through the town and onto a green lane alongside birch trees and vivid emerald fields. As we weaved our way up and down, we passed a *Castro* and other ancient looking stone buildings. The path was narrow, with little room for passing, so we ambled along enjoying the scenery as we clambered down stone steps towards the river. At times we came to a complete standstill as the crowds backed up, but eventually we popped out onto a village road. Here we wound downhill, passing derelict stone houses and yellow-painted modern ones until we reached the river Miño itself.

The walk alongside the river was pleasant and shaded, the sunshine having long since heated up the pathway in the open areas.

We followed the river into Os Peares, the village of the three rivers, passing by the railway station with its collection of Victorian buildings and walked as far as the river Búbal where we had swum the previous summer. We expected that to be the end of the walk as there were people milling about and organisers taking numbers. But no.

The sinuous line of walkers crawled up an almost vertical track towards the sports centre, perched on a hill high above the town. There we collapsed in a heap to await our coach back to the starting point. I couldn't help reflecting on the fact that a sports lover in Os Peares would have to be fit to reach the sports hall in the first place.

When our coach finally arrived, we all piled on for the winding road back to A Peroxa. At one especially narrow defile we met another coach coming the opposite direction to collect the next lot of walkers. The two vehicles couldn't pass. The second coach refused to give way despite having marginally more space to manoeuvre so our driver, huffing and puffing as he did so, reversed and squeezed into the rock wall so hard I felt sure he left paint scrapings behind.

CHESTNUT, CHERRY & KIWI FRUIT SPONGE

By the time we reached A Peroxa it was 1.30pm. The organisers were kindly handing out goody bags of sandwiches and orange juice, but it was my dinner time. We had left Mum that morning to make her own dinner so we stopped at the Rio Búbal, a hotel and restaurant on the way home, for a very well-deserved steak and chips.

Diary Wednesday 27th April Hot in the sun
S laying the floorboards in the living room around the new wood-burning stove and marble plinth. L sowed pumpkin, courgette and squash seeds, then carrots, leeks and basil in the afternoon.
Lunch: Roast squash, parsnips, carrot, onion, and red pepper with pesto dressing. Egg custards with cherries. Yum!
S put Carmen's roof tiles back on her barn where the cats have knocked them off.
Both walked up to the next village and back to keep in shape!
Drinks in Taboada.

It was Yoda who gave Clarence his voice. She was so vocal that our previously silent tomcat started to copy her, and eventually we heard him purr for the very first time. Often at morning tea break, S would sit with a cat either side of him vying for his attention and purring loudly as he tickled their ears. Clarence seemed as surprised as us with this purring phenomenon but once found, his voice remained.

Beautiful and clever Yoda was only with us for 18 months. A cat who was virtually never at ground level – much preferring the tops of trees or a comfortable chair, and who hardly ever left the confines of our garden, was run over just outside our gate. A gate leading to a tiny road which sees maybe four cars a day.

Our feisty feral tomcat, Clarence, we lost to kidney failure the very week I was editing this

APRIL 2016

chapter. He would have been around eleven years old. Losing Clarence made me think about all the animals we have lost over the years, both those mentioned in this book and beyond.

Whether they were with us for a few short weeks, like Feliz the orphan chick; a few months, like beautiful Yoda; or almost ten years, like our patriarch cockerel Buzz Lightyear and our handsome cross-eyed tomcat, Clarence – each and every one of them was special to us.

I'd like to dedicate this chapter to all those animals everywhere who have crossed the rainbow bridge – thank you for enriching our lives in so many ways.

MAY 2016
A home of her own

May 2016 started off deliciously hot and sunny. It was so warm that S reconnected the solar water heating at our house, and I was surprised how quickly the hot water tank in the loft began to heat up. It was also prime planting time, so I was busy in the allotment when not working on the *Casita*.

I put up the stakes for my tomatoes, sowed late brassicas (cabbage and swede) and planted out peppers in the polytunnel where I hoped they would be safe from any further frosts. It was so hot and dry that first week in May that I was already watering the vegetable plot daily.

S, in the meantime, was laying the new sweet chestnut floorboards in the final room (for now), the living room. It was a tricky room because of the odd angles. There was Tony's seat in one corner, and the marble hearth at the other end necessitating much cutting and measuring of boards. As S laid floorboards at one side, I followed on sanding the ones he had finished. It worked well, our team effort, and made the whole job much more streamlined.

Diary Wednesday 4th *May Hot, 27°C on terrace.*
Prepped lunch, made cakes, and picked veg. First broad beans for lunch and first peas from the polytunnel. Showed Mum how to mortar the back wall of the Casita barn. She wants to help so S set her up with a bucket of cement, trowel, and stool

MAY 2016

to sit on plus another bucket full of small stones to fill any holes. Left her wearing her sunhat and happily poking the mortar in the holes.
Lunch: Tortilla with bacon. Salad of fresh broad beans, fresh raw peas, sun-dried tomatoes, pumpkin seeds and mixed leaves from the polytunnel. Feels like summer is on the way.
Into town in the evening for drinks. Still showing 21°C on the pharmacy thermometer at 10pm.

I was a bit premature thinking summer had arrived. I should have known that Galicia is nothing if not erratic when it comes to weather, especially spring weather. It started raining the following day, and by the weekend the steady drizzle had turned to gales.

On the Saturday there was a fiesta at the Club Nautico where S had his stag do almost six years earlier. The club had changed hands at least twice since then. Although the setting is beautiful, it is too far from any town to be profitable year-round. Even in summer, the dammed section of the river Miño which forms the reservoir often sinks too low for easy access to the slipway with boats, the mainstay of the club's income. Next to the boat club itself is a large hostal complete with solar roof panels and stunning views.

Our friend Jorge had tried to persuade me to apply to the council to run the place and I had toyed, very briefly, with the idea of running a cookery school there with my friend. I didn't really want to have a full-time job to be perfectly honest. I loved my busy life but my hours were my own, dictated by the weather rather than a timetable. If we wanted to take a day off to explore, or laze about by the municipal pool in summer, we could. I declined my friend's persuasions.

The fiesta was a great idea though. We'd invited some friends along and we all ate at our local

CHESTNUT, CHERRY & KIWI FRUIT SPONGE

restaurant in Taboada, Bar Mencia, before driving the few miles to the river.

By the time we arrived it had been raining a while. There was a large marquee set up on the grass with benches inside and a long bar. The grass was trampled and sodden underfoot and we watched in amazement as the giant lorry for the evening's 'orchestra' skidded and eventually bogged down in the mud outside. It had to be pulled out by a tractor (of which there is always one handy in Galicia) and I wondered how he was ever going to get back up the waterlogged slope to the road.

The entertainment started with one of our local music troops.

Galician dance and music is in the folk tradition and some of the 'instruments' were agricultural tools such as hoes and forks. I asked Kath to translate some of the words they were singing.

"I'm going to plant my potatoes. I'm planting my potatoes now…" she intoned.

"You are kidding?"

"No, a lot of Galician songs are about agriculture."

"I guess!"

Soon I forgot to worry about the words as the music transported me and had my feet twitching. Suddenly the group split apart and started to drag spectators into the circle. Kath was whisked away, grabbing my hand at the last minute to ensure I had to follow her. As I whirled and laughed, I noticed even my reluctant hubby had been coerced onto the 'dance floor' as someone began a conga line. It was great fun and warmed us up nicely. The weather was soon, if not forgotten then at least ignored, as we chatted, danced and supped beer and vino under the rain drenched canopy. By the time we left at 8pm we were content; our boots only slightly squelching, and our clothes gently steaming.

MAY 2016

On the Sunday, S and I went for our customary walk after lunch. The weather was fine when we started, the sky an intense blue. By the time we were at the furthest point from home, it was hammering it down. My hair was plastered to my head and my shoes squelched. I think the locals at that village thought we were weird... then again, they'd probably already heard of us.

The rain continued all that week. I put up bean poles in the rain, planted crops in the rain, cut the grass at the *Casita* in the rain, and hid from the rain sanding the floorboards in the living room.

Diary Thursday 12th May Wet
S off to Lugo to collect the worktop for the utility-bathroom. L sanded the final floorboards in the living room and swept up.
After lunch, S connected the water heater and the electric cooker.

The damp weather did mean we were forging ahead inside the *Casita*.

We had ordered the worktop for the utility-bathroom the previous day. It was 2.4 metres in length and 60 centimetres wide. Even our Ruby wouldn't fit that size load with passengers too, so S had to collect it alone. We'd bought a stainless-steel sink unit to fit into the worktop and planned to fit shelves and a cupboard below to create useful storage.

Fitting the wooden framework for the worktop run and storage shelving was not as easy as it should have been. As usual, the oddly angled walls in the *Casita* caused problems. In this case we needed space for Mum's washing machine to fit in the corner of the room. The only place was behind the door but the wall there is a rather acute angle, meaning it was an almost impossible task to squash it in.

CHESTNUT, CHERRY & KIWI FRUIT SPONGE

We only found out just how impossible when we had to pull the washing machine out some years later after it developed a leak. Like a ship in a bottle, it was suddenly bigger than the space it occupied. It took us an hour of manoeuvring to inch the thing out so we could see the pipework. Probably not one of our better design ideas. But in fairness there wasn't much choice.

Diary Friday 13th May Drizzle
Cleaned up in the living room again. It takes a while for all the dust to settle and I don't want any bits on my varnished floor. S fitted a new ceiling inside the dining room cupboard so the woodworm dust won't fall onto Mum's crockery.
Lunch: Cod, chips and peas. Apple pancake and honey.
Bathnight. To the swimming pool via the paint shop for yet more varnish.

The chap in our local paint shop thinks I'm strange. (Yes, another one.) I buy so many tins of varnish he must think we drink it. He once asked me how many coats I used.

"Three," I replied.

His eyebrows shot up. "*¿Tres capas?*"

"Yes, for a floor, it needs three coats. I want it to be hardwearing," I replied, amused.

"And how many floors have you?" he asked.

"Two houses now," I laughed.

Every time I visited afterwards, I would take photos in to show him our progress. I don't think he had ever sold so many five litre tins of varnish to one individual. I did once suggest a discount from Titan, the varnish company, at which point he discounted the two tins I'd just bought. He is no doubt quite disappointed we didn't buy more houses.

MAY 2016

Our local building suppliers must be as disappointed as I am, now that S says he is hanging up his building hat forever. My hints to buy number four, next to the *Casita*, have gone unheeded and my hubby is enjoying his rather late retirement, albeit one with plenty of projects in it.

Diary Sunday 15th May Hot pm
The firewood arrived while we were in bed... on a Sunday! Spent most of morning barrowing it out of the way. At least we will be ready for next winter.
Lunch: Pork heart, sausages, and mash. Creamed spinach (Carmen's). Lemon curd sponge.
L painted the second coat of varnish on the living room floor leaving S to barrow wood in peace haha.

We also increased the business for our local firewood merchant once *A Casita* was up and running. Before, we would buy three tractor loads a year to service all the wood-burners at *A Casa do Campo*. Once Mum moved into the *Casita*, this doubled. It also doubled our workload of course as we have twice the amount of firewood to barrow and stack each year.

S generally stacks our firewood himself as he can take his time and get it how he wants (extremely neat and squared off). The *Casita* is different – the only place to dump the load is on the track past the house. Although it's not a main thoroughfare, that track is access for our neighbours and their tractor, so we need to move the wood as quickly as possible. It usually takes us a day to barrow and stack the wood when it arrives. It would be ideal if we had Workawayers for wood-stacking days but delivery rarely seems to coincide with us having help. It keeps us fit, though.

CHESTNUT, CHERRY & KIWI FRUIT SPONGE

Diary Monday 16th May Sunny and warm
Planted out the final 25 tomatoes on the allotment. 58 in all.
Lunch: Rabbit and pork burgers with apricots and olives. Rice, tomato sauce, peapods (first huge haul) and asparagus. Homemade Spanish flan
L sanded and revarnished the living room floor. Final coat. S fitted the new worktop in the bathroom-utility. Another two rooms almost finished.

That was the end of my varnishing for the moment. Now we just had to wait for it to dry hard and cure. I had learnt quite a bit during my mammoth varnishing task. The most important was to wear a hat...

I had been carefully varnishing the wooden surrounds in front of the *cocina* housing one day when I swung my pony tail out of the way, inadvertently dipping it into the varnish tin. As I turned, I trailed varnish across the kitchen floor.

"Oh, great!"

I ran out of the *Casita*, squeezing as much varnish from my hair as I could, leaving an easily followed golden trail along the track. In our barn where we keep the cleaning products, I grabbed the turpentine bottle and lathered it generously into my sticky hair.

Luckily the hosepipe had been still attached to the well, not yet removed for the winter. I took the bottle of turpentine and one of shampoo and spent the next 20 minutes alternating between the two and rinsing my hair using the hose. Eventually, I felt the varnish had probably all dissolved and my hair no longer felt sticky. It was particularly shiny, though, and had a most interesting aroma, which took days to wear off. I was even more reluctant than normal to allow anyone to smoke near me, fearing my strawberry locks would go up in flames.

MAY 2016

Diary Thursday 19th May Hot
All to town for shopping and tea in Bar Scala.
L plastered the edges where the wall and floor meet in the living room while S filled any gaps and generally tidied the room.
Second load of leña had arrived when we got back from town so S spent the afternoon barrowing firewood again. I bowed out, claiming important business elsewhere.
Enjoyed our evening swim and sauna!

We went swimming a day early that week as Friday was yet another fiesta – our local *Papeiros* fiesta. Last year we had shared Luis' family meal. This time we sat in the large marquee, erected for the purpose, with dozens of our *vecinos*. It had been another hot day and the temperature was hovering around 28°C in the afternoon. This meant there was no danger of freezing that evening in the canvas-sided marquee on the market square. There was however a rather unexpected danger – from plastic cutlery.

This year the giant paella was supplemented by barbecued beef – specifically, beef skirt or *falda*. This cut is used in Britain for stews or braising: long cooking renders the connective tissue silky and tender. Galicians tend to use skirt on the barbecue which can leave it a little tough to my mind. Galicians also like large chunks of meat. Instead of the chef cutting the meat into strips, each person was handed a fist-sized piece on a flimsy plastic plate together with a plastic knife and fork.

Have you ever tried to cut a well-charred slab of beef with a plastic knife? My neighbour to my right at the long table was muttering to himself when a sliver of something white shot past my nose.

"¡*Perdone!*" he shouted as I ducked instinctively. In his right hand he was brandishing the handle of his demised plastic utensil. "These knives are *fatal*," he complained.

CHESTNUT, CHERRY & KIWI FRUIT SPONGE

I made an effort with my piece of plastic before sticking my hand in my pocket to retrieve my penknife. To my left, S had done the same. All around the table, knives were flicked open and meat cut into bite sized pieces. The same knife was then used to ferry the meat to the mouth. To an observer we must have looked like a medieval banquet. It only needed some bones to throw to the town dogs, loitering hopefully, for the authenticity to be complete.

I must point out once more that carrying a penknife or a hunting knife on one's person is perfectly normal in Galicia and I have never heard of a knife fight or a stabbing taking place locally. And they are much more useful than a plastic knife for attacking *falda*.

The paella was much easier to shovel in with our plastic forks, though Mum wasn't keen on the giant prawns leering up at her. We quickly moved them to our plates and collected the discarded heads for our chickens, who fight for the privilege of eating our leftovers. The whole meal; paella, beef, bread and lashings of local red wine cost 7€ a head. The music afterwards was of course free - the dancing was the entertainment.

Galegos are, almost without exception, excellent salsa dancers. They twirl and step as if born to it - which they probably are. Even young children join in, taking a partner and twirling with the best of them. We enjoy watching and I mentally give out my rosettes for the best couple. There is one local couple who 'win' my rosette most years. They are so in tune with each other that they never miss a beat, but I am fascinated by their facial expressions which seem to be of disinterest and boredom. Instead of smiling into each other's eyes as they salsa around the floor, they stare over the other's shoulder into middle distance as if they want to be anywhere but here.

MAY 2016

That particular night we had a new contender for my rosette. An elderly man in a battered trilby was dancing alone near to the stage. He twisted and circled, did Michael Jackson moon walks and break dancing. It was all most bizarre, and most entertaining.

We of course avoided the floor.

When I met S, I was amazed to find another person who danced like me – on the rare occasions that he allows himself to be persuaded. We cleared the dance floor on a memorable evening at a local pub in England, and our single outing in Galicia is still talked about some 13 years on.

You see we both need a lot of space, and I mean a *lot* of space. No dancing round bags or genteel steps for us: we jump and bounce and windmill our arms, and generally cause mayhem. It's great fun but best taken very occasionally.

Mum and Dad were great ballroom dancers in their day. I suggested Mum accompany one of the old chaps in a turn round the floor that warm spring night, but she sadly declined.

Diary Sunday 22nd May Sun pm, warm
L made lunch after scrummy boiled eggs and soldiers. Promised Mum she could still have Sunday boiled eggs with us after she moves to live in the Casita.
Painted the living room walls together. L cut in, and S rollered. Malva suave, whatever that is. Looks very nice. Cleaned up the speckles from the floor then all to lunch with Kath and Jorge.

We were now racing to the finish with our work on the *Casita* and it was nice to have the time to visit with friends and to eat out once more.

We had just sat down in the restaurant when in walked my Bryan Ferry look alike. I hadn't seen 'Bryan' since a memorable party in town some five

CHESTNUT, CHERRY & KIWI FRUIT SPONGE

years earlier. He really was the spitting image of a young Roxy Music lead singer, down to the long dark hair and the chiselled features. On this occasion he was accompanied by his wife and daughter.

I nudged Kath and inclined my head towards the door.

"Wow, he's a dead ringer for…"

"Love?" I mumbled.

"Bryan Ferry," replied Kath, grinning at me. "He is cute though. Wonder if he can sing?"

"That's what I said last time we saw him."

I explained to Kath how he was serving up the food at a fiesta and what a fabulous dancer he was. And how I hadn't noticed his tight bum at all while he was strutting his stuff, honest!

Bryan and family sat down behind us. Kath and I were still giggling when Jorge decided to explain everything to the bemused Galicians behind us.

"Who?" asked Galician Bryan.

Obviously British 80s pop was not popular in Galicia – or our Bryan was too young. Quick as a flash, though, his daughter was on Google finding some early Ferry photos which showed our imaginations weren't lying.

Sadly, Galician Bryan said he couldn't sing a note, and his voice when he spoke was nothing like the silky deep real deal. It was a good giggle, though, and I still thought he could make a killing on the circuits.

Mum loved going out and enjoyed our *menús del dia* as much as we did. She was a favourite of everyone; shopkeepers, our friends and neighbours, and of course the local bars.

On that Sunday, we dropped Mum back home before setting off on a new walk.

From Taboada we had seen signs for the *Ruta de Fuente Mouros*, or Mouros fountain route. This turned out to be a glorious walk along narrow tracks through chestnut woods. Down a steep slope

MAY 2016

covered in leaves, with the spring flowers blooming at its margins, the woods opened to a clearing. In that clearing was a small fountain with a water wheel created from an old bicycle wheel. The water was pure and clear and tasted delicious after a walk in the sunshine. Through a gateway nearby was an old mill which begged to be used for a picnic one day. The route climbed back up to Taboada, coming out at the top end of town in the village of San Pedro with its grand *Pazo* and church.

> *Diary Monday 23rd May Sunny*
> *L and S moved Mum's furniture into the living room then L and Mum unpacked what felt like 100s of boxes of ornaments and knick-knacks. S was cleverly otherwise occupied in the bathroom-utility.*
> *Lunch: Meat & 'tater pie. Peapods and asparagus. Sponge with lemon curd sauce.*
> *L and Mum continued emptying boxes! S mowed the lawns and hung Mum's pictures.*

Once all her knick-knacks were in place, Mum announced that she would stay overnight at the *Casita* that week.

On Saturday the 28th of May, we finished fitting the utility sink and had a grand turn on of the hot water. We had decided on a 50-litre electric hot water heater for the *Casita*. There is little attic space near to the bathroom for a large tank and this was a cheap and easily fitted option. The little tank was surprisingly efficient and soon heated more than enough water for a shower. The weather had regressed to heavy rain that day so Mum made her first meal at the house for us all – sandwiches and tea.

It was perfect sitting in the cosy kitchen with the *cocina* lit, our backs to the warmth of the chimney, listening to the rain on the skylight windows in the

CHESTNUT, CHERRY & KIWI FRUIT SPONGE

dining room and remembering all the hard work we and our Workawayers had put in. It had been tough at times, but oh so worth it.

We found Mum's bedding and aired her quilt. The following evening, we again adjourned to the *Casita* for a scrabble evening and a few vinos.

When we walked home, Mum remained, locking her door behind us. She slept the night away and said that, although she had enjoyed staying with us, it was lovely to wake up in a home of her own again.

JUNE 2016
Full circle

So, that was it. We had done the almost impossible and turned a derelict ruin into a cosy home for a soon to be 85-year-old. By June 2016, Mum was living full-time in the *Casita*. And what a different little cottage it was…

In place of the mouldering, soot-stained kitchen, she had a warm airy room with a wood-burning range cooker, a new corner sink and a safely capped, but unused, well. The dark bedroom, with its rain-soaked, dangling ceiling and man-trap floor, was transformed into a beautiful light room. That bedroom had a sort-of-stable door to the steps and balcony outside, and a lovely iris window at the other end.

There was a new bathroom. With a large, level access shower, complete with tiled wave design on its walls, a recently installed worktop and sink, and hot water, it was a far cry from the long, dark, ivy strewn 'ironing' room.

The living room had Mum's furniture and knick-knacks in it and only needed a new sofa, once she found one she liked. The view from this room across the fields to the river was lovely. Before, that room had huge holes in the floor and ceiling, no view at all through the bramble infested window, and rats living in the old bedding.

CHESTNUT, CHERRY & KIWI FRUIT SPONGE

The dining room was (and still is) my favourite room in the *Casita*. With that soaring ceiling; skylights which let in the summer sunshine and reflect rainbows from Mum's crystal pendant, hanging below the roof light; and with Mum's old oak furniture, it is perfect. And could not look more different from the old, low-ceilinged, dim central room we first saw in June 2014.

June 2016 dawned hot. It was 29°C outdoors and the new *cocina* was not needed in the kitchen. Neither was the new wood-burner in the living room. But it didn't matter because Mum was home.

Although we had 'finished' *A Casita* for the moment, we decided to carry on inviting Workawayers to our home. We enjoyed their easy company and there is always plenty of outdoor work to do here over the summer. Mark arrived on a day when the mercury hit 32°C, and fit in with our little household immediately.

Diary Friday 3rd June Escorchio!
L prepped lunch while S did some small jobs in the Casita, like screwing Mum's radio shelf on in the kitchen and fixing wood beading along the worktop. Collected our new Workawayer. Mark is probably the most polite chap I've met. Everything is Ma'am and Sir and nothing is too much trouble. Love him already!
Lunch: Sardine and pesto pie (good, huge) with chips and pea pods. Mum's bread and butter pudding.
Set up Mum's TV and DVD player. Of course, without an aerial it will be DVDs only. Still, we have plenty of those. Mum was worried it would only play in Spanish now. Reassured her... I think!
Got Mark cutting the grass on the allotment for me – by hand using the hoe as I have no power over there. Must buy a petrol or battery strimmer one day.

JUNE 2016

Bathnight. Booked Mum onto imserso for the coming year at the travel agency in town.

Getting Mum onto the imserso programme was another tick for our 'completed' column. We had failed the previous year, trying to do it ourselves online. This time we happily paid the travel agency their miniscule fee to ensure it happened.

Mark was a young, 20-something, American lad: very good looking and with that Deep South politeness that I never hear elsewhere. He was with us for two weeks and immediately got stuck in helping.

Having Mark around meant we could complete a few other things; like mortaring the wall behind the house, which Mum had started but got quickly bored with, and of course cut all the elephant-eye height grass.

Diary Sunday 5th June
Eggs a tad hard. Due to so many in the pan according to the chef!
Kath and Jorge arrived for lunch and S and Jorge attempted to undo the door to Mum's Welsh dresser which seems to have lost its key somewhere en route!
Lunch: Mixed tapas. Pork stew with olives. Lemon magic sponge, and chocolate tart.
Chatted 'til about 6pm then left Mum to wash up while we took Mark on a walk to see the countryside.

Signs of summer were everywhere that week and the scent of newly-cut grass mingled with our usual aromas of eau-de-cow and chopped firewood. We took Mark on our usual circuit.

We are the last house in our tiny village. If one turns left out of our gate, the tarmac village road peters out to packed earth, winding beneath the

CHESTNUT, CHERRY & KIWI FRUIT SPONGE

boughs of ancient chestnut trees. In summer these trees provide welcome shade and I love to gaze at them, wondering what tales they could tell in their 200-year-old lives.

A few hundred metres along the track, it turns sharply left over a small stream. In spring and autumn there is a tiny waterfall here. In winter this waterfall becomes a torrent, often washing away the track itself. In summer, it is no more than a trickle. Beyond is my favourite tree – a huge oak which stands regally at the top of the slope, alone and aloof.

As the track twists again there are two red, square markers partly buried in the ground. This is where the new motorway bridge will begin. Thankfully in the 14 years since we heard the devastating news, no more has been done. Those markers are almost invisible now and I remain optimistic that the necessary money will never reach its destination. (As I write this in summer 2021, I recently heard on the grapevine that the motorway project has been suspended indefinitely due to a lack of funds. I can't help but ponder whether I have at long last found an actual 'Brexit' benefit!)

Beyond the red markers, the chestnut woods give way to low rocky cliffs on the right and a steep-sided valley of birch and gangly oak trees on the left. Down beyond the trees is the river which runs along the bottom of our valley. And down a track to the left is the second water mill on that *rio*, now with a brand-new roof, though it is sadly not a working mill.

Beyond the mill turn off, the vista opens up again with fields either side of the track and, in winter, a view back towards our house – the red chimney of *A Casa do Campo* the only thing visible through the trees.

The fresh scent of pine heralds a dense wood on the left, the ground below the conifers thick with needles. Further still, the track crosses a concrete bridge over yet another stream before climbing to the little village above us.

It's a pleasant walk around the village with its stone-built church and granite houses. The views from this height are spectacular on a clear day and the water in the village trough is fresh and cool.

The tarmac village road crosses back over the *rio* as the latter passes beneath. Just beyond, a quiet track turns off to the left, paralleling the river on the south side of our little valley. The huge field on the right used to have the best display of field mushrooms I've ever seen in autumn. Sadly, it was ploughed up some years ago and they have not yet reappeared, though I remain hopeful.

At the top of the hill on that June afternoon, the wayside was full of gorse, broom, and heather. In spring there are bright flowers along the centre of the track, and in autumn the colchicums, or autumn crocuses, flourish here. Further along, below the chestnut woods, woodland spring flowers such as primroses and wild daffodils are followed by tall stately asphodels in early summer.

From the top of a large sloped field, we could finally see our village, laid out below us across the river. *A Casita* was to the right of the group, the skylight windows glinting in the sunshine. Our own *A Casa do Campo* was off to the left, screened from view by a line of too tall eucalyptus trees.

From here we made our way downhill through the long dry grass of the *finca*, in need of a trim in the late spring, back to the *rio* and the first water mill – the one we can see from our house. That house sits some 30 metres higher up the valley. As we clambered up the final, and steepest, section of the track, I crossed the stone stile to the right to check my tomatoes on the allotment. The others climbed the stone steps, inset into the high boundary wall on the left, to the house and a welcoming cup of tea.

CHESTNUT, CHERRY & KIWI FRUIT SPONGE

Our circuit is a pleasant, hour and a half, amble with plenty of time to photograph and observe nature all around us. It reminds us how lucky we are.

That week, I planted out my melons and squashes, picked my mangetout and asparagus, and day-dreamed on the allotment whilst peering over the wall across Carmen's *huerta* to the back of Mum's new house. It was less than 50 metres as the crow flies from my allotment to the back wall of the *Casita,* and slightly over 100 metres by road to the front door.

Everything was perfect.

Diary Wednesday 8th June Even hotter
Decommissioned the cocina at A Casa do Campo. Can't bear to be in the kitchen with the heat, though I shall miss it as ever. Finished the tiny mosaic splashback tiles in the utility-bathroom and S put in the shaver socket we bought in England all that time ago.

The following day we took Mark on an outing to Lugo. I never tire of showing visitors our wonderful Roman city and on a sunny June day it couldn't be bettered. Mum dragged us around furniture shops until she found a sofa she liked for her living room, whilst my back enjoyed sitting in some deliciously comfortable reclining chairs. We had cold drinks outside the bars, still stunned by the size of some of the tapas even after nine years in Galicia.

At one bar we were presented with a slate platter with four hamburgers on it.

"But we are eating lunch soon," I said to our charming waiter.

"This is only an *aperitivo*," he replied.

Saturday 11th June Hot
Taboada had one of its 'one off' festivals today – a beer festival which seemed to consist of just three

JUNE 2016

stalls by the time we arrived mid-afternoon, all selling beer more expensive and less flavourful than the stuff we normally buy in Bar Scala. As Mum doesn't like beer anyway, we retired to said bar for further refreshment.

That evening was another of our local village fiestas. As it is a pretty walk on a sunny evening, we took Mark along to experience a country festival.

Another tiny village which sits at the top of the hill on the south side of our valley, San Xulian has a miniature village square and space for a well-manoeuvred *orchestra* lorry to park. There was the usual bar set up for food and drink, and neighbours mingled, chatting and mainly ignoring the poor band who were playing to the children running round in front of the stage and dancing to the beat.

The walk there is once more uphill, through woodland and past green fields full of wild flowers. The moon was only a crescent that weekend, but full darkness doesn't really descend until after 11pm in midsummer so we could see enough to follow the strobe lights ahead of us and orientate ourselves by the sounds of the salsa-playing band.

Unfortunately, we arrived at the village just in time for the interval between bands. That interval was filled by comedy acts, the like of which I hadn't seen since my schooldays' revues – with dressing up and incomprehensible in-jokes. It was so bad it was hilarious and I was rather chuffed that I even 'got' a couple of the jokes, dreadful though they were. We drank wine, ate grilled meats and laughed together until almost 3am. By then we adjudged Mark had experienced enough Galician culture for one day and walked home in the warmth of a summer's night.

In between fiestas that weekend, we were all trying to fit that washing machine of Mum's into

CHESTNUT, CHERRY & KIWI FRUIT SPONGE

the impossible space in the bathroom. It was an interesting exercise and kept us amused for the whole two days.

Diary Tuesday 14th June Cloud and drizzle
...obviously now the cocina is off. Decided on a trip to Ourense pools as it's not gardening weather. Ramón met us in the Maria Andrea for lunch which turned into a tussle when Mum insisted on paying for everyone.
Lovely afternoon whiling away time sitting in the thermals and pondering on the meaning of life.

While S was busy cementing glass bricks into the cat escape hole in the utility-bathroom, I decided to cement up some of the wall in the second bedroom. Although we didn't plan to do anything with this room in the near future, it did need some serious TLC to make it weather proof over winter.

The second bedroom was tiny, but had an en suite bathroom when we bought the house: an en suite which had been demolished and its ancient fittings removed by Roy and Francesca so we had a dry storage space for Mum's furniture.

Our two Workawayers had also removed the bathroom wall tiles. This may not have been quite such a good idea as we found the external wall of the bathroom was one of those wonderful Galician 'miracle' walls. These are constructed of a single thickness of thin bricks, full of holey chambers, stood on end. It is a miracle of engineering that they stand upright at all. Most are held together by cement render; this one was held together by ceramic tiles. Removing the tiles had left just the measly, thin brick wall. But worse still, a run for the bathroom pipework had been chiselled into the five-centimetre-thick brick. This meant that in places the 'wall' was a whole half a centimetre thin: a swift kick would have brought the lot crashing down.

JUNE 2016

I filled in bits of the wall with cement render to hold it together until we could rebuild it. I was no Tony, but the whole of this weedy wall would eventually be demolished and rebuilt in plasterboard so it just needed to last until then.

Diary Thursday 16th June Wet all day
Mark shelled walnuts for me (always a good rainy-day job) while Mum made him a Roman toga for Arde Lucus, from an old bed sheet and lots of imagination.
S is back in our Big Barn cutting laths for the plasterboard ceiling. L back in the kitchen making ice cream and cakes. Life continues onwards.

We had gone full circle.

That weekend we took Mark to the Roman festival of Arde Lucus in Lugo. It was exactly one year since Mum had moved to Galicia to live amid chaos. And almost two years since we had bought *A Casita do Campo* on a sunny June morning, just two days after viewing it with the lovely owners, Pepe and Mercedes. With the help of our veritable rainbow army of Workawayers from all over the globe we had turned an abandoned derelict cottage into a cosy living space for a soon to be 85-year-old.

There was still work to do on the *Casita*: there was that second bedroom with en suite to create, overlooking the *alpendre* from its own balcony; and there was the dressing room to finish. But for now, we returned to our own Big Barn project.

Our sofas had been squatting, swathed in plastic, for over two years: and were destined to remain that way for a further four years until spring 2020. That year, as Covid raged through the world, we finally moved into our stunning Big Barn. It is a large, full height space with a cosy snug, a dining area, and my own writing space on the mezzanine, where I am sitting now, typing this. Completing the Big Barn brought our self-renovation of *A Casa do Campo* to an end only 13 years after buying it on that spring day in May 2007.

A Casita do Campo was finally decreed finished in February 2018, with the completion of the dressing room and the balcony off the second bedroom. That guest bedroom was inaugurated by Mum's sister, Aunty Jan, when she visited in May of that year.

We totally rebuilt that second bedroom, although in the image of the original. The weedy brick wall was demolished and replaced by a sturdy double thickness, insulated, plasterboard wall. We moved the doorway to the middle of the outside wall to allow a bed to be fitted in the far corner where the original door had been. S cleverly designed a snazzy built-in headboard which takes advantage of the angle of the wall to provide shelving behind on one side. There is a large window at the side of the bed and the new door opens out onto the remade balcony. This space overlooks the *alpendre* and has a couple of chairs and a small coffee table for guests to sit and enjoy the peace of our little village. There are two of our skylight windows in this area: one in the bedroom above the dressing table, and the second in the newly rebuilt en suite.

We had fun designing that bathroom. We needed space in the bedroom for Mum's second dressing table: one I remember helping Dad to strip down and repolish many years ago and which held special memories We also needed space in the bathroom to fit a shower. That needed to be at least 70 centimetres wide, and it had to be at the opposite end to the chest of drawers due to the slope of the roof. The doorway was 69 centimetres wide – the old original outside door reused, cleaned and varnished. The total width of the room was 210 centimetres. With the three 'set' widths, we were a centimetre short.

JUNE 2016

S, brilliant mathematician that he is, managed to set the doorway at a very slight angle, just enough to fit a quart into our pint pot.

The en suite has a large walk-in shower, WC, vanity unit and tall free-standing cupboard. The shower is tiled in white with stripes of cream and moss green – the second batch of tiles our friends Al and Debs had donated to us.

The old smoke room is now a fully furnished walk-in dressing room. Mum had a large wardrobe of her own from England and together we bought a second, three-door flat-pack, one locally for her winter clothes. That was possibly a mistake. The thing had to be made lying down for some bizarre reason, but once flat on the floor it took up the entire remaining floor space in the room. There was no way to lift it upright.

S, as I've possibly mentioned, is good at spatial puzzles. He tried every which way – but the sloping ceiling, the low central beam, and that one metre block of stone which comprises the back of the old well, defeated us.

At one point we had the wardrobe entirely blocking the doorway, unable to go one way or the other. We told Mum it had to stay there, to her horror. S finally decided it was possible to get the thing upright if we lifted it sideways over the stone back of the well. The wardrobe was incredibly heavy, but as ever our Workawayers at the time got stuck in. Between the four of us we had it fitting within a few minutes – I just hope it never needs moving again.

We continue to have Workawayers to help around the garden and allotment, and enjoy their company. In 2019, S and I went on our own Workaway trip around the world: from Japan to Singapore to Australia to Chile, for his 70th birthday and my 55th. We enjoyed it so much we repeated the experience, journeying to New Zealand in spring 2020 just

CHESTNUT, CHERRY & KIWI FRUIT SPONGE

before Covid hit the world. And that, as they say, is another story...

Mum loves Galicia, and our small part of it. In July 2016 we had a recreation of our wedding breakfast at Bar Mencia for Mum's 85th Birthday. We invited family, and our friends here in Galicia, for a fabulous afternoon of eating, drinking, and laughing. That August, we took her to the Viking festival in Catoira where we all stayed in a most 'interesting' motel where there were strange comings and goings all night, and where both Mum and I could have made a few 'shillings' had we known. Mum was rather bemused by the long, narrow 'shower caps' in the mirrored bathroom though.

Since she arrived in Galicia, Mum has partaken in our pensioner holidays, fancy dress parties, and more fiestas than I care to remember. This July, 2021, we had a delicious lunch for 12 of our and Mum's friends at the lovely restaurant Pitón, near to Ourense. We sat together on a flowery terrace, eating and drinking, for some four hours to celebrate Mum's 90th birthday.

We have visited many, many places since Mother made three in Galicia. Some of these trips will be in my next travelogue memoir, a collection of stories highlighting some of the fabulous things Galicia has to offer. I hope you will join us.

Coming next: Pulpo, Pig & Peppers
– Travels round Galicia, and beyond.

More fun and more adventures in the new travelogue memoir from Lisa Rose Wright

Galicia, in the remote northwest of Spain – a land of mists and mysteries, green fields and greener forests; of vines and vistas, rivers and rias; of erratic weather and warm welcomes.

Galicia is a surprisingly well-kept secret to those of us who live here. Except for the Camino de Santiago pilgrim route and the coast near to Santiago, Galicia is not known as a tourist destination. This means that the inland areas in particular are unspoilt and definitely off the beaten track. Even the beautiful coastline is all but empty outside the July-August high season. One can potter around much of Galicia without any crowds to spoil your enjoyment of everything she has to offer.

Although there are no more letters home, Lisa, S, and Mum, Iris, continue to have many adventures in beautiful green Galicia. In *Pulpo, Pig & Peppers – travels round Galicia, and beyond*, Lisa invites you to join *los tres* as we visit some of our favourite places and events in this wild and unspoilt part of the Iberian Peninsula.

From Viking festivals to undiscovered beaches, Celtic roundhouses to Galician peppers, and from mountain villages to ancient forests – each chapter is devoted to one trip, one experience, one more enjoyable adventure here at the end of the world.

Want a sneak peek? For a FREE downloadable, bonus e-chapter just join my subscribers' list at
https://lisarosewright.wixsite.com/author/

If you enjoyed this book, please consider leaving me a review on Amazon or Goodreads. Reader support is important to indie authors and I really appreciate your feedback.

Thank you,

Lisa

https://www.goodreads.com/author/show/20423710.Lisa_Rose_Wright

https://www.smarturl.it/ChestnutCherryKiwi

To download your free photo album which accompanies the stories in this book month by month just follow the link below:

https://www.flipsnack.com/65E9E6B9E8C/album-3-cherry.html

For updates and free offers follow me at
http://www.facebook.com/lisarosewright.author
http://www.twitter.com/galauthor_lisa

THE RECIPES

July: *Arroz con leche*

Spanish rice pudding is a regular on *menú del dia* boards throughout Galicia. It is always served cold with a shaker of *canela* (cinnamon) on the side. It is sweet and delicious, and Mum's favourite dessert – though where she puts it after a huge three-course meal is anyone's guess.

Ingredients for six people:
100g round/pudding rice
1litre milk
A piece of orange rind, a piece of lemon rind, and a cinnamon stick to flavour the milk.
70g sugar

Put the milk into a saucepan with the rice and flavourings. Cook very slowly for 45 minutes, stirring occasionally to prevent the rice sticking. Once it begins to thicken, add the sugar and continue to cook until the rice is tender. Remove the flavourings before pouring into glass coupes or dishes to serve.
Cool in the fridge for at least one hour.
Serve with cinnamon for diners to add to their taste.

CHESTNUT, CHERRY & KIWI FRUIT SPONGE

August: *Tarta de manzana*

Apple tart is another regular menu dessert here in Galicia and combines Galegos love of custard-based desserts with crisp sweet apples. It was always my favourite at the Lugo based restaurant, Recatelo. Sadly, the proprietor, Andrés, has since retired, though the *tarta manzana* can still be bought from the nearby bakery on the same street, Rúa Recatelo.

Ingredients for a 25cm (10") tart tin:
For the pastry.
8oz (250g) flour
A tsp baking powder
A pinch of salt
2tsp caster sugar
5oz (75g) cold, unsalted butter
1 egg

Heat the oven to 200°C
Sift the flour and baking powder with the sugar and a pinch of salt. Rub in the cold butter until the mixture resembles breadcrumbs. Break in the egg and mix with a knife until the dough comes together, (you can, of course, make the dough in a food processor if you prefer). Chill in the fridge for 30 minutes before rolling out on a floured surface. Bake blind to keep the shell crisp. Paint the cooked shell with egg white and return to the oven briefly to set. Leave to cool.

For the custard filling.
2 eggs
1tbsp sugar
1tbsp cornflour
½ pint/400ml whole milk or a mixture of milk and cream
Tsp vanilla essence

THE RECIPES

6 crisp eating apples
2 tbsp redcurrant or grape jelly

Mix the eggs, cornflour, sugar and vanilla in a heavy bottomed saucepan. Boil the milk (in the microwave if you prefer) then pour over the egg mix stirring all the time. Reheat gently, stirring constantly until the mixture thickens. Cover with paper and leave to cool
Peel the apples. Cut each one in half and remove the core. Slice each half into eighths neatly. Put into acidulated water (with the juice of a lemon in it) until ready to use
Pour the cooled custard into the pastry case.
Arrange the apples slices in concentric rings on top of the custard. Bake until the apple is browned and soft.
Melt two tablespoons of grape or redcurrant jelly. Brush the baked tart with the jelly and leave to cool.

CHESTNUT, CHERRY & KIWI FRUIT SPONGE

September: *Almejas a la marinera*

This is my take on one of the dishes we had at Pepe and Mercedes' anniversary lunch. Clams in paprika sauce are a regular dish in Galicia, and quite delicious.

Ingredients for 4 people as a starter or part of a multi-course meal:
5 onions, cut very finely
A tbsp of olive oil
60 fresh clams, cleaned
A bottle of dry white wine
A tbsp of wine vinegar
A tbsp sweet paprika
A tsp of spicy paprika (optional)
salt

Heat the olive oil in a lidded pan, add the onions and cook, covered, very slowly until golden and soft but not burnt. Approx. 10 minutes. Add the paprika, the vinegar, a teaspoon of salt and the wine, then the washed clams. Cover the pan and cook until the clams have opened, approx. 10 minutes, agitating the pan occasionally. Discard any clams which remain closed and serve the dish with fresh crusty Galician bread to mop up the sauce.

THE RECIPES

October: *Cocido*

There are many different recipes for Cocido; as many as there are cooks really. Traditionally cocido is a winter stew, often cooked after *matanza*. It uses all parts of the pig including ears, tail and head. Some restaurants serve the pig's head cooked whole and chopped in half.

This recipe is from a dear friend of ours. We first ate it at her brother's house one October and I thought it was the best cocido I'd ever tasted (and still do)

1kg of beef skirt
Half a medium sized free-range chicken, cut into pieces
½ kg pancetta semi-cured, cut into chunks
½ rack salted pork ribs, cut into ribs
2 chorizos semi-cured, cut into chunks
I pointy cabbage and a good bunch of greens, chopped
12-16 medium potatoes, cut into chunks
50-100g *unto*

Unto is the fat from around the pig's intestines which is traditionally salted and layered following the yearly pig slaughter. Chunks are cut off to add to soups and stews throughout the year. You can use lard though the taste is not the same and you may need extra salt.

Put a big pot with water on the stove with the beef, chicken, ribs and *unto*. Let it boil for 15 minutes then add the pancetta and chorizos. Let it boil another 30 minutes before adding the cabbage and greens. Add the potatoes after a further 15 minutes. Test the stock and if necessary, add salt. Boil for a further 20-30 minutes until the potatoes are ready.

If the chicken is smallish and not homegrown, add it at the same time as the pancetta as it will not take too long to cook

CHESTNUT, CHERRY & KIWI FRUIT SPONGE

November: *Chocolate caliente*

Spanish style hot chocolate is nothing like the weak drinking chocolate of my youth in England, nor is it anything like the sickly-sweet, runny, marshmallow topped confection found in certain internationally known coffee chains. If you like those sorts of drinks then that's great – enjoy and turn to the next recipe. If, on the other hand, you like a cup of melted chocolate that your spoon can stand up in and which you need a spoon to eat, then read on...

I've given two versions of Spanish hot chocolate here. In the interests of experimentation S and I had to try a lot of recipes before we were happy with either version!

The huge blocks of *'chocolate de taza'* or literally 'chocolate for the cup', are great presents to give to loved ones. They make the best *chocolate caliente* to my mind and are so simple to use.
400g bar of *chocolate de taza*
1L/ whole milk
Pinch of salt
50g sugar, or to taste
15g cornflour (optional)

Mix the cornflour (if using) with a little cold milk. Heat the remaining ingredients together in a heavy-bottomed saucepan until the chocolate has dissolved. Add the mixed cornflour, if using, and heat, stirring constantly until thickened.

Chocolate caliente can also be made with cocoa powder but make sure it's pure cocoa not the sweetened drinking chocolate as it will be disgustingly sweet before you have enough to make the chocolate drink thick.

THE RECIPES

So, if you don't have a block of *chocolate de taza*, or any kind relatives or friends to bring you some, or if you want a gluten and dairy free version, then try this recipe.

1litre whole milk or dairy free milk (soya milk thickens well)
200g pure cocoa powder (Valor is an excellent Spanish brand)
Sugar or honey to taste

Whisk the milk and cocoa together then bring to the boil, stirring until the mixture begins to thicken. Add sugar or honey to taste and continue boiling until thick and rich.

As an aside, I remember being at the airport with Mum on our way home and asking the man at the drinks concession how much cocoa he put in his hot chocolate. He lifted a teaspoon up and said; 'this much.' Spanish chocolate needs way more than that per cup!

CHESTNUT, CHERRY & KIWI FRUIT SPONGE

December: *Filloas*

Traditional *filloas* were made around *matanza*, or pig killing time, using some of the blood from the pig. They are dark brown and deliciously sweet/savoury but rarely found on a menu any longer as tastes have changed. It's also pretty difficult to get hold of pigs' blood nowadays unless you are killing your own. However, in the interests of authenticity I've given the blood pancake recipe below. For 'normal' pancakes, replace the blood and the water with milk.

250g milk
250g water
250g fresh pigs' blood
6 eggs
Pinch salt
400g flour
100g sugar
2tsp cumin
1 tbsp pig fat, or lard, to fry.

Mix the liquids in a large jug
Put the flour into a large bowl with the salt, sugar, and cumin. Make a well in the centre and add the eggs one by one, drawing the flour into the middle and whisking until well combined.
Pour in the liquid slowly, whisking as you go until everything is smooth and combined.

Melt a tsp of lard in a heavy bottomed pan.
Pour in a little of the batter. It needs to be thick enough to coat the pan but not heavy. The first couple are usually experimental pancakes (or cook's treat, as I call them).
Fry until the batter has set then flip and fry the other side.
Stack the pancakes as you go.

THE RECIPES

These are best eaten hot so this is a good dessert if you are eating in the kitchen and can flip each pancake onto a diner's plate as you go, chef style.

Eat smothered in local honey.

CHESTNUT, CHERRY & KIWI FRUIT SPONGE

January: *Roscón*

Traditionally served for *los reyes* (the kings, epiphany) on January 6th each year, this is a sweet, decorated sponge, very typical of Galicia.

Ingredients for eight to ten people:
350g strong flour
100g sugar
70g softened butter
100ml tepid water
1 sachet quick bake yeast or 20g fresh yeast
1 egg
20ml rum, or other liqueur
30ml milk
Zest of an orange
Salt
Flaked almonds, candied fruits, sugar and 1 egg (beaten) to decorate.

Put the flour and sugar in a bowl. Rub in the butter. Dissolve the yeast (if using fresh) in the tepid water then add to the flour mix. If using dried yeast, add it to the dry ingredients first and mix, then add the warm water. Add the rest of the ingredients except the decorations and combine well.

Knead on a floured board until the dough is elastic and no longer sticky (ten minutes). Form the dough into a circle on a floured tray then make a hole in the centre of the dough. Stretch and widen the hole until the dough forms a large ring approximately 20cm (8") across. Pop the tray into an oiled plastic bag and leave to rise in a warm place for at least an hour (or overnight in the fridge).

Paint the risen dough with beaten egg. Decorate with the almonds and candied fruit and sprinkle with sugar before baking for 15-20 minutes in a hot oven (200°C)

THE RECIPES

February: Pork with apple sauce

This is my take on the delicious dish we ate on the way back from the ferry that snowy February. It is really quick and simple, especially if you have a jar of unsweetened apple puree to hand.

Ingredients for four people:
Four large pork chops
4oz/100g apple puree*
1pint/400ml pouring cream

*Nothing tastes better than homemade apple puree, so if you can get hold of some cooking apples or are lucky enough to have a tree in your garden then this can be made cheaply from scratch. If not just substitute a 4oz/100g jar of unsweetened apple puree.
Peel and core the apples then cook in a tiny amount of water until they turn to fluff. Cooking apples really are beautiful to cook as the flesh very quickly turns to a lovely fluffy puree with no work whatsoever. Beat with a wooden spoon to remove any lumps.
Mix the puree with the cream and warm gently in a saucepan, bring to the boil and bubble until thickened slightly. Stir occasionally to make sure it doesn't stick.

In the meantime, grill the pork chops on both sides until cooked through and caramelised on the outside.

Pour the sauce over the chops and serve with potatoes and vegetables.

CHESTNUT, CHERRY & KIWI FRUIT SPONGE

March: *Caldo de ósos*

The Taboadan 'bone stew' fair is held on the first Sunday in Carnival. This is seven weeks before Easter so can vary from early February to early March. There is fierce competition between establishments to make the best *caldo de ósos* each year in Taboada. This is the famous recipe of Mari Luz at *Casa Descalzo* the oldest restaurant in Taboada. The brains can be omitted but do add a sweet note to the dish.

Take the spine pieces of pork (ham is pretty good too) cut into sections and boil with onions and chickpeas (soaked overnight) for 1-2 hours until the chickpeas are tender. Add potatoes cut into chunks plus a grated parsnip. Once the potatoes are cooked add the pig brains cut small and continue cooking until everything is tender.
Make a refrito of oil, garlic and sweet paprika. Mix into the stew and serve immediately.

THE RECIPES

April: Spanish fried liver

This is a typically Spanish way of cooking liver, involving marinating the liver overnight which is ideal for the stronger pig or ox liver. Even if you are not a fan of liver, do try it this way as it's quite delicious.

Ingredients for 4 people:
6 cloves of garlic
125ml olive oil
125ml wine vinegar
1tsp spicy paprika
750g liver (pig or ox) sliced thinly
Oil for frying

Chop the garlic very finely, or mince. Mix with the olive oil, vinegar and paprika in a non-metallic lidded bowl. Add the sliced liver, cover and refrigerate overnight.
The next day, remove the liver from the marinade, pat dry then fry until golden on both sides but still tender, around five minutes.
Pour the marinade into the pan and cook for another minute until the sauce is hot.
Sprinkle with sea salt and extra paprika before serving.

CHESTNUT, CHERRY & KIWI FRUIT SPONGE

May: Garlic Prawns

These are another staple on Galician *menús*. Simple and delicious

Ingredients for 4 people as a starter:
4-6 cloves of garlic chopped finely
100ml olive oil
1 small green chilli chopped very finely
Juice of one lemon
1tsp rough sea salt
500g peeled prawns, tail left on.

Heat the oven to 180°C.
In a dish* mix all the ingredients and stir until the prawns are well coated.
Cook in the oven for 20 minutes. Serve in the dish sprinkled with parsley and with lots of crusty bread.

*The Galician shallow earthenware *cazuelas* are perfect for this dish. You can use one large dish or four smaller ones.

THE RECIPES

June: Chestnut, cherry & Kiwi fruit sponge

I have to admit that this was by far the easiest recipe of my book titles in this series.
Sweet chestnuts make a delicious flour to use in this roulade recipe and the cherries and kiwi fruit make a very pretty filling. All in all, a lovely summer dessert. Oh, and it's gluten free and dairy free too

Ingredients for six people:
For the roulade.
75g/3oz roasted chestnuts, ground, or chestnut flour
1tsp cornflour
1tsp vanilla extract
1tsp white wine vinegar
4 egg whites
140g/5oz caster sugar

Heat the oven to 160ºC and line a shallow oblong tin with greaseproof paper.
If using freshly roasted chestnuts, grind to a powder in a food processor or coffee grinder. Blend the cornflour, vanilla and wine vinegar to a smooth paste in a cup. Whisk the egg whites until stiff. Whisk in the caster sugar, a tablespoon at a time, adding a little of the cornflour mixture each time. The meringue should be very thick, white and shiny. Fold the ground chestnuts into the meringue with a metal spoon.
Spoon into the prepared tin and spread evenly over the base.
Bake for around 25 minutes until pale golden. It should feel dry to the touch but slightly springy.
Lay a sheet of greaseproof paper onto the worktop and invert the tin onto it. Peel off the lining paper. Cover with a just damp tea towel and leave to cool.

CHESTNUT, CHERRY & KIWI FRUIT SPONGE

For the filling.
Whipped cream or soya cream or pastry cream.
4 ripe kiwi fruit, peeled and chopped finely
100g/4oz fresh cherries, halved and destoned

Mix the cream with the chopped kiwis and spread on the cooled roulade. Sprinkle over the cherries and roll carefully from one short end.
Dust with icing sugar if liked

Enjoy eating this book!

A GLOSSARY OF ENGLISH WORDS

I write in British English, and at times, to Mum, in Midland's slang.

Despite quickly discovering that not everyone on the other side of the pond knew what a courgette was (about three days after publishing *Plum, Courgette & Green Bean Tart*), I continued to confound non-British speakers with *Tomato, Fig & Pumpkin Jelly*.

Luckily one of those very nice but confused people agreed to help me compile a glossary for my second memoir and, with little arm twisting from me, to do likewise for this third memoir.

And here it is; again, with my special thanks to Eileen Huestis for not only taking the time to write to me in the first place but for volunteering to help her fellow countrymen and women understand 'Lisa' speak.

Allotment – A remote piece of land for growing vegetables. A *huerta* in Spanish
Aubergine – eggplant
Barrowed/barrowful – wheelbarrowed or wheelbarrowful
Beetroot – beets
Biscuit – a biscuit is a hard sweet cookie
Boiled eggs and soldiers – soft boiled eggs in their shells with toast fingers (soldiers)
Boot – trunk of a car
Builder's tea – strong tea (because British builders like it strong)
Bum – informal English for the bottom, butt
Bunked off – skipped class
Bused – late, or specifically late for the bus/coach to school/work. A Midlands expression.
Butties/butty – a sandwich, or bread and butter
Chawl – pressed pigs' head meat pate. Very tasty, honest

CHESTNUT, CHERRY & KIWI FRUIT SPONGE

Chips – fries, hot chips
Chuffed – very pleased
Chuntering – muttering
Colliery – coal mine
Courgette – zucchini
Cuppa – a cup of (usually) very British tea. Or in our case normally a large mug
Faff – bother or fuss
Gammon – a side of bacon usually cooked in thick slices or as a joint
Gas hob – gas burner
Hosepipe – garden hose
Jemmied – jimmied
Jumper - sweater
Katy-corner – kitty corner, catty corner. Corner-wise on
Kerfuffle – commotion
Kiwi vines – Chinese gooseberries
Lorry – semi-trailer
Marrow – a vegetable marrow. A type of pumpkin or gourd, usually long, green and striped
Mash – mashed potatoes
Moggies – informal British word for cats, and for the Morris Minor motor car.
Mortaring – to push mortar into the joints of a brick or stone-built house
Nosey – being a busybody
Petrol – gasoline
Pensioner, OAP (old age pensioner) – retiree
Postman – mailman
Potty – traditionally a ceramic chamber pot kept under the bed for night time use.
Pressie – present, gift
Promenade – a walkway along the seafront
Pudding – a sweet or sometimes savoury dish. In Britain we have a sweet sponge pudding or chocolate pudding but also savoury black (or blood) pudding. The explanation for this term, in my Collins English Dictionary, covers half a page!

A GLOSSARY OF ENGLISH WORDS

Scrummy – delicious, yummy
Skip – a yellow metal container for waste, delivered to the house, a sort of dumpster
Snug – a cosy intimate warm space
Stag do – bachelor party
Strimmer –grass cutter, weed eater
Swimming baths – swimming pool
Swineherd pie – shepherd's pie but made with pork
Swish – fashionably smart or posh
Tarmac – tarmacadam, a trade name for blacktop used on roads
Tip – municipal rubbish dump
Toad in the hole – sausages cooked in a batter pudding (that word again!)
Tweeny – a servant 'between the stairs'
WC – water closet... another name for a toilet
Wellies – rubber boots
Windscreen wipers – windshield wipers

Spanish/Galician words used throughout this book
Augardente (*aguardiente* in Spanish) – a Galician firewater, or moonshine, of varying quality and strength
A Casa do Campo – the country house. The original name of our stone farmhouse
A Casita do Campo, or A/La Casita – the country cottage/little house. Our recent buy
Alpendre – slat-fronted or open barn
Casa nosotros – our house
Churrasco – a huge Galician mixed grill of sausages, pork ribs and beef steak, often including seconds, thirds or even fourths should you manage it.
Cocina – a wood-fired range cooker
Empadronamiento – proof of residency in a particular council area
Galego/a – a person from Galicia, a Galician male/female
Horno – a wood-fired stone-built oven, usually outside and used for baking bread

CHESTNUT, CHERRY & KIWI FRUIT SPONGE

Hórreo – grainstore. In central Galicia these are usually stone-built with wooden slatted sides and a stone overhang at the base to prevent mice and other pests spoiling the grain
Huerta – a vegetable garden, as opposed to *Jardín*, a flower garden
Jefe/jefa – the boss (man/woman) often used in a light hearted way as to Mum.
Jamón/jamones – Spanish cured ham(s)
Lareira – open fireplace, mainly for smoking the hams and chorizos
Vecino/a – neighbour (male/female)

ACKNOWLEDGEMENTS

An Indie author can never succeed alone so here's my chance to say a great big thank you to all those wonderful people who have helped this book come to fruition.

To my beta readers, Julie Haigh, Beth Haslam, Val Poore, and Alyson Sheldrake. Thank you for daring to read the first draft and for your incredibly helpful comments. I hope this final version meets all your approvals.

To my special US beta reader, Eileen Huestis, for helping once more compile the glossary. I have learnt much of our common language!

To [100covers](#) for stepping in to provide the beautiful cover artwork at the last minute and literally saving my sanity.

To the friendliest group on Facebook, [We Love Memoirs](#), for support, and for lots of fun-filled hours when I should have been working but was instead online. If you love reading memoirs (or writing them), enjoy competitions and chatting with like-minded people, then I highly recommend this wonderful group. We can be found at http://www.facebook.com/groups/welovememoirs

To Mum for keeping eight years' worth of letters home. As ever, without you this book would not have been possible – even though transporting boxes of said letters back to Galicia with you was... interesting!

To S, my blue-eyed husband, for alpha, beta and omega reading, and for being there, always.

And to you, my readers – without you this book would just be another dream.

ABOUT THE AUTHOR:

In 2007 Lisa left a promising career as an ecologist catching protected reptiles and amphibians, and kissing frogs, to move to beautiful green Galicia with her blue-eyed prince (now blue-eyed husband).

She divides her time equally between growing her own food, helping to renovate two semi-derelict houses and getting out and about to discover more of the stunningly beautiful area she calls home.

Lisa is happiest outside in her *huerta* weeding; watching the antics of her chickens; or in her kitchen cooking interesting recipes on her wood-burning range.

Chestnut, Cherry & Kiwi Fruit Sponge is the third in the *Writing Home* trilogy. The series is available in paperback, eBook and free with Kindle Unlimited at Amazon stores worldwide.

For more details about Lisa, her life in Galicia, and her writing, go to her website at
http://www.lisarosewright.wixsite.com/author
or follow her on
Facebook
http://www.facebook.com/lisarosewright.author
Twitter
http://www.twitter.com/lisarosewright.author

Printed in Great Britain
by Amazon